Leisure, citizenship and working-class

men in Britain, 1850–1945

Manchester University Press

STUDIES IN
POPULAR
CULTURE

Leisure, citizenship and working-class men in Britain, 1850–1945

BRAD BEAVEN

Manchester University Press

Manchester and New York

distributed exclusively in the USA by Palgrave

Published by Manchester University Press
Oxford Road, Manchester M13 9NR, UK
and Room 400, 175 Fifth Avenue, New York, NY 10010, USA
www.manchesteruniversitypress.co.uk

Distributed in the United States exclusively by
Palgrave Macmillan, 175 Fifth Avenue,
New York, NY 10010, USA

Distributed in Canada exclusively by
UBC Press, University of British Columbia, 2029 West Mall,
Vancouver, BC, Canada V6T 1Z2

British Library Cataloguing-in-Publication Data is available

Library of Congress Cataloging-in-Publication Data is available

ISBN 978 0 7190 6028 1 paperback

First published by Manchester University Press in hardback 2005

This paperback edition first published 2009

Printed by Lightning Source

STUDIES IN
POPULAR
CULTURE

There has in recent years been an explosion of interest in culture and cultural studies. The impetus has come from two directions and out of two different traditions. On the one hand, cultural history has grown out of social history to become a distinct and identifiable school of historical investigation. On the other hand, cultural studies has grown out of English literature and has concerned itself to a large extent with contemporary issues. Nevertheless, there is a shared project, its aim, to elucidate the meanings and values implicit and explicit in the art, literature, learning, institutions and everyday behaviour within a given society. Both the cultural historian and the cultural studies scholar seek to explore the ways in which a culture is imagined, represented and received, how it interacts with social processes, how it contributes to individual and collective identities and world views, to stability and change, to social, political and economic activities and programmes. This series aims to provide an arena for the cross-fertilisation of the discipline, so that the work of the cultural historian can take advantage of the most useful and illuminating of the theoretical developments and the cultural studies scholars can extend the purely historical underpinnings of their investigations. The ultimate objective of the series is to provide a range of books which will explain in a readable and accessible way where we are now socially and culturally and how we got to where we are. This should enable people to be better informed, promote an interdisciplinary approach to cultural issues and encourage deeper thought about the issues, attitudes and institutions of popular culture.

Jeffrey Richards

This book is dedicated to my parents,

Gail and Martin Beaven,

my partner Becky and our son

George Isaac Beaven

Contents

General editor's foreword

Brad Beaven's wide-ranging, readable and impressively researched book constitutes a major contribution to the ongoing debate about the nature and scope of working-class male leisure in the period 1850–1945. Recently class has been downplayed by scholars in favour of gender, generation and income as principal determinants in the nature of working-class leisure. Dr Beaven does not deny the importance of these factors, but powerfully argues for the continuing importance of class and in particular an active engagement in and contestation with popular culture by working-class males.

To make his case, he analyses the efforts of a succession of essentially middle-class interventions aimed at promoting improving pastimes and creating a sense of responsible citizenship in the working-class male. They included the rational recreation advocates from Salvationists to socialists, paternalist employers providing company-based activities, uniformed youth movements and government agencies like the wartime Council for the Encouragement of Music and the Arts. He examines the successive debates about and inquiries into such concerns as youthful hooliganism, suburban neurosis and the Americanisation of inter-war teenagers, and considers the moral panics about the deleterious influence of various aspects of popular culture.

In parallel with this strand of investigation, Dr Beaven charts the growth of the commercialised leisure industries: mass-produced literature, the music hall, association football, cinema and wireless. He assesses the extent and nature of working-class male participation in such activities.

Throughout the book, Dr Beaven engages thoughtfully and constructively with a wide range of secondary literature, including the most recent scholarship. He also deploys a mass of fresh primary research, particularly in the hitherto comparatively neglected areas of the Midlands and Southeast, to support his argument. The whole adds up to a fresh, vivid and thought-provoking interpretation of a subject central to the history of popular culture.

Jeffrey Richards

Acknowledgements

First I would like to thank Jeffrey Richards, who has provided me with invaluable support and constructive criticism throughout this project. Thanks also to Alison Welsby, Jonathan Bevan and the anonymous readers at Manchester University Press for all their hard work on the project.

I am fortunate to work with a team of social historians who specialise in popular culture and have found them a constant source of advice and discussion. Thanks particularly to Dave Andress, who meticulously read through the entire manuscript, and to Ken Lunn, who has offered invaluable advice on this and many other projects throughout my time at Portsmouth. I am also grateful to Sue Harper, Matt Taylor, Bob Kiehl and Heather Shore, who all read draft chapters. I have also worked extensively with John Griffiths of Massey University, New Zealand, on a number of projects through the years and have benefited from both his historical expertise and his uncanny ability to find a public house on leaving an archive. Donna Loftus of the Open University, Mark Jenner, Dorian Harris and Rob Shardlow also provided helpful comments on earlier drafts of the manuscript. I must also thank my father, who, since his retirement, has been commandeered into helping me in the archives. Although this was a dramatic change of career, he has shown that an old dog can learn new tricks! Thanks also to the students who have taken my Special Subject and Group Research Project strands, as they have consistently made me reflect on the material and themes contained in this book.

xiiAcknowledgements

Over the last few years I have given papers on themes related to the book at a number of venues. Thanks particularly to the organisers and contributors to the discussions at the following events: Hawaii Conference for Social Sciences 2003; Economic History Conference, Oxford 1999; International Conference on the Crowd, De Montfort University 1996. The research and travel costs for the book were generously funded by the University of Portsmouth, while some overseas conference expenditure was met by a British Academy Award.

Finally, I would like to thank my partner Rebecca Denyer for all her love and support. Becky not only had to witness the trials and tribulations of historical writing but, in addition, was often burdened with my personal ordeal of following Coventry City Football Club.

Introduction

During the 1930s a series of conferences were held in Britain to discuss the 'problem' of leisure and citizenship. 'Tell me how a man spends his leisure time and I will tell you what sort of a man he is' was the common cry from the platform.[1] Such a statement would not have been out of place in the mid-nineteenth century as leisure and citizenship had long been elevated to a position of national importance. To be precise, it was male leisure which generated the most concern. The 1867 Reform Act, which allowed a proportion of skilled working men to vote, propelled the male citizen to the heart of the ongoing discourse on the foundation of democratic principles and their subsequent development in Britain. During the late nineteenth century it was decreed that 'elevated' recreation would stave off the degenerate influences that seemed to accompany a 'mass' society.[2] By the interwar period, social reformers began to worry that 'passive' leisure pursuits had helped create a 'dull' and 'apathetic' working class, circumstances which they feared could provide a fertile ground for fascism.[3] Thus, for those in society keen to create a bond between individual and nation during this mass democratic age, the diffusion of appropriate leisure activities became a means to achieve a more incorporated and civic-minded population. Although the creators of social citizenry enthusiastically extolled the virtues of their schemes, established working-class leisure habits proved a stubborn barrier to change. Thus, more often than not, the issue of male leisure became enmeshed with contemporary debates on the nature of work, urbanisation and the diffusion of political and civic principles. This book, then, will analyse the development of male leisure against the changing notions of citizenship which underpinned perceptions of society during this period.

Although in assessing the relationship between leisure and citizenship evidence will be drawn from a variety of British regions, special attention will be paid to the Midlands city of Coventry. It was a city which entered the twentieth century with new industries and a new relatively affluent workforce, a transformation which encapsulated many contemporary anxieties over the relationship between leisure and citizenry. Coventry's changing industrial economy, from the traditional craft industries of silk weaving and watchmaking to the new mass-produced industries of bicycle and motor manufacture, attracted not only a new semi-skilled workforce to the city but also greater capitalisation of leisure facilities by the interwar period.[4] The pioneering work of George Singer, who began producing the world's first safety bicycle in the city, ensured that Coventry became the centre of Britain's bicycle industry, boasting over forty-six firms by 1896.[5] In the same year, Coventry gained the reputation as the early home of the motor car industry when Harry Lawson, a company speculator, sited Britain's first car factory in the city. The city's pool of semi-skilled workers and plethora of engineering firms proved so attractive to the new motor car entrepreneurs that by 1914 Coventry was known in some quarters as 'Britain's Detroit'.[6] Such was the expansion of the motor industry in the city, one American visitor reported that 'the people in Coventry walk quicker than other Englishmen. Everyone seems prosperous. There is a briskness in the very air of the place. Your factories are growing as fast as the factories in Detroit – and I cannot say more than that. Everyone is busy.'[7]

Alongside this industrial transformation, leisure opportunities also expanded. One historian has noted that in Coventry during the interwar period 'cinemas, dance halls and social clubs increased in number and size in response to the vitality of the local economy'.[8] These new developments did not go unnoticed by contemporaries. In 1934, J. B. Priestley observed that there were in Coventry 'whole new quarters, where the mechanics and fitters and turners and furnace men live in neat brick rows, and drink their beer in gigantic new public houses and take their wives to gigantic new picture theatres'.[9] Indeed, for most of the period under study, Coventry can genuinely be labelled an industrial boom-town for, as Thoms and Donnelly have argued, 'the new generation of Coventry workers were not only better paid than their predecessors, but in general by 1914 enjoyed substantially improved living and working conditions'.[10] To place this in context, Waller noted that Coventry was one of a number of cities involved in the new industries which underwent at least one period of exceptional growth between 1860 and 1914.[11] Between 1901 and 1911, the city's population grew by 50 per cent to 106,349, a demographic trend that continued during the interwar period when, by 1939, Coventry's population stood at 224,267.[12] Significantly, Coventry's industrial and demographic transformation raised questions about whether modern leisure activities were an obstacle to the dissemination of 'good citizenship'. For example, the demand by civic elites for a greater sense of citizenship to combat the corrosive affects of commercial leisure, youth culture and suburban isolation were particularly acute in cities like Coventry which had experienced rapid socio-economic change. Surprisingly, however, the Midlands has largely have been overlooked by historians. Most historiography on working-class leisure has drawn evidence from the North of England, communities which, though fairly stable, suffered from bouts of severe poverty. Thus, Pat Thane has noted the growing commercial leisure pursuits of the late nineteenth century 'were more readily accessible to the more affluent workers of more prosperous expanding towns, such as Coventry, but just occasional treats for many in Salford'.[13] Furthermore, historians charting the early development of social citizenship in Britain have perceived the movement as the civic elites' response to the poverty-stricken people of the inner-city slums.[14] However, working-class males in the Midlands were also subjected to a plethora of social citizenship schemes, even though they experienced very different material conditions to their counterparts in the North. The Midlands experienced significant economic booms and an associated influx of migrants throughout the late nineteenth and early twentieth centuries.[15] The rise of the 'new' industries helped nurture the first relatively 'affluent' workers, a process which brought its own 'problems' for the local civic elites. A large influx of young male semi-skilled workers, with money in their pockets, proved as much a headache for the local civic elite as the 'slum dwellers' in other parts of the country.

Recent approaches to male leisure

Popular leisure became an academic subject in its own right during the 1960s with the emergence of the 'new' social history and the identification of 'culture' within the disciplines of sociology and anthropology.

Since those historians investigating leisure invariably came from a labour history background, it was perhaps inevitable that leisure was perceived as an essential factor in the formation of a 'standardised' working-class culture towards the end of the nineteenth century. Much of the literature here placed leisure in a pivotal role in determining the political characteristics of working people between 1870 and 1939. For some labour historians such as Hobsbawm, class-specific leisure institutions such as the Working Men's Club and the Cooperative movement provided a foothold for Labour politics that helped engender a sense of class consciousness by the turn of the century.[16] This perspective elicited a more sceptical response from historians who suspected that popular leisure was little more than a culture of consolation which had fostered conservative and inward-looking traits.[17]

These competing models of working-class culture, however, were sensitive neither to less formal leisure activities nor to the diversity of the working-class experience. According to Davies, previous historians' preoccupation with leisure's impact upon political behaviour has obscured significant varieties of working-class leisure that were shaped by gender, generation and poverty.[18] In this important corrective to the 'homogeneous working-class culture' model, Davies persuasively demonstrates in his case study of Salford and Manchester that participation in leisure was structured by profound inequalities of gender. The primacy of male leisure in working-class communities meant that women's recreation was severely restricted on financial, domestic and moral grounds. The issues of generation and poverty also diversified the working-class experience of leisure, with teenagers often shunning adult forms of entertainment, while the longstanding issue of poverty ensured that regional variation would also be a factor in prohibiting the uniformity of working-class leisure. The continued existence of poverty also prompted Davies to question the assumption that commercial leisure had played a central role in working people's lives, as many of the traditional informal leisure activities found in the public house and the neighbourhood could be traced back to the mid-nineteenth century.[19] Elsewhere, Davies has concluded that the considerable diversity of leisure within working communities has 'reinforced a growing recognition of the limitations of a class-centred approach'.[20] Taking this lead, a number of historians have produced a flurry of recent studies on Lancashire which have vigorously argued that working people's experience of life and leisure was fragmented and atomised to the point where class became submerged beneath more pressing identities such as gender, ethnicity and generation.[21]

The exploration of gender, generation and poverty has produced some important contributions to understanding how ordinary people, detached from formal clubs or political affiliations, spent their leisure time. Indeed, these histories have made significant strides in breaking the causal relationship between working-class leisure and working-class politics that had underpinned previous models of traditional working-class culture. However, highlighting the diversity of experience to illustrate the unwieldy nature of the 'standardised and homogeneous' model of working-class culture does not necessarily relegate class as an outmoded concept. A methodological approach which dissects working-class culture in isolation almost certainly exaggerates the nuances and divisions within a community. Without doubt, greater attention must be levelled at the contesting principal categories of gender, generation and poverty in the mapping of leisure patterns between 1850 and 1945. This book will argue that a more pluralised working-class culture does not preclude the importance of class relations in helping shape the male leisure experience. Indeed, Bailey has recently acknowledged that while gender, generation and poverty were important, 'class has to be retained in any reworked agenda'.[22] The research and interpretation of working-class leisure here embraces the 'diversity' approach, acknowledging that gender, generation and poverty certainly had a bearing on leisure patterns and behaviour. In contrast with women's domestic duties, a working man's day was often distinctly divided between work and non-work activities – developing a 'consciousness' of leisure time for males which was reinforced by male-only working men's clubs and public house bars. Undoubtedly, gendered leisure patterns led to conflict and sometimes male violence towards women in working-class households. However, although gender-based inequality was a significant feature of working-class family life, it should not obscure the consensus and mutuality between the sexes that also emerged in working-class communities. Abendstern reminds us that 'women-only' neighbourhood gossip, clubs and outings were not simply a response to exclusive male leisure activities but that many women preferred the company of other women and wished to exclude men.[23] Thus identities were not fixed or constant as within one class, and at certain times gender could seem the more significant determinant of activity. For example, class identities may have been submerged beneath more pressing gendered conflicts within the domestic sphere, particularly since male leisure spending patterns took precedence in working-class families. Social class takes on a greater importance once working-men's leisure activities are contextualised against the changing notions of citizenry between 1850 and 1945. Indeed, it is argued here that notions of what constituted citizenship often propelled class issues to the forefront of social relations and contemporary discourse. However, due to the plurality of working-class culture, it can no longer be pigeonholed in either the 'incorporation' or 'resistance' models of class relations that featured in the social control debates of the 1970s and 1980s.[24] Working-class culture was not a consistent entity; it was both competitive and communal, there were gendered and generational tensions, and middle-class interventions were at times accepted, manipulated or overtly challenged.[25] Indeed, August has recently argued in his analysis of working-class communities in late-nineteenth-century London that 'we should be careful to avoid the replacement of one overly simplistic view of an apathetic and passive population with an equally one-dimensional image of an heroic resistant one'.[26] Thus though working-class males may have demonstrated a remarkable propensity to manipulate their environment, it was in a fashion that often disappointed contemporary socialists and subsequent historians. This is particularly the case when we turn our attention to leisure's relationship with citizenship, which was perceived by the urban elite, across the political spectrum, as an opportunity to improve and acquiesce working-class male opinion and behaviour.

Recent approaches to citizenship

In historiographical terms, analyses of citizenship have largely featured in studies exploring the urban elites' response to a perceived moral and social 'degeneration' of the late-nineteenth-century city.[27] Croll has argued that, although the uniform application of social class to all scenarios is inappropriate, it cannot be jettisoned altogether. Thus he states that 'many of the popular cultural pursuits that so upset civilised middle-class opinion, and so problematised public space, were pastimes enjoyed exclusively by members of the working class. So frequently was this the case that to deny that the civic project was, in key respects, a class project would be curious indeed'.[28] Indeed, Otter has persuasively argued that narratives of citizenship were fostered by the 'bourgeois visual environment'. The 'civilised' city inhabitants, who mastered their baser instincts, were open to civil scrutiny in the respectable public sphere of parks, squares and wide streets. The uncivil's activities, however, were shielded from public gaze by the labyrinth of backstreets, dens and courts of the inner city. Otter notes that 'this environmental polarity is clearly a heuristic simplification, but for the purposes of my argument the equation runs thus: the inhabitants of "anti-bourgeois visual environment" could not be trusted with social and political freedom. The moral, physical and biological fears they aroused were inseparable from the spaces in which they lived.'[29] The 'civic project', then, stimulated discourse on who qualified for citizenship which, often class expressive, sheds light on the contestations over popular leisure and public space in the late-nineteenth-century city. Only recently have historians begun to project their analysis of national and local citizenry into the early to mid-twentieth century.[30] The Second World War, in particular, has been perceived as an era which invited greater scrutiny of 'good citizenship' as civilian duty became increasingly important during this national crisis.[31] However, this crucial period 1850–1945 still lacks a consistent analysis of the development of citizenship in Britain, a gap this book addresses through an examination of its relationship with the theme of male leisure.

At a very basic level, social citizenship was an attempt to forge a link between the individual and the authorities at either a local or a national level, though the nature of citizenship changed according to the circumstances of time.[32] In effect, social citizenship defined desirable patterns of behaviour in both public and private life which interlocked with the cultural norms of a burgeoning liberal democracy. In 1949, the philosopher T. H. Marshall argued that deep economic inequalities had been offset by an 'amplification' of citizenship rights. It was contended that successful schemes of social citizenship encouraged a tacit agreement between the state and those who fulfilled the criteria of citizenship, a relationship that if extended to the rest of society could cultivate a degree of social cohesion.[33] This study, however, argues that concepts of citizenship in Britain developed four distinct phases between 1850 and 1945. During the first three-quarters of the nineteenth century, citizenship was perceived as a series of rights based on status with only limited obligations. During the mid-nineteenth century, at this high water mark of Victorian liberalism, the prevailing philosophy of an individualist and atomised society defined citizenship as the engagement with only basic civic duties such as voting and the payment of taxes. The widening of the franchise in 1867 and 1884, along with a perceived growing crisis in Britain's cities, saw narratives of citizenship enter a new phase during the late nineteenth century. This period was also a turning point in how the concept of citizenship was disseminated since it was no longer confined to a small academic elite. The foundation of the social sciences and public administration as academic disciplines gave the movement a practical dimension which it had hitherto lacked. Urban elites, social workers, political activists and the national and local press became drawn to the concepts of citizenship emerging from academia, disseminating the message in a popular form.[34] Moreover, the late-nineteenth-century revival of interest in classical idealism gave the movement a solid intellectual framework. Both academics and urban elites became influenced by Hegelian philosophy, which believed citizenship could help nurture the socially integrated city. In this scenario, citizenship was not the embodiment of a series of rights or an indication of status; rather it was a dynamic entity which cemented real moral and spiritual bonds between the individual and the state. The historian R.H. Tawney and social reformers like Samuel Barnett saw 'social' citizenship as an activity that obliged the individual to engage in 'public spiritedness' and carry out wider social and civic duties.[35] Thus, according to Arnold Toynbee, a prominent advocate of social citizenship in the late nineteenth century, class antagonism was to be replaced by 'the gospel of duty'.[36] It was presumed that 'active citizenship' would encourage a healthy democracy at both a local and a national level and that working people would at least possess a stake in a society where poverty and destitution were never far away. Significantly, social citizenship could also be employed to define the nation's 'other', which might have been the undeserving poor, the overindulgent pleasure seeker or the delinquent youth. Indeed, in the Edwardian period, anxieties over the 'stock of Britain's youth' and the future of the Empire gave the citizenship movement an added impetus. Although citizenship continued to be regarded as an energising activity, national duty rather than civic duty increasingly dominated discourse on the nature of citizenry. Indeed, it was a notion of citizenship which was ideally suited to meet the demands of the First World War, and only fell from grace when the true horrors of the conflict emerged in the postwar period. Notions of citizenship underwent further changes in emphasis between 1918 and 1939, a period that represents the third distinct phase in its development.[37] Although citizenship continued to strive to create bonds between the individual and the state, the Victorian and Edwardian 'civic gospel' emphasis was superseded by the desire to maintain 'national efficiency'. In a period of increasing suburbanisation, modern paternalist employers such as Sir Alfred Herbert replaced the civic elite as the moral guardians of popular leisure pursuits.[38] In a period of increased domestic and international tensions, employers justified their involvement in their immediate local community on a number of levels. The 'humanitarian' employee who provided extensive leisure facilities and advice on good citizenry to his employers was essentially making the moral as well as the economic case for 'enlightened capitalism' during an era in which the system was under sustained criticism by the hostile ideologies of fascism and communism.[39] Furthermore, an employers' investment in wholesome out-of-work entertainment could only aid 'national efficiency' since a physically and mentally fit workforce would boost labour productivity during a period of economic uncertainty. The final phase of citizenship during this period was triggered by the Second World War. This was unlike any other war as, for the first time, a large proportion of the civilian population was under the threat of enemy bombardment. In contrast to the First World War, where the emphasis was very much on 'imperial national duty', 'total war' drew civilian activities under increasing observation. In such unusual circumstances it is perhaps not surprising that notions of citizenship became enmeshed with civilian morale and social cohesiveness.[40] Leisure in the public sphere, clearly important before the war, took on a new significance since the government perceived it as one of the few indicators of 'good' civilian morale during the conflict. During a period of national crisis, notions of citizenship stressed class harmony and a sense of common purpose, values that were amplified through the repeated message that Britain was engaged in a 'Peoples' War'.[41]

Research parameters: themes, chronology and structure

During the late nineteenth century the term 'pleasure seekers' became a fashionable phrase bandied about by disgruntled philanthropists and political activists alike to describe the vast majority of the working class's out-of-work activities. According to these providers of rational leisure, the working class seemed more interested in 'play' than the more serious matters of civilisation and political salvation. Although the term had derogatory overtones, it did signify the point of leisure: enjoyment.[42] This may seem an obvious point, but it has sometimes been lost beneath historiographical debates on working-class political apathy and the hegemonic role of rec-reation. Leisure was principally to be enjoyed and was not viewed by its participants as a consolation for an inequitable society or a symptom of their political deficiencies. However, leisure was not a depoliticised activ-ity in itself; it was important enough, as we shall see, for working men to challenge various levels of authority over their right to engage in their own forms of entertainment in the public sphere. Leisure between 1850 and 1945 was neither independent nor autonomous but wedded to the socio-economic structures of society and should not be compartmentalised and analysed in isolation.

The chronology encompassed in this particular study opens with the period commonly marked out as the key era in the 'remaking' of the Brit-ish working class. The core mass leisure institutions, which had become commonplace by the interwar years, first emerged towards the third quarter of the nineteenth century. This period also saw significant socio-economic, political and cultural changes that had repercussions on leisure patterns. The regular five-and-a-half-day working week, new working arrangements organised around the principles of mass production, the incremental en-franchisement of working men, the growth of large cities and working-class 'suburbia' all appeared during this period. Although many of the issues that underpinned schemes of social citizenship changed between 1850 and 1945, the 'problem' of male leisure remained a constant. This book, then, will not attempt to survey male leisure patterns in their entirety between 1850 and 1945, but will instead identify key working-class male leisure pursuits that interfaced with questions of citizenship.

Chapters 1–3 focus broadly on the years 1850 to 1918, a period which witnessed wholesale changes to urban life, a burgeoning mass society and the growth of an Empire, which, though vast and rapidly expanding, had worrying tensions and weaknesses. The book opens with an examination of the 'leisure' problem of the middle decades of the nineteenth century. After the defeat of Chartism and associated challenges to the employers' right to organise the workplace, factory owners, the clergy and philan-thropists established schemes of rational recreation designed to attract and educate working-class males.[43] Chapter 1 explores how schemes of rational recreation attempted to create the model citizen and the impact of these strategies on male working-class leisure. Chapter 2 focuses on the growth of commercial leisure and initiatives by class-specific and class-collaborative movements to forge 'good citizenship' as an alternative to this new mass leisure. Taking three influential leisure activities – drink, the music hall and association football – this chapter will explore their impact on both concepts of citizenship and male leisure patterns. In addition, commercial leisure also highlighted the marked gender divides in leisure activities found within working-class households. Regardless of the economic constraints, 'spends' for males were often prioritised, allowing them to extend participation in new commercial leisure forms beyond the public house. Chapter 3 investigates the generational issues that shaped male working-class leisure. The increase in non-apprenticed semi-skilled work, particularly in the 'new' industry regions, raised fears that monotonous working practices and new leisure activities were a dangerous social cocktail. Moreover we shall investigate how, during the late Victorian and early Edwardian era, the problem of a 'degenerate' youth became entwined with anxieties over the future of empire.

Chapters 4–7 contextualise male leisure against the dominant concerns between 1918 and 1945. This era saw the suburbanisation of British cities, continued anxieties over male citizenry and increased international tensions that led to war. Chapter 4 will analyse specifically how working-class male leisure activities often shifted from the hearts of cities to the self-contained new housing estates that mushroomed in Britain, particularly in the Midlands and Southeast. The trend of firms establishing factories on the outskirts of cities created new working-class suburbs that were served by a proliferation of work-based clubs and societies. Here, the original objectives of the clubs will be explored to establish the extent to which the participants shaped the clubs' subsequent development. Chapter 5 tracks the issue of male youth culture between the wars, examining these leisure patterns against contemporary debates on the youth 'problem' and subsequent historiography which has proclaimed that this generation of youths were Britain's 'first teenagers'. The interwar period also witnessed technical innovation in the realm of leisure and, with it, the growth of more sophisticated propaganda techniques. Indeed, by the 1930s, the era of mass communication had arrived. Chapter 6 examines the explosion of commercial literature, the cinema and the inception of public broadcasting to establish whether working-class males really did embrace a more 'homogeneous', less class-specific culture as some historians have argued. Finally, Chapter 7 concentrates on the Second World War and explores why government intelligence officers perceived working-class leisure activities and citizenry as important variables in sustaining 'good' morale during a period of national crisis. An important question addressed in this chapter is whether 'total war' and the ensuing national crisis created the conditions in which working people were more willing to conform to government-defined 'acceptable' modes of citizenry and leisure.

Notes

1 W. Boyd, *The Challenge of Leisure* (London, New Education Fellowship, 1936), p. 167; E. B. Castle, A. K. C. Ottaway and W. T. R. Rawson (eds), *The Coming of Leisure. The Problem in England* (London, New Education Fellowship, 1935).

2 P. Bailey, *Leisure and Class in Victorian England. Rational Recreation and the Contest for Control 1830–1885* (London, Methuen, 1978), ch. 5.

3 S. G. Jones, *Sport, Politics and the Working Class. Organised Labour and Sport in Inter-War Britain* (Manchester, Manchester University Press, 1992). Sir Ernest Simon, a Manchester businessman, provides a good example of a social reformer who feared that working people were vulnerable to the mass appeal of fascism; see A. Olechnowicz, 'Civic leadership and education for democracy: The Simons and the Wythenshawe estate', *Contemporary British History*, 14 (2000), 3.

4 For a general history of Coventry, see K. Richardson, *Twentieth Century Coventry* (Bungay, Chaucer Press, 1972); for a more thematic account, see B. Lancaster and T. Mason (eds), *Life and Labour in a 20th Century City. The Experience of Coventry* (Coventry, Cryfield Press, 1986).

5 D. Thoms and T. Donnelly, *The Coventry Motor Industry. Birth to Renaissance* (Aldershot, Ashgate, 2000), p. 18.

6 B. J. Beaven, 'The growth and significance of the Coventry car component industry, 1895–1939', Ph.D. dissertation, De Montfort University, 1994, p. 81.

7 *The Times*, 17 January 1916.

8 J. Crump, 'Recreation in Coventry between the wars', in Lancaster and Mason (eds), *Life and Labour in a 20th Century City*, p. 261.

9 J. B. Priestley, *An English Journey* (1933; Harmondsworth, Penguin, 1977), p. 71.

10 Thoms and Donnelly, *The Coventry Motor Industry*, p. 3.

11 P. J. Waller, *Town, City and Nation. England 1850–1914* (Oxford, Clarendon Press, 1983), pp. 3–4.

12 B. Lancaster, 'Who's a real Coventry kid? Migration into twentieth century Coventry', in Lancaster and Mason (eds), *Life and Labour in a 20th Century City*, pp. 61, 67.

13 A. Davies, *Leisure, Gender and Poverty. Working-Class Culture in Salford and Manchester, 1900–1939* (Buckingham, Open University Press, 1992), p. ix.

14 H. Meller, *Leisure and the Changing City, 1870–1914* (London, Routledge & Kegan Paul, 1976); R. A. Evans, 'The university and the city. The educational work of Toynbee Hall', *History of Education*, 11 (1982); A. Vincent and R.

Plant, *Philosophy, Politics and Citizenship. The Life and Thought of the British Idealists* (Oxford, Blackwell, 1984); H. Meller, 'Urban renewal and citizenship: The quality of life in British cities, 1890–1990', *Urban History*, 22 (1995); T. Thomas, 'Representation of the Manchester working class in fiction, 1850–1900', in A. J. Kidd and K. W. Roberts (eds), *City, Class and Culture. Studies of Social Policy and Cultural Reproduction in Victorian Manchester* (Manchester, Manchester University Press, 1985).

15 B. Beaven, 'Shop floor culture in the Coventry motor industry, *c.* 1896–1920', in D. Thoms, L. Holden and T. Claydon (eds), *The Motor Car and Popular Culture in the 20th Century* (Aldershot, Ashgate, 1998), p. 197.

16 E. J. Hobsbawm, 'The making of the working class 1870–1914', in E. J. Hobsbawm, *Worlds of Labour. Further Studies in the History of Labour* (London, Weidenfeld & Nicolson, 1984). Hobsbawm's thesis was later revised and defended by M. Savage and A. Miles, *The Remaking of the British Working Class, 1840–1940* (London, Routledge, 1994), and N. Kirk, *Change, Continuity and Class. Labour in British Society, 1850–1920* (Manchester, Manchester University Press, 1998).

17 G. Stedman Jones, 'Working class culture and working class politics in London 1870–1900: Notes on the remaking of a working class', *Journal of Social History*, 7 (1975); P. Johnson, 'Conspicuous consumption and working-class culture in late Victorian and Edwardian Britain'', *Transactions of the Royal Historical Society*, 38 (1988); C. Waters, *British Socialists and the Politics of Popular Culture, 1884–1914* (Manchester, Manchester University Press, 1990). These competing models of working-class culture were reflected in histories that focused entirely on the nature of leisure. See the seminal work of P. Bailey, *Leisure and Class in Victorian England. Rational Recreation and the Contest for Control 1830–1885* (London, Methuen, 1978), and H. Cunningham, *Leisure in the Industrial Revolution, 1780–1880* (London, Croom Helm, 1980).

18 Davies, *Leisure, Gender and Poverty*, p. 2.

19 Davies, *Leisure, Gender and Poverty*, p. 171.

20 A. Davies and S. Fielding (eds), *Workers' Worlds. Cultures and Communities in Manchester and Salford, 1880–1939* (Manchester, Manchester University Press, 1992), p. 10.

21 Davies and Fielding (eds), *Workers' Worlds*; S. Fielding, *Class and Ethnicity. Irish Catholics in England 1880–1939* (Buckingham, Open University Press, 1993); D. Fowler, *The First Teenagers. The Lifestyle of Young Wage Earners in Interwar Britain* (London, Woburn Press, 1995) T. Griffiths, *The Lancashire Working Classes, c. 1880–1930* (Oxford, Clarendon Press, 2001); C. Langhamer, *Women's Leisure in England, 1920–1960* (Manchester, Manchester University Press, 2000).

22 P. Bailey, 'The politics and poetics of modern British leisure', *Rethinking History*, 3 (1999), 159.

23 M. Abendstern, 'Expression and control: A study of working-class leisure and gender, 1918–39. A case study of Rochdale using oral history methods', Ph.D. thesis, University of Essex, 1986, p. 28; see also Kirk, *Change, Continuity and Class*, p. 223.

24 L. Senelick, 'Politics as entertainment: Victorian music-hall songs', *Victorian Studies*, 19 (1974); J. Clarke, C. Critcher and R. Johnson (eds), *Working Class Culture. Studies in History and Theory* (London, Hutchinson, 1979); R. Gray, 'Bourgeois hegemony in Victorian Britain', in T. Bennett et al. (eds), *Culture, Ideology and Social Process* (London, Batsford, 1981); B. Waites, T. Bennett and G. Martin (eds), *Popular Culture. Past and Present* (Beckenham, Croom Helm, 1981).

25 A. August, 'A culture of consolation? Re-thinking politics in working-class London, 1870–1914', *Institute of Historical Research*, 74 (2002), 200.

26 August, 'A culture of consolation?', 218.

27 W. Picht, *Toynbee Hall and the English Settlement Movement* (London, G. Bell & Sons, 1914); J. A. R. Pimlott, *Toynbee Hall. Fifty Years of Progress* (London, Dent, 1935); G. Stedman Jones, *Outcast London* (Oxford, Oxford University Press, 1971); A. Briggs and A. Macartney, *Toynbee Hall. The First Hundred Years* (London, Routledge, 1984); S. Meacham, *Toynbee Hall and Social Reform 1880–1914. The Search for Community* (New Haven, Yale University Press, 1987); J. Davis, 'Slums and the vote 1867–90' *Historical Research*, 64:155 (1991); S. Pennybacker, *A Vision for London, 1889–1914. Labour, Everyday Life and the LCC Experiment* (London, Routledge, 1995). For a wider perspective on educational settlements, see M. Freeman, '"No finer school than a Settlement": The development of the Educational Settlement Movement', *History of Education*, 31:3 (2002); R. J. Morris, 'The middle class and British towns and cities of the industrial revolution, 1780–1870', in D. Fraser and A. Sutcliffe (eds), *The Pursuit of Urban History* (London, Edward Arnold, 1983), p. 303; S. Gunn, 'The "failure" of the Victorian middle class: A critique', in J. Wolff and J. Seed (eds), *The Culture of Capital, Art Power and the Nineteenth Century Middle Class* (Manchester, Manchester University Press, 1988); see also H. Meller, *Leisure and the Changing City, 1870–1914* (London, Routledge & Kegan Paul, 1976); M. Hewitt, *The Emergence of Stability in the Industrial City. Manchester 1832–67* (Aldershot, Scolar Press, 1996); A. J. Kidd and K. W. Roberts (eds), *City, Class and Cultures. Studies of Cultural Production and Social Policy in Manchester* (Manchester, Manchester University Press, 1985).

28 A. Croll, 'Street disorder, surveillance and shame: Regulating behaviour in the public spaces of the late Victorian town', *Social History*, 24 (1999), 268; A. Croll, *Civilizing the Urban. Popular Culture and Public Space in Merthyr c. 1870–1914* (Cardiff, University of Wales Press, 2000).

29 C. Otter, 'Making liberalism durable: Vision and civility in the late Victorian city', *Social History*, 27:1 (2002), 2–3.

30 R. Weight and A. Beach (eds), *The Right to Belong. Citizenship and National Identity in Britain 1930–1960* (London, I. B. Tauris, 1998); L. Black et al., *Consensus or Coercion? The State, the People and Social Cohesion in Post-War Britain* (Cheltenham, New Clarion Press, 2001).

31 D. Morgan and M. Evans, *The Battle for Britain. Citizenship and Ideology in the Second World War* (London, Routledge, 1993); G. Field, 'Social patriotism and

the British working class: Appearance and disappearance of a tradition', *International Labor and Working-Class History*, 42 (1992); S. O. Rose, 'Sex, citizenship and the nation in World War II Britain', *American Historical Review*, October 1998.

32 For classic definitions of citizenship, see A. C. Pigou, *Memorials of Alfred Marshall* (1925; New York, Augustus Kelley, 1966); T. H. Marshall, *Class, Citizenship and Social Development. Essays* (Garden City NY, Doubleday, 1964). For useful analyses of changing notions of citizenship and community, see: Vincent and Plant, *Philosophy, Politics and Citizenship*; D. Gilbert, 'Community and municipalism: Collective identity in late Victorian and Edwardian mining towns', *Journal of Historical Geography*, 17:3 (1991), 262; R. Pearson, 'Knowing one's place: Perceptions of community in the industrial suburbs of Leeds, 1790–1890', *Journal of Social History*, 27:2 (1993), 236; Field, 'Social patriotism and the British working class', 30; H. Meller, 'Urban renewal and citizenship'; Rose, 'Sex, citizenship and the nation in World War II Britain', 1168.

33 T. H. Marshall, *Citizenship and Social Class* (Cambridge, Cambridge University Press, 1950). For a discussion of social citizenship in a contemporary setting, see Black et al., *Consensus or Coercion?*, p. 6.

34 B. Beaven and J. Griffiths, 'Urban elites, socialists and notions of citizenship in an industrial boomtown: Coventry *c.* 1870–1914', *Labour History Review*, 69:1 (2004), 300.

35 H. Meller (ed.), *The Ideal City* (Leicester, Leicester University Press, 1979), p. 58.

36 Quoted in S. Joyce, 'Castles in the air: The People's Palace, cultural reformism, and the East End working class', *Victorian Studies*, 39 (1996), 526.

37 Weight and Beach (eds), *The Right to Belong*, pp. 1–19.

38 J. McG. Davies, 'A twentieth century paternalist: Alfred Herbert and the skilled Coventry workman', in Lancaster and Mason (eds), *Life and Labour in a 20th Century City*.

39 S. Jones, *Sport, Politics and the Working Class. Organised Labour and Sport in Inter-War Britain* (Manchester, Manchester University Press, 1992), p. 62.

40 Morgan and Evans, *The Battle for Britain*, p. 23.

41 B. Beaven and J. Griffiths, 'The blitz, civilian morale and the city: Mass-Observation and working-class culture in Britain, 1940–1', *Urban History*, 26 (1999).

42 Recently Annette Kuhn has highlighted the 'enjoyment factor' of the cinema; see A. Kuhn, *An Everyday Magic. Cinema and Cultural Memory* (London, I. B. Tauris, 2002), p. 147.

43 For Chartism and the challenge to the employers' right to govern the workplace, see C. Behagg, *Politics and Production in the Early Nineteenth Century* (London, Routledge, 1990).

Rational recreation and the creation of the model citizen, c. 1850–1914

The period 1850–1914 was an age in which working-class males benefited from an unprecedented diversity in leisure opportunities, from the traditional 'spit and sawdust' public house to the new and lavish music hall that promised excitement and escapism at a modest price. In short, this was the era which witnessed the first of Britain's mass 'pleasure seekers'. Moreover, the combination of trade-union agitation, half-day holiday movements and government legislation in the 1860s and 1870s reduced working hours and established prescribed breaks from work during the week. It is during this period that the recognisable 'working week' emerged in many industries and trades, with the Saturday half-holiday gradually replacing the tradition of 'Saint Monday'.[1] The Bank Holiday Act of 1871 was also an attempt to impose greater regulation, designed to encourage employees to observe a legitimate day off work, as opposed to the rather haphazard traditional holidays associated with Wake Weeks in the summer.[2] With the emergence of regularised breaks from work, it became inevitable that working-class recreation would attract the interest of social reformers and philanthropists. Accordingly, during the mid-nineteenth century, clubs, societies and leisure activities were founded by urban and rural elites anxious to provide civilising recreation for the masses. Although this was not a coherent or organised movement, schemes such as these became known collectively as rational recreation. This chapter will investigate the impact that rational recreation had upon working-males' leisure, during a period in which there was a heightened awareness of citizenship with the dawning of a newly democratic age. Initially, enthusiasts of rational recreation set about attracting working-class males into bourgeois establishments to teach them, through a mixture of instruction and amusement, the political and economic laws and certainties of the day. Clearly, a 'properly' educated artisan would be first to qualify for the vote from the disenfranchised multitude. It will be argued, however, that rational recreation underwent a major shift in emphasis after 1870, with moral reformers becoming less confident that their own prized civilised culture would survive the onslaught of modernity. This modernity came in the guise of rapidly growing cities, rising poverty and expansion of 'low' forms of leisure. The intelligent artisan was becoming lost beneath the degenerate semi-skilled 'pleasure seekers' that characterised the era. Moral reformers from across the political spectrum began to pursue more aggressive and coercive forms of rational recreation, with leisure provision and notions of citizenship reflecting a more anxious and insecure climate in British society.

The rational recreationalists' desire to create the model citizen through the reformation of working-class leisure habits stemmed from a number of factors. Male leisure had certainly been most visible to social observers and was often deemed the more threatening to the social order, particularly when public houses and social events became a means of disseminating radical politics during the first half of the nineteenth century.[3] Moreover, it was no coincidence that programmes of rational recreation, which stressed instruction and education, were at their most intense prior to the enfranchisement of the artisanal class of working men in 1867. In the same year, the underlying assumptions of many rational recreation schemes were encapsulated in a *Times* editorial:

> Who would not be the English working man? He is the spoilt child of the great British family. Though very well able to take care of himself, and with strong notions of independence, we are all striving to take him by the hand and do him some good or other. We build institutions for him, we present him with books, pictures and models, we read to him and preach to him, we teach him to make societies, we are bringing the franchise to his door and laying it on his table if he will but rise from his chair and take it.[4]

The Times, thus, portrayed the working-class male as the child of the British family, who, after his flirtation with irrational and dangerous Chartist ideas, was finally maturing, until, by the 1860s, he was in a position to accept the friendly hand of his social superiors. The provision of rational recreation, then, was designed to eliminate the last vestiges of a brutal culture and recast the working man as an active citizen participating in an embryonic pluralist state.

The period 1850–70 witnessed a steady growth of literature devoted to the reformation of male working-class leisure which reflected this desire. Female exclusion from this new democratic process ensured that interest in their out-of-work activities was minimal. For example, when Walter Besant, the social observer and novelist, wrote a long and detailed study on British leisure time, his only comment on female leisure was that he had 'never been able to find out anything at all concerning their amusements'.[5] Generally, advice on women's out-of-work activities was largely confined to a role as the domestic linchpin of family life.[6] Social reformers also believed that many working-class women were already exposed to civilising influences through domestic service and their daily contact with cultural values of the upper classes, and that this would eventually filter down into working-class home life.[7] However, even women's domestic commitments were not to disrupt working-class male leisure patterns. In 1860, one account of working-class leisure described the difficulties that working men could experience when their wives undertook the weekly 'cleaning and swilling of the house and children'. J. Erskine Clarke, a vicar in Derby, noted that 'as a general rule, many causes combine to make the poor man's house, on Saturday evening, an especially noisy and uncomfortable place – and one where the master, if he has by chance a taste for reading the newspaper or a book, would find himself very much in the way of what was going on.'[8] This 'uncomfortable' atmosphere could be avoided if women undertook the housework on a more convenient day that would allow the husband to enjoy his leisure time in the confines of his house and avoid the dangers of the taproom. The message was clear, women's leisure was not largely an issue for the rational recreationists. Only when women's out-of-work activities affected either the domestic sphere or men's leisure time did female recreation merit attention.

The origins of rational recreation lay in the instruction and improvement societies that were formed as an antidote to the emergence of working-class political agitation during the 1830s and 1840s.[9] Generally, the guiding principle of these societies was to instruct, rather than entertain, the more 'respectable' working class in religious and secular ideas. By the 1840s most towns and cities possessed societies that were designed to 'improve' the working class. However, organisations such as the Useful Knowledge Society, the Mechanics Institute, and the Mutual Improvement

Society all shared an unwelcome feature: a near total rejection by both artisans and the rest of the working community. Despite being designed for artisan instruction, the societies' survival into the second half of the century owed most to the continued patronage of middle-class members. This unpopularity among working-class males can be explained by the organisers' insistence that 'entertainment' was kept to a minimum and that teaching and discussion should be monitored along strict guidelines. For example, the Mechanics Institute in Coventry was established in 1828 and formed to teach the city's artisan weavers a variety of 'safe' natural sciences, banning the discussion of politics, religion and plays and novels deemed too controversial.[10] Seven years later, the Useful Knowledge Society was formed to 'help import religious and useful knowledge to the industrious classes', and, noting the distinct failure of the Mechanics Institute to reach the working class, adopted a more proactive approach to securing membership. Members of the Useful Knowledge Society visited artisans in their local factories in a recruitment drive which, once again, failed with the chairman candidly declaring that the strategy 'did not succeed to any extent'.[11] By 1855 the Mechanics Institute and the Useful Knowledge Society had reluctantly merged to become the Coventry Institute, dropping their founding aim of educating the artisans and instead concentrated on securing membership from the ranks of the middle class.[12] The failure of social reformers and philanthropists to penetrate a rather impervious working-class culture was not unique to the Midlands. Bailey's analysis of Bolton and, more recently, August's study of London during this period have revealed similar patterns of failure.[13] However, the 1860s marked a turning point in the fortunes for the organisers of rational recreation – remarkably, given the poor reception of earlier forms, events began to attract large working-class audiences. Some historians have interpreted the working class's patronage of rational recreation as a sign of their increasing adoption of 'respectable' or bourgeois values.[14] However, when we take a closer look at the type of entertainment on offer in the 1860s, it is clear that it was the organisers rather than the audiences who had reassessed their whole approach to rational recreation.

Rational recreation: towards amusement, 1850–70

The failure of Chartism and the decline in the associated industrial unrest saw the 1850s–1860s emerge as a relatively stable political and economic period, a context which gave the drive to improve popular leisure patterns added impetus. Since, in this 'progressive age', the moral reformers and philanthropists had successfully taught the working man the futility of radical Chartist politics, it was now necessary to turn attention to his leisure time. The failure of educational clubs that offered a scientific curriculum led philanthropists to explore 'lighter' forms of recreation that would ultimately pave the way for a greater understanding between the classes. In most towns and cities, philanthropists founded small clubs and societies which sprinkled dry lectures with a little amusement such as music, singing or coffee soirées. Although it is difficult to gauge the success of these small ventures, the surviving evidence suggests that the events were far from a meeting of minds and manners. In one event in London, local manufacturers and dignitaries organised for working men an evening of music and readings from the 'great poets'. Crucially for the working-class men, however, the evening also involved a slap up meal. The social discord and shared embarrassment between the organisers and their guests was captured by a local newspaper. The reporter noted that the working men came to the party en masse, 'looking in at the door, and grinning and nudging each other as though they thought all along that it would be a "lark" and that now they were sure of it'. They were seated on separate tables from the rest of the visitors and consumed their food in their own fashion, oblivious to the other party guests:

> They ate silently, with downcast eyes, and their throats at ease in their voluminous wrappings. The only time when they evinced any emotion was when the musicians struck on an uncommonly lively key, and then they looked up with sudden pleasure in their eyes and in the act apparently bolted half a slice without mastication.[15]

Although the reporter regarded the event as a success, as 'there had not been a single fight among them', he had reservations about the attempt to import an element of instruction into the proceedings. After the tea, a number of 'gentlemen' took the platform to recite literature, a segment of the evening which was met with indifference from the workers.[16] The reporter's account of the event reinforces the notion that, despite attending a rational recreation event, the invited guests had no wish to interact or learn from their 'social superiors'.

A form of rational recreation which proved extremely popular throughout Britain and attracted working-class audiences in their thousands were Penny

Readings. According to Rose, Penny Readings emerged in the Midlands when Samuel Taylor, the secretary of Hanley's Mechanics Institute, began in 1854 to read aloud extracts of *The Times* in the market square. Taylor found that by adding literary and musical entertainment to his programme he could boost attendances and charge one penny admission. The scheme proved an outstanding success, as between October 1857 and April 1858 nine Staffordshire towns were hosting Penny Readings, attracting audiences of between 60,000 and 70,000 in a district population of 100,000.[17] Penny Readings proved equally popular elsewhere. In Derby it was deemed the most successful organised philanthropic venture, while the Coventry Penny Readings were so popular that a local newspaper described them as the most 'striking feature of social history of the city'.[18] However, a simple head count of those attending Readings or an investigation of the readings recited would not be an adequate measure of whether the organisers had at last found a successful formula of amusement and instruction. The critical issue which determined whether the organisers achieved their aims of elevating a 'brutal culture' was the extent to which the values and social mores that ran through the entertainment were received, understood and adopted by the working-class audience. Thus, in the case of the Penny Readings, the three-way interaction between the organisers, the working-class audience and the performers was of paramount importance.

An observer well placed to gauge the success of the Penny Reading movement was Thomas Wright, a journeyman engineer. Wright, who was compelled to travel due to his profession, was in a unique position of visiting a large number of readings that were staged in the principal manufacturing towns in England. Wright noted:

> I am glad to find that they [Penny Readings] are exceedingly popular all over the country ... The many thousands of working men and boys who frequent them give unmistakable evidence of the appreciation of them; and from this consideration, I know, from constantly mingling with the working men of densely populated manufacturing towns, that the penny readings are immensely popular with them.[19]

Invariably, the readings would be organised by a group of philanthropists, sometimes in connection with a working-men's association, and held at a local corn exchange or theatre. Initially, these events were targeted at males, though usually the organisers relented and by the end of the first series most Penny Readings admitted women. The Readings proved a great attraction as they were organised around recognisable working-class leisure traditions. For example, Wright noted that Readings were staged either on Monday or Saturday nights and organisers were 'careful to notify in their bills that there are "No Reserved Seats"'. In contrast to the theatre and opera house, this marked out the Penny Readings as a working-class form of entertainment which followed the traditional entrance procedures of the Penny Gaff or Singing Saloon. This was confirmed by Wright's experience of actually trying to enter the hall, as he observed that, although the hall seated 1,500, 'there were more than that number waiting outside'. Wright joined the mêlée, which involved a good deal of pushing, shoving and elbowing; this he did quite effectively, as he successfully found a seat, leaving the more 'timid' members of the original crowd outside. Once inside, Wright observed the general conduct of the audience and noted that traditional forms of audience response, usually found in the Singing Saloons and the Penny Gaffs, survived in this new form of rational recreation. Although the Penny Reading programme forbade the audiences' use of the encore, Wright observed that it was a common practice among the working-class audience, as was 'coughing' or 'stamping' down an unpopular act. There is also evidence that readings were attended by male youths out to impress their male and female friends. Wright complained that young swells go to readings 'in the hope of impressing the audience with the idea that it is simply for a lark that they come there[;] they bawl out all kinds of senseless slang, under the impression that they are wittily "chaffing" the performers'.[20]

Wright's observations demonstrate that significant traits of traditional working-class behaviour continued to be exercised within an event organised by middle-class philanthropists. Indeed, the continuation of these behavioural traits casts doubts on the assumption that popular rational recreational events successfully diffused the organiser's 'civilised' values to an expectant public. Much depended on the readings' organisers and the content of the entertainment offered. In Derby, although initiated by middle-class philanthropists, the Penny Readings were organised in conjunction with the local Working Men's Association. Working men had considerable autonomy over the proceedings since they acted as doorkeepers and seem to have had some influence over the type of entertainment on offer. Readings were kept to a minimum while music and acts such as ventriloquism and conjuring formed the night's staple entertainment. In effect, although these were amateur performers, the organisers were staging acts that would not have been out of place in the Penny Gaffs, a point not lost on some critics of the series. Moreover, the Penny Readings had also failed in their original aim in keeping working men from the 'pot-house', starting sufficiently early for the audience to enjoy a post-performance drink at a nearby public house. The Derby case illustrates how some of the working-class organisers were able to include entertainment that had a resonance for the working class, a clear departure from the philanthropists' original aim of 'providing musical and literary entertainment of a high order of merit'.[21]

In areas, such as Coventry, where rational recreationalists failed to include working-class involvement in the organisation of Penny Readings, the event sometimes evolved into a contestation over the control of the entertainment on offer. The Readings were organised in the winter of 1862 by a group of middle-class benefactors that included the local MP, clergymen and schoolmasters. Significantly, although they operated under the title 'The Coventry Working Men's Club', unlike their Derby predecessors, working-class men were not given any role in the management of the club or the readings. At first the Readings were held in a small civic hall and consisted of approximately fifteen recitations of 'higher literary works', attracting about a hundred working-class people.[22] However, in a bid to attract a larger working-class audience, musical entertainment was introduced, a move which split the entertainment committee. The slight alteration proved so popular that the Readings were moved to the larger Corn Exchange and, by the end of the first series, the event attracted full houses of over 2,000 people.[23] Critics of the Readings focused their attention on the crowd's 'disgraceful' behaviour, demanding that the management committee forbid the audience's use of encores and 'ironical clapping'. Observers at the Readings claimed that the audience were 'inflicting their vulgar tastes' on the proceedings, dragging 'all down to their ignorant level'.[24] During the third series of Readings a former committee member declared that the organisers must improve the literary and musical works on offer. However, he added:

> I am quite aware that to carry this out the managers must first get the command of their own hall. Now they are servants of the mob … The chairman at present is a mere sign post – an illumination for the programme instead of being there to direct the meeting and to keep order – the order arranged by the committee … If he finds it impossible to keep order, let him at once dissolve the meeting and leave the chair, and let the Police clear the room. When this has been done once, the committee will for the future have, what they ought to have, the command of their own hall.[25]

On the completion of the third season of Penny Readings, even the most enthusiastic 'rational recreationalist' had been persuaded to abandon the venture. The evolution of the Coventry Penny Readings from the recitation of 'high' literature to music and comic entertainment highlights the ability of the audience to manipulate the proceedings set by their 'social superiors'. In addition, this contestation for control did not take place in a typical working-class institution such as the public house, but within the Coventry Corn Exchange, a building that symbolised middle-class authority and civic responsibility. In effect, within the heart of Coventry's 'civilised' enclave, the organisers had succeeded in creating a Frankenstein's monster that displayed the very elements of working-class culture they had been eager to eradicate.

By the early twentieth century, Penny Readings had been sanitised and resembled a form of entertainment that mid-nineteenth-century philanthropists would surely have approved of. William Woodruff recalled his Lancashire childhood experiences in one of the few Penny readings that struggled on after the First World War:

> When money was short we went to the 'penny readings', where we sat on a hard bench in a cold warehouse. The reader, Mr Peck, was a grey haired, gaunt-faced elderly gentleman who wore a threadbare suit and a winged collar and whose teeth kept slipping. He first told us in his own words what the story was about, and then filled in by reading from the text. I only recall the hard seat and the cold.[26]

The few Penny Readings that limped into the twentieth century, then, still retained their Victorian moralising essence and had become outdated, unpopular and a refuge for the poor who were unable regularly to afford commercial entertainment.

Penny Readings, in their purest form, represented the first attempt to shift from dry instruction into a form of recreation which would provide sufficient amusement to attract working men from the public house. The Coventry Penny Readings' deviation from literature to music reflected a national trend among rational recreationalists who, by the mid 1860s, recognised that they faced new competition from the increasingly popular music hall circuit.[27] Surveying popular amusement in the 1870s, Florence Marshall noted that there had been a marked rise in 'People's Concerts' during the winter months in Britain. In the first four months of 1879, Marshall noted that sixty-six concerts were given in the poorest areas of

London alone, while in Birmingham the local musical association gave a series of concerts attracting 3,000 people on each occasion.[28] In contrast to earlier social reformers who excluded music from 'rational' leisure on the grounds that it was not the purest form of recreation, philanthropists of the late 1860s regarded cultivated music as a 'softening' and 'elevating' form of recreation.[29] In a typical analogy, one middle-class organiser of a series of Penny Entertainments in the Midlands claimed that 'the very beasts of the forest would sit entranced when music's gentle strains were heard'.[30] The belief that music could both tame and distract the working class from their traditional leisure patterns continued into the 1870s. Indeed, as late as 1880 Marshall still held out hope that 'People's Concerts' would replace the entertainment that was on offer elsewhere, for 'when a working-man sings his songs or plays his tunes to his companions in the public house, no doubt the situation is fraught with some peril to say nothing of the temptation to undue vanity of the performer!'[31] Despite Marshall's enthusiastic call for popular concerts, they reached their high-water mark in the late 1860s and early 1870s and acted as a transitional phase in mass entertainment between the Penny Reading movement and the music hall. By the late 1870s, the music hall was accessible to most working-class people and was firmly embedded in their culture.[32] Mass entertainment was left to the commercial sector, which had none of the dilemmas over content and form that wracked the philanthropic conscience.

Clearly, the attempt to provide rational recreation on a mass scale had failed. However, although philanthropists shied away from staging mass entertainment, recreational clubs for working men were formed throughout the 1860s. The loose array of clubs were given some direction after the founding of the Club and Institute Union (CIU) in 1862, which set about encouraging, supervising and coordinating Working Men's Clubs across the country.[33] Under Henry Solly, a middle-class Unitarian minister who had developed a sympathy with the 'moral force' dimension of Chartist politics in the 1830s and 1840s, the CIU grew rapidly. In 1862 there were 23 affiliated clubs, a figure that had increased to 245 by 1883. Despite the swift formation of clubs, change was initially fairly slow due to an alcohol ban imposed by the early patrons, which was eventually lifted in the 1870s. The introduction of alcohol into clubs confirmed the CIU as the most successful and rapidly expanding working-class club movement as the number of clubs had increased to 550 in 1883 and had topped the 1,000 mark by 1904.[34] Solly placed amusement at the centre of club activities in the belief that within a civilised environment working men would become attracted to the more elevating forms of leisure. Thus:

> what working men wanted was a place of intercourse and fellowship. If a working man heard a good lecture or concert, played a game of cricket or chess – thus passing a pleasant hour – the great possibility was he would make his home happy ... there was music – they were all aware of its elevating and refining influences. He believed the readings of Dickens, Shakespeare and other celebrated authors, would be very attractive and useful.[35]

The strategy of offering working men facilities for largely secular entertainment had certainly proved extremely successful by 1914. The uniform nature of 'club-life' in England by the beginning of the twentieth century has prompted a number of historians to consider the extent to which clubs were able, for the first time, to penetrate and influence working-class culture. Price has argued that it was no accident that it was the aristocrats, industrialists and clergymen who propagated the movement with the clear intent of 'trying to impose its ideology upon the working class'. Indeed, Price concludes that the clubs can be viewed as subtle agencies of social control, 'the largest and most successful of all the efforts which Victorian England set out to ensure an assimilated and acquiescent proletariat'.[36] However, the relatively progressive management of the clubs allowed working-class participation in the organisation and eventually management of clubs. In addition, by the mid-1870s a number of clubs were established by working men with 'no patronage', while others turned to self-governance and jettisoned their 'sluggish' gentlemen patrons. It was in this context that the alcohol ban was eventually lifted in the 1870s, which boosted membership considerably. Significantly, the funds raised by the bar allowed clubs to operate independently from the patronage of their social superiors who had been instrumental in founding the movement. For example, the local Working Men's Club of Maidstone calculated that the profit on beer was approximately 30 per cent, a sum double what they had to pay in rent. Moreover, Bailey has shown the intense debate within clubs on the prohibition of alcohol, and Solly's eventual concession demonstrated that the 'bourgeois patrons had come closer to an informed and committed tolerance of that culture than the great majority of their fellows, for they had after all been prepared to modify social patterns to accommodate behaviour that others tried simply to eradicate'.[37]

The working-class committees that had wrestled control of their clubs from the grip of their middle-class patrons only heightened concern among social reformers that their efforts in civilising the urban poor were becoming increasingly futile. Alongside attempts by philanthropists to provide alternative forms of leisure, more aggressive versions of rational recreation emerged which attempted to confront working-class males about their leisure activities in their own environment. Simultaneously, concerns regarding the 'degeneration' of the urban working class were addressed by local councils through the provision of recreational facilities that would create the model working-class citizen for the twentieth century.

Social intervention and rational recreation: the working class and the city, 1870–1914

The Times's optimistic 1867 editorial which predicted that the working man would, with middle-class guidance, mature into a 'civilised' member of the community lay in ruins by the late 1880s. The rapid growth of the city was perceived as the great stumbling block for middle-class initiatives designed to improve popular leisure patterns. What use was the hand of civilised friendship if the working class could not be found within the dark and degenerate 'rabbit warrens' of the modern city? *The Times*, only ten years after the self-confident predictions about the future of the British work-ing-man in a socially cohesive society, began to question whether the urban working class could ever be left to its own devices. The problem was, in great measure, to do with 'modern English society itself' and the fact that towns were 'the natural receptacle of everything that is discontented or disorderly, or that wishes, from what ever reason to hide itself'. In 1877, *The Times*'s editor was clearly overwhelmed by these modern developments and was at a loss to explain how a city, which 'by virtue of its name' was the 'germ of civilization', should have fostered conditions which were 'the most opposite of all those of civilized life'. In a striking contrast with the tone and language of the 1867 editorial, *The Times* concluded that,

> as long as these frightful dens exist in which a large part of our city popu-
> lation is now crowded we shall go on breeding a new criminal population
> every year. It is a mere physical necessity. As long as children are born and
> brought up in human rabbit-warrens, they will grow up into a kind of human
> vermin. We may catch a few of them and put them in cages, moral or legal;
> but the mass of them will remain in their savage condition.[38]

The Times reflected a growing pessimism in British society, which was ag-gravated by both domestic and foreign affairs during this period. Alongside a growing anxiety about the decline of Britain's industrial strength and apprehensions regarding the political role of the working class, intellectuals began to demand the abandonment of the laissez-faire policies on poverty, housing and urban living.[39] The social elites' attitude to leisure was not immune from the new mood for active social intervention. Clearly providing rational alternatives was not enough; some form of intervention into working-class male leisure had become desirable.

From the late 1870s the urban crisis prompted social reformers to focus on the location and nature of working-class communities themselves by establishing rational recreational initiatives within the heart of 'slum dwelling' neighbourhoods. No longer was it tenable to wait until curious, usually skilled, working-class males visited the events staged in the bourgeois spheres of the Corn Exchange, the Mechanics Institute and (initially) the Working Men's Club. Civilised culture had to be delivered to working-class districts. It is at this point that the rational recreation movement began to develop along two distinct lines, which ran concurrently into the twentieth century. The first strand comprised philanthropists, usually unattached to any formal organisation, keen to expose the working class to the civilising qualities of high culture through the opening of museums and exhibitions in working-class districts. The second strand adopted an altogether more aggressive strategy of attempting to impose a civilised culture on the working class in a bid to neuter an indigenous culture that was perceived as degenerate and dangerous. This second strand was fed by the growing paranoia of the late-nineteenth-century city and the quest for national efficiency in the face of international competition.[40]

The moral panic surrounding the city in the late nineteenth century was symbolised by London's expanding East End. For many social observers, London's East End was a microcosm of the social problems endemic in modern society. Furthermore, this urban degeneration was taking place in the heart of the world's greatest empire. The startling pace of demographic change and urban development in the East End ensured that large homogeneous working-class suburbs developed, housing the mainly semi-skilled labourers who had migrated into the area. Many social observers from West London viewed the new developments in the East with a mixture of fascination and anxiety. The *Spectator* described the East End in 1906 as 'isolated, individual, alien in colour and temperament, in London, and yet, not except economically and politically, of London'.[41] Perhaps, though, the most disturbing aspect for social observers was that working-class residents in these new districts were largely left leaderless as entrepreneurs began living at some distance from their businesses, caring little for the local civic development and generally shunning their social responsibilities. This perceived vacuum in social leadership prompted philanthropists to venture into the East End to establish colonies of high culture in a bid to stem the tide of degeneration. In 1880 Samuel Barnett, the parish vicar of Whitechapel and keen exponent of the civilising nature of the ideal city, began exhibiting art in school buildings that adjoined his church.[42] *The Times* noted that by dispersing civilised culture to the East End 'no greater contrast could well be imagined than that between the squalid streets, the dreary surroundings, and the dismal life of Whitechapel, and the walls of the school rooms in their new and unaccustomed splendour.' In addition, once the working-man had been introduced to these civilising works it was envisaged that he would, at some level, join the middle class in a shared appreciation of the paintings. It was hoped that the greater understanding of aesthetic beauty would eventually extend to the social relations between the classes. Thus *The Times* commented that the working class

> should see what a good picture is – and generally in these gatherings there are some kindly educated folk present who explain the pictures to willing groups of listeners – it is something that they should feel the emotions which a work of ISRAELS or BRETT will call up; it is something that in spite of our enormous social inequality they should see that the rich owners of pictures are ready enough to give a share in their pleasures to the poor.[43]

Exhibitions and museums set up in the heart of the East End did not, however, prove a success in attracting and influencing visitors. Walter Besant condemned Barnett's art exhibitions and similar ventures for providing little in the way of guidance and instruction in the interpretation of the arts for the working-class visitors. In 1884, Besant mused that attempts to encourage working men to visit libraries and museums had largely failed. Despite the fact that in London there was a ratio of half a million working-class people to every free library, Besant noted that 'one has yet heard no complaints of overcrowding', while the museums to the working class were 'cold and dumb'. Besant concluded that the working-class visitor understood little and took away with him nothing at all; 'those glass cases, those pictures, those big jugs, say no more to the crowd than a cuneiform of a Hittite inscription … it is to them [the working class] simply a collection of curious things which is sometimes changed'.[44] For Besant, the solution to the problem was to generate a more active learning environment that would integrate education and amusement facilitated through the construction of an institution in the heart of the East End. Besant's campaign for the construction of a People's Palace finally came to fruition in 1887.

The People's Palace of the East End was the archetypal philanthropic gesture to the urban poor of the late nineteenth century. This project represented the first and more dominant strand of thought among rational recreationists, which held that only through siting enlightening institutions within the heart of the urban sprawl could working-class culture be elevated. Although there was some dispute as to who actually devised the idea of creating a People's Palace in Whitechapel, the popular novels and articles on working-class leisure by Walter Besant were certainly influential in generating support for the venture. In common with many philanthropists, Besant consistently remarked that the working class lacked the opportunities and knowledge to 'play' since he did not recognise anything worthy in the working class's preferred leisure pursuits.[45] Consequently, for Besant, the working-class man did not possess the cultural education with which to appreciate the finer arts that were open to the public-school boy. Character-building sports like fencing, gymnastics and cricket mixed with an academic grounding in subjects such as history, philosophy and poetry had encouraged an appreciation of the development of civilisation and importantly instilled a discipline lacking in the working class. Thus the public-school boy

> learns to be obedient to law, order, and rule: he obeys, and expects to be obeyed ... And this discipline of self, much more useful than the discipline of books, the young workman knows not. Worse than this, and worst of all, not only is he unable to do any of these things, but he is ignorant of their uses and their pleasures, and has no desire to learn any of them, and does not suspect at all the possession of these accomplishments would multiply the joys of life.[46]

Significantly, like many middle-class commentators, Besant believed that this cultural discipline would only be adopted by the working class if they had a recognisable role model. For this he turned to the artisan worker who 'pursues knowledge for its own sake'. The leisure that Besant attributed to the artisan was temperate, individualistic and had horizons beyond the tightly packed housing and urban encroachment that made up the East End. Thus this largely mythical self-taught artisan would wander in the country lanes on a Sunday 'botanizing, collecting insects, moths and butterflies in the fields'.[47] However, to middle-class contemporaries, the gentle leisure pursuits of the artisans were, to some extent, a reflection of their experience in work. The work that this imagined artisan was engaged in was one which required education, skill and intelligence since it was a craft that would result in an individual and unique product. The work process was also supposed to have instilled discipline in the skilled worker. In other words, this was a form of work which brought discipline, contentment and fulfilment both in and outside the workplace.[48] This analysis was extended to the East End worker who was largely engaged in monotonous semi-skilled mass production, a work process which was thought to lead to unhealthy and irrational leisure pursuits.

The economic changes of the late nineteenth century had seen the decline of the artisan in the East End and, in their place, the influx of the uneducated semi-skilled worker.[49] Furthermore Besant, like many social commentators, perceived that the artisan's demise had engendered a leadership vacuum within the working-class community that local employers were reluctant to take up. Besant, along with Edmund Currie, the heir to a distillery fortune, was determined to fill this perceived vacuum and encourage the 'lowest' members of the working class to pursue rational recreation and learning through the creation of a 'People's Palace' situated in the heart of the East End.

Fundraising for the People's Palace began slowly and it was not until after the 1886 London riots that donations from wealthy employers met the £100,000 building costs.[50] The bourgeoisie's sudden willingness to donate large sums of money to East End causes provoked George Bernard Shaw to remark during the period of the Whitechapel murders that only direct threats of violence seemed to stir the middle-class conscience. 'The riot of 1886 brought in £78,000 and a People's Palace: it remains to be seen how much these murders may prove to be worth to the East-End in *panem et circenses*'.[51]

The People's Palace was finally opened in 1887 and boasted a concert hall, gymnasium, library, winter gardens, art gallery, theatre, dance hall and reading room. However, the lavish design with its mix of classical and gothic styles resembled the Victorian town halls that had come to symbolise middle-class power and authority in mid-Victorian Britain. Indeed, in providing leadership to the working class in the heart of the East End, the People's Palace resembled an East End manor house from which an urban squirearchy could teach among the poor. It is perhaps, then, of little surprise that the Palace failed to break down the social barriers and attract the 'slum-dwellers' of the East End. Despite keeping prices down to attract 'only the very poorest', the most regular users of the Palace were the lower middle class. The author Arthur Morrison had a unique insight into the running of the Palace as he worked as an administrator for the organisation between 1887 and 1890.[52] By the time Morrison resigned from the People's Palace it was in financial crisis and there was a serious question mark over whether the massive financial outlay had successfully 'reformed' any of the targeted social groups. This scepticism was captured in Morrison's novel *A Child of the Jago*, which satirises the attempts of West End philanthropists to 'elevate' their working-class neighbours through the creation of the 'East End Elevation Mission and Pansophical Institute'. Morrison described how, in celebrating the opening of a new wing at the Institute, the middle-class subscribers descended on the institute and were pleasantly surprised at how the rational entertainment on offer had transformed the degraded classes into respectable and neatly attired citizens. Drawing heavily upon his experience of the People's Palace, Morrison describes how, in fact, the recipients of this rational recreation were clerks, artisans, tradesmen and small shopkeepers and their families. Indeed, Morrison only identifies one working-class East Ender at the event, Dicky Perrott, a youth who slipped into the Institute unnoticed as it was his belief that 'celebrations at such large buildings were accompanied by the consumption, in the innermost recesses, of cake and tea'. While the dignitaries stood drinking tea and congratulating themselves on the virtues of rational recreation, it became clear that Perrott had taken more than a yearning for intellectual stimulus away from the Institute. In the midst of conversation the local bishop reached to his waistcoat for his watch and found 'there hung three inches of black ribbon, with a cut end. The Bishop looked blankly at the Elevators about him. Three streets off, Dicky Perrott, with his shut fist deep in his breeches pocket, and a gold watch in the fist, ran full drive for the Old Jago.'[53] This fictional account of the working class's uneasy relationship with a philanthropic institute reflected the missionaries' experience of working in the People's Palace. During the early events staged at the Palace, observers noticed that 'authentic' working-class men only attended specific performances of a light or comic character. When there were attempts to instil a serious lecture alongside the light entertainment, organisers discovered that the events attracted 'two distinct audiences each unappreciative of part of the programme'.[54] Eventually the comic and light entertainment was phased out of the programmes and with it went the working class's brief interest and involvement in the Palace. By the mid-1890s, the Palace had become less the institute of rational recreation envisaged by Besant and more a polytechnic with an emphasis on dry academic learning.[55]

The call for intervention into working-class leisure patterns did not fall on deaf ears.[56] Between 1880 and 1914 two organisations, the labour movement and the Salvation Army, made consistent assaults on popular leisure patterns. Although the labour movement and the Salvation Army had different objectives, they both sought to save the working class from the uncivilising influences of urban working-class leisure and used similar methods to 'convert' the degenerate. The socialists, who had once defended the less fortunate from an unjust economic system, now condemned the poor for their leisure excesses and moral negligence.[57] Moreover, Victor Bailey has shown that there were strong membership links between the organisations during the late nineteenth century, since founding socialist leaders, such as George Lansbury, were formerly Salvation Army members. In addition, during the 1880s both organisations united in opposition against the London authorities who had threatened to ban processions and open air meetings through fear of public disorder.[58] Both organisations also saw their message as life changing and sought to embark on missions into the urban sprawl to 'convert' and, in the case of the labour movement, 'make socialists'. Taking a strikingly similar approach to the Salvationists, socialists embraced their ideology as a way of life, for, in almost a spiritual sense, it was an experience that could only be appreciated after conversion.[59] The Salvation Army and socialists also shared an anti-urbanism which not only ran through William Booth's *Darkest England* (1890) but also found support in works by William Morris, *News from Nowhere* (1890), and Robert Blatchford, *Merrie England* (1894). Indeed, the arts-and-crafts movement, where wholesome work and leisure could be enjoyed in a rural setting, was one socialist solution to combat the uncivilising influences of the modern city.[60]

Not all socialists, of course, shared this rather prescriptive notion of what constituted a civilised culture amidst the rapid urbanisation.[61] However, this anti-urban streak in late-nineteenth-century socialism was most apparent in towns and cities that had experienced a rapid population growth which had not been matched by increases in housing and accommodation. These problems were acute in the Midlands and Southeast, where the 'new' industries had brought economic boom and an influx of workers during the late nineteenth century. The census data for 1891 and 1901 reveals that a significant number of workers from the traditional industrial northern areas migrated to the Midlands and South, with at least eleven key towns and cities in this region boasting an average 25 per cent increase in population in this period.[62]

Coventry, which had attracted a consistent stream of migrants taking work in the city's bicycle industry in the 1890s, was further boosted by the emergence of a viable motor industry during the early twentieth century. It was estimated that between 1901 and 1911, Coventry's population increased by 51 per cent due to immigration of workers primarily to work in either the bicycle or the motor industry.[63] With such a rapid increase in population, coupled with a housing crisis in the city, it was perhaps no surprise that an overtone of anti-urbanism figured strongly in Coventry's socialist movement. The small band of Coventry socialists, who had fervent religious and temperance links, were particularly concerned with the mass immigration of young semi-skilled workers who had little interest in the civic development of the city. These new bicycle workers contrasted with traditional perceptions of the skilled Coventry weaver of the first half of the nineteenth century, who had taken an active role in municipal affairs.[64] A major concern for the socialists was that the 'residuum' working class from the slum dwellings of London and Birmingham were being drawn to Coventry for work and replacing the politically conscious and respectable artisan weaver. The socialist response to the bicycle worker's cultural deprivation was to link pride in civic values and local patriotism with working-class self-improvement. For example, Roland Barrett, who launched the *Coventry Sentinel*, a short-lived socialist newspaper, was an avid teetotaller who could often be found 'preaching' on the fusion of socialism and temperance from a wagon in the centre of Coventry.[65] Similarly, Hugh Farren, another pioneer of the Coventry labour movement, was also secretary to the Coventry Temperance and Band of Hope Association, who would play music in the 'allies and courts' of Coventry to 'elevate and brighten the dreary, dull routine lives of the dwellers in these places'.[66] Another important influence in Coventry's socialist network was the Christian Socialist League led by the Rev. P. E. T Widdrington, whose St Peter's vicarage became the home of the city's Fabian society.

The religious and temperance dimension, then, gave Coventry socialism a reforming zeal which attempted to confront and transform a 'low' popular culture and encourage working-people to embrace an enlightened socialist vision of society. However, the attempt to instil a socialistic civic pride in the bicycle worker consistently failed. The newly formed Independent Labour Party in Coventry regularly made a loss due to low membership and poor attendances at public lantern lectures.[67] Speaking in 1912, Widdrington viewed the outlook as 'gloomy' since the masses 'see no way out of their misery and are not convinced that socialism is the remedy'. Widdrington laid the blame for the failure of socialism squarely at the feet of the bicycle worker, as the high wages being earned were 'too largely expended on crude and trivial satisfaction by the population with little experience to guide them to a wiser outlay'.[68] These sentiments were echoed in early socialist meetings when attempts were made to strengthen local support for the Labour Representative Committee. In 1903, James Walsh, a member of the Labour Representative Committee, complained that,

> if there was a place where men could be accused of being apathetic and indifferent to their own interests he thought Coventry claimed that description. He did not know of a place where men seemed so very dense, if they would excuse the term, or so very dull to their own absolute interest, as the average man in Coventry. This he attributed largely to the fact that many men living in Coventry had been drawn from other places because they had obtained employment here. For some reason or other there was a lack of local patriotism on the part of many of those which he had never been able to understand.

Walsh concluded by reminding Coventry workers that wherever a man might go for employment 'the duties of citizenship followed him'.[69] The Coventry socialists' disillusionment with the semi-skilled worker was shared by socialists at a national level. Writing in *The Clarion*, Leonard Hall complained that socialists had made the mistake of appealing 'exclusively to the manual labouring classes, who, stupefied by generations and lives of oppression turn a perfectly deaf ear'. Hall appealed for socialists to turn to the lower middle class and skilled working class for support since this section of the community were more open to new ideas.[70] The socialists' strategy of street processions and zealous preaching in working-class neighbourhoods sometimes provoked violent responses from working-class communities. For example, George Lansbury recalled how socialist activists in the East End of London were attacked in the 1880s, while Robert Noonan, writing under the pen name Robert Tressell, drawing from his own experiences, included an account of a socialist demonstration broken up by a working-class crowd in his Edwardian-era novel *The Ragged Trousered Philanthropists*.[71]

Attacks on socialists, however, were not as numerous as those on the Salvation Army in the 1880s. In 1882 alone, 643 Salvation Army members were attacked by protesting crowds.[72] The movement was founded in 1878, when William Booth renamed his Christian Mission a 'Salvation Army' and embarked on an aggressive soul-saving drive, which grew beyond its East End origins. Booth identified key slum areas across the country and appointed officers (clergy) to establish colonies with the help of local religious or temperance organisations. In tune with the intellectual climate of the time, Booth also likened the officers' forays into the dark and undiscovered cities to the imperial explorers in Africa, delivering the same civilising agenda and zeal to the degenerate masses.[73] Moreover, the whole terminology that Booth employed, from naming his clergy 'officers' and ordering them to 'invade hostile areas', evoked a militaristic tone not only to the Salvationists themselves but also to the subjects they were intent on saving.

The first organised response from a working-class neighbourhood was recorded by 'Captain' Payne of Whitechapel who reported that an opposition army had formed entitled the 'Unconverted Salvation Army', which organised open air meetings, processions and was designed to intimidate the Salvation Army.[74] Within two years organised groups calling themselves 'Skeleton Armies' emerged in opposition to the Salvation Army in cities and towns in England. Places as diverse as Sheffield, Coventry, Honiton and Worthing all experienced violent clashes between Salvationists and Skeleton Armies during 1880–82.[75] There is little doubt that Skeleton Armies were predominantly young males, described by one historian as 'pre-Edwardian Teddy Boys', recruited from the working-class areas that the Salvation Army had attempted to colonise.[76] A typical Skeleton Army response to the Salvation Army was captured by *The Times* in Weston-super-Mare in 1881. It was reported that

> The Salvation Army formed its procession and paraded the streets and places, accompanied by a disorderly and riotous mob of over 2,000 persons which seems to have assembled chiefly for the purpose of molesting the salvationists. The gathering gave rise to fighting and great disturbance, stone throwing and noise. For a time the police were overpowered, but on their being reinforced the mob dispersed.[77]

The Skeleton's success in raising a crowd of 2,000 and their rapid response to Salvationist processions indicated that there was considerable planning and organisation in their demonstrations. Furthermore, there was an element of ceremony incorporated as the Skeletons would often wear elaborate costumes and parody aspects of the Salvationist's movement. Indeed, Bailey has argued, 'through subscriptions from publicans, beersellers and other tradesmen, the Skeleton Armies became a well-organised secular imitation, and a unique instrument of social pressure.'[78]

Where there has been less agreement among historians is over the extent to which these disturbances represented a working-class resistance to attempts to undermine their traditional leisure patterns. Murdoch, for example, identifies a robust response to the Salvation Army from Liverpool's Irish working class, which, he argues, eventually led William Booth to pursue less confrontational strategies. In contrast to this combative interpretation of the disturbances, Victor Bailey has maintained that the analysis of disturbances in the southern counties demonstrated that both the Salvation Army and the Skeleton Army were not class-loyal organisations.[79] Indeed, the Salvationists had large numbers of working-class recruits, while Skeleton Armies often had the backing of sections of the petty bourgeoisie in the guise of publicans and breweries. However, in many respects, the working-class members of the Salvation Army no longer frequented working-class institutions as many of the traditional leisure patterns were renounced on conversion. Furthermore, the Skeleton Armies' alliance with the local publican was hardly unique, since through much of the nineteenth century the public-house landlord had played a key role in organising, sponsoring and accommodating working-class activities.[80] In addition, although undoubtedly there was some social integration, it does not detract from the contestation over urban space, which, due to its geographical location, took on class dimensions. The Salvation Army's assault on working-class leisure *within* working-class neighbourhoods was a significant departure from previous attempts at providing rational recreation for the masses in middle-class venues. This new development saw the Salvation Army attempt to colonise traditional working-class leisure by establishing their own sanitised versions such as teetotal 'free and easies' and providing religious lyrics to music hall songs. Given that these recognisable events were staged within their own communities, a significant number of working-class men felt sufficiently justified to reclaim their leisure through brute force.

Although the zealous policy of conversion was toned down after 1890, the Salvation Army continued to attack working-class leisure patterns and provoke contestations over urban space. As late as 1905 the Salvation

Army in Dunstable embarked on a rather ambitious temperance campaign in which they would attempt to persuade drinkers of the evils of alcohol by visiting public houses just prior to closing time. However, on almost every occasion, the Salvation Army were obliged to leave the public house earlier than they intended as the drinkers 'showed their hostility to such a marked degree that the party had, in many cases, to withdraw in order to prevent a disturbance'.[81] After one particularly hostile evening, the Salvation Army decided to carry on their programme in the safety of their barracks. The procession marched silently back to the barracks, on account of the belligerence shown by local residents who objected to the Army's musical demonstrations in their neighbourhoods. Hounded out of the local public houses and stripped of their musical accompaniment, the beleagued Salvation Army were sadly mistaken if they thought that things could not have got any worse. The *Luton Reporter* recorded that the meeting in the barracks had been opened in the usual way, but then

> the building was invaded by a hostile crowd who seemed determined that no meeting should be held. Some disgraceful scenes ensued. When the revivalists endeavoured to sing a hymn the hostile section drowned their efforts with comic songs. Language heard on all sides was disgusting although not exactly used against the religious section. In fact on the whole, the crowd were, to some extent good humoured, but for all this nonetheless determined to have their own way. At one time 'the glory song' and 'Blue Bell' were both sung together. Under these circumstances all hope of holding a meeting was abandoned.[82]

The organised 'Skeleton Armies' and the more informal resistance shown by the Dunstable drinkers illustrates a combative strand that threads through much of working-class culture in the late nineteenth and twentieth centuries. The Salvation Army, then, provoked a contestation for urban space which previous forms of rational recreation had shirked away from. In contrast to the conservative, inward-looking working class described by some historians, aggressive forms of rational recreation provoked equally defiant responses from working men. Robert Roberts remembered that at weekends in Salford the Salvation Army would congregate at the end of a street in the heart of a working-class neighbourhood challenging residents not to enter a nearby public house. Roberts recalled how working men saw it as their 'duty' to push through the Salvation Army ranks with a jug of beer in each hand. Roberts's father would visit the 'beer-house himself, returning with a quart vessel through the ring of singing Salvationists, their leader, a large ginger man, staring hard and bawling across'.[83] The centrality of drink and the public house to male working-class culture elicited responses that turned violent in the Skeleton Army cases, or forceful and ironic in the Dunstable example. Indeed, just as the Skeleton Army was a parody of the Salvation Army, the Dunstable drinkers took it upon themselves to imitate the local Salvation Army by going to the heart of their barracks and imposing their own drinking and music hall culture on the bewildered Salvationists. In an ironic twist and within the sanctity of the Salvation Army barracks, the Dunstable crowd reimposed the traditional lyrics of a music hall tune that William Booth had commandeered.

Conclusion

The early rational recreation schemes heralded the first concerted attempts to foster a 'civilised' worker that could be deemed sufficiently qualified to assume an active role in the emerging pluralist society of late Victorian Britain. By the 1880s, mass democracy beckoned and contemporaries worried that the new sprawling cities were breeding a new degenerate working class that pursued the 'lowest' forms of leisure, a situation far removed from the 'intelligent' artisan. It was during this period that the mood and tone of rational recreationalists shifted from the confident air of welcoming new family members into the fold to the family under siege, anxious to lock out distant cousins who they feared might not only steal the family silver but also bring the house crashing down. From the socialists to the Salvationists, a common strand of thinking materialised which believed that only through aggressive forms of rational recreation, taken to the heart of working-class communities, could the modern citizen be fostered. However, another perhaps unwelcome feature that pervaded most schemes of rational recreation was their failure, regardless of political colour. As August has argued, at the root of many conflicts between the working class and the authorities were the issues of control over space and regulation of behaviour.[84] The Penny Reading crowd and the Dunstable drinkers demonstrated that struggles were not confined to the usual arenas of the street or the public place, but were sometimes played out in the civilisers' own environment, a particularly worrying development for the social reformers themselves. Thus, working men showed a remarkable propensity to manipulate the entertainment offered to coincide with their own cultural preferences. Therefore these actions did not emerge from a passive, conservative or inward-looking culture, since aggressive rational recreationalists who attempted to colonise their neighbourhoods were met with indifference, irony or even violence. Indeed, traditional male working-class leisure not only emerged unscathed by the moral reformist onslaught but was bolstered by new and popular forms of commercial leisure. It is to the emergence of this mass leisure that we now turn.

Notes

1 For an analysis of the St Monday holiday, see D. A. Reid, 'The decline of St Monday, 1766–1876', *Past and Present*, 71 (1976).

2 P. Bailey, *Leisure and Class in Victorian England. Rational Recreation and the Contest for Control 1830–1885* (London, Methuen, 1978), p. 91.

3 C. Behagg, *Politics and Production in the Early Nineteenth Century* (London, Routledge, 1990), pp. 134–6.

4 *The Times*, 2 May 1867.

5 W. Besant, 'The amusements of the people', *Contemporary Review*, 45 (1884), p. 347.

6 J. Belchem, *Industrialization and the Working Class. The English Experience, 1750–1900* (Aldershot, Scolar Press, 1990), p. 173.

7 R. McKibben, *The Ideologies of Class. Social Relations in Britain 1880–1950* (Oxford, Oxford University Press, 1991), p. 183.

8 J. Erskine Clarke, 'The working man's Saturday night; its bane and an antidote', *Transactions National Association Promotion Social Science*, 1860, p. 807.

9 Behagg, *Politics and Production in the Early Nineteenth Century*, ch. 5.

10 B. Poole, *Coventry and its Antiquities* (London, John Russell Smith, 1869), pp. 327–8.

11 Coventry Record Office (hereafter CRO), Acc 128/2, 'Coventry Religious and Useful Knowledge Society Minute Book 1839–1860'.

12 Poole, *Coventry and its Antiquities*, pp. 327–8.

13 Bailey, *Leisure and Class*, ch. 4; A. August, 'A culture of consolation? Rethinking politics in working class London, 1870–1914', *Historical Research*, 74 (2001).

14 For two differing interpretations on how 'respectable' leisure was adopted by the sections of the working class, see G. Best, *Mid-Victorian Britain 1851–75* (Glasgow, Collins, 1971); J. Foster, *Class Struggle and the Industrial Revolution. Early Industrial Capitalism in Three English Towns* (London, Methuen, 1974).

15 J. Greenwood, *The Wilds of London* (London, Chatto & Windus, 1874), pp. 121–3.

16 Greenwood, *The Wilds of London* p. 124.

17 J. Rose, *The Intellectual Life of the British Working Classes* (Yale University Press, New Haven, 2002), p. 84.

18 *Coventry Herald*, 8 April 1864.

19 T. Wright, *Some Habits and Customs of the Working Classes by a Journeyman Engineer* (London, Tinsley Brothers, 1867), p. 174.

20 Wright, *Some Habits and Customs*, pp. 170, 181.

21 Clarke, 'The working man's Saturday night', pp. 808–10.

22 *Coventry Herald*, 23 September, 25 November 1864.

23 *Coventry Herald*, 10 April 1863.

24 *Coventry Herald*, 4 December 1863, 11 November 1864.

25 *Coventry Herald*, 16 October 1865.

26 W. Woodruff, *The Road to Nab End. An Extraordinary Northern Childhood* (London, Abacus, 2002), p. 113.

27 See Chapter 2.

28 F. Marshall, 'Music and the people', *Nineteenth Century*, 8 (1880), 923–7.

29 Marshall, 'Music and the people', 923. For a commentary on how rational recreation developed from instruction to entertainment, see W. McG. Eagar, *Making Men. The History of Boys' Clubs and Related Movements in Great Britain* (London, University of London Press, 1945), pp. 148–81.

30 *Coventry Herald*, 21 October 1864.

31 Marshall, 'Music and the people', 930.

32 Bailey, *Leisure and Class*, ch. 7.

33 Bailey, *Leisure and Class*, p. 118; H. Cunningham, *Leisure in the Industrial Revolution, 1780–1880* (Beckenham, Croom Helm, 1980), p. 121; G. Tremlett, *The First Century* (London, Twentieth Century Press, 1962), ch. 2.

34 R. N. Price, 'The Working Men's Club movement and Victorian social reform ideology', *Victorian Studies*, 17 (1971), 124.

35 Quoted in Price, 'The Working Men's Club movement', 122; For a similar speech by a founder-member of the CIU, see W. Cowper's address to the first annual general meeting of the CIU, *The Times*, 13 July 1863.

36 Price, 'The Working Men's Club movement', 147.

37 Bailey, *Leisure and Class*, pp. 127, 132.

38 *The Times*, 30 November 1877.

39 G. Stedman Jones, *Outcast London. A Study in the Relationship Between the Classes in Victorian Society* (1971; London, Penguin, 1984), p. 296.

40 E. J. Yeo, *The Contest for Social Science. Relations and Representations of Gender and Class* (London, Rivers Oram Press, 1996), p. 223.

41 *Spectator* 29 September 1906.

42 H. Meller (ed.), *The Ideal City* (Leicester, Leicester University Press, 1979).

43 *The Times*, 26 March 1883.

44 W. Besant, 'The amusements of the people', *Contemporary Review*, 45 (184), 344, 351.

45 C. Waters, *British Socialists and the Politics of Popular Culture, 1884–1914* (Manchester, Manchester University Press, 1990), p. 347.

46 Besant, 'The amusements of the people', 351.

47 Besant, 'The amusements of the people', 348. An important attribute that the older worker was purported to have held was an interaction with the

countryside, since a fear of encroaching urbanisation was developing and the perception of a gulf between town and country was an important aspect of middle-class uncertainty by the 1890s. This was a fear reflected at a national level. For a middle-class fear of urbanisation and a rural antidote, see M. J. Wiener, *English Culture and the Decline of the Industrial Spirit* (Harmondsworth, Penguin, 1981), pp. 55–64. Also Marsh notes that 'The visible decline of the countryside prompted a sudden rush of nostalgia for rural life … Love of the country became an article of faith as essential to respectability as the belief in manners or morality'; see J. Marsh, *Back to the Land. The Pastoral Impulse in Victorian England, 1880–1914* (London, Quartet Books, 1982), p. 4.

48 B. Beaven and J. Griffiths, 'Urban elites, socialists and notions of citizenship in an industrial boomtown: Coventry, *c.* 1870–1914', *Labour History Review*, 69:1 (2004), 302.

49 Stedman Jones, *Outcast London*, part 1.

50 A. Chapman, 'The People's' Palace for East London: A study of Victorian philanthropy', M.Phil. dissertation, University of Hull, 1978, p. 67.

51 S. Joyce, 'Castles in the air: The People's Palace, cultural reformism and the East End working class', *Victorian Studies*, 39 (1996), 529.

52 A. Morrison, *A Child of the Jago* (London: MacGibbon & Key, 1969), p. 19.

53 Morrison, *A Child of the Jago*, pp. 54–7.

54 A. Chapman, 'The People's Palace', 234.

55 D. E. B. Weiner, 'The People's Palace. An image for East London in the 1880s', in D. Feldman and G. Stedman Jones (eds), *Metropolis London. Histories and Representations since 1800* (London: Routledge, 1989), p. 53.

56 Godfrey Turner advocated government intervention to curb 'the villainous language of the gallery-folk, whose obscene oaths, yelled forth at full pitch'; see G. Turner, 'Amusements of the English people', *The Nineteenth Century*, 2 (1877), 830.

57 Belchem, *Industrialization and the Working Class*, p. 174.

58 V. Bailey, '"In darkest England and the way out". The Salvation Army, social reform and the Labour movement 1885–1910', *International Review of Social History*, 29 (1984), 139.

59 S. Yeo, 'A new life: The religion of Socialism in Britain, 1883–1896', *History Workshop Journal*, 4 (1977).

60 Waters, *British Socialists and the Politics of Popular Culture*, p. 173.

61 Waters, *British Socialists and the Politics of Popular Culture*, p. 102.

62 D. Read, *England 1868–1914* (London, Longman, 1979), p. 220.

63 B. Lancaster, 'Who's a real Coventry kid? Migration into twentieth century Coventry', in B. Lancaster and T. Mason (eds), *Life and Labour in a 20th Century City. The Experience of Coventry* (Coventry, Cryfield Press, 1986), p. 61.

64 V. E. Chancellor, *Master and Artisan in Victorian England. The Diary of William Andrews and the Autobiography of Joseph Gutteridge* (London, Evelyn, Adams & Mackay, 1969), p. 149.

65 CRO, Acc 135, Roland Barrett, 'Socialism made plain'.

66 CRO, Acc 835/2, Hugh Farren, 'Newspaper cuttings', 24.

67 J. A.Yates, *Pioneers to Power. The Story of the Ordinary People of Coventry* (Coventry, Coventry Labour Party, 1950), p. 31.

68 K. Richardson, *Twentieth Century Coventry* (Suffolk, Coventry Council, 1972), p. 162; M.B Reckett, *P. E. T. Widdrington. A Study in Vocation and Versatility* (London, SPCK, 1961), pp. 55, 69.

69 CRO, Acc 836/2, Hugh Farren, 'Newspaper cuttings', p. 46.

70 *The Clarion*, 8 February 1896.

71 Bailey, 'In Darkest England', 137; R. Tressell, *The Ragged Trousered Philanthropists* (London, Flamingo, 1993) p. 430.

72 Belchem, *Industrialization and the Working Class*, p. 227.

73 M. Valverde, 'The dialectic of the familiar and the unfamiliar: "The jungle" in the early slum travel writing', *Sociology*, 30:3 (1996), 494.

74 V. Bailey, 'Salvation Army riots, the "Skeleton Army" and legal authority in the provincial town', in A. P. Donajgrodzki (ed.), *Social Control in Nineteenth Century Britain* (Beckenham, Croom Helm, 1977), p. 233.

75 B. Harrison, *Drink and the Victorians. The Temperance Question in England, 1815– 1872* (Staffordshire, Keele University Press, 1994), p. 129.

76 Belchem, *Industrialization and the British Working Class*, p. 227.

77 *The Times*, 14 June 1882.

78 Bailey, 'Salvation Army riots', pp. 233–4.

79 N. H. Murdoch, 'Salvation Army disturbances in Liverpool, England 1879– 1887', *Journal of Social History*, 25:3 (1992), 576; Bailey, 'Salvation Army riots', 247.

80 Behagg, *Politics and Production*, p. 135.

81 *Luton Reporter*, 23 March 1905.

82 *Luton Reporter*, 23 March 1905.

83 R. Roberts, *The Classic Slum. Salford Life in the First Quarter of the Century* (Manchester, Manchester University Press, 1971), p. 122.

84 A. August, 'A culture of consolation? Rethinking politics in working class London, 1870–1914', *Institute of Historical Research*, 74 (2001), 209.

2

The era of mass leisure:
the pleasure-seeking citizen

The rise of mass commercial leisure in the late nineteenth century profoundly influenced the nature and development of popular culture in Britain. The emergence of the modern city with its crowded living and working conditions ensured that mass leisure became a potent symbol of the age. New populist and heavily capitalised commercial leisure events offered no 'rational' self-improvement, and in turn attracted vast numbers of 'pleasure seekers'. With few moral restraints, leisure entrepreneurs capitalised on traits within working-class culture and recast them into appealing commercial ventures. The male worker, who was the chief beneficiary of an increase in surplus income, was in the front line of this new commercial entertainment. By 1900 both the skilled and, in some places, semi-skilled working man, saw the regular expenditure from the household budget on at least one aspect of commercial leisure as a 'right' rather than a luxury.[1]

Many, however, remained uncertain of how civic responsibility could be encouraged in the city. The heady mix of drink and the hedonistic delights of commercial leisure were all too much for some social observers, who lambasted the suppliers of this new form of leisure and the people who regularly supported it. In a climate of international anxiety social reformers from across the political spectrum wondered what would become of a nation that spent its leisure hours in the public house or slavishly attached to the vulgar entertainment offered by the music hall. A tinge of disappointment with the development of popular culture can also be detected in the subsequent historiography that has developed around the subject, with some historians arguing that an authentic working-class culture was replaced by a mass culture shorn of its class identity.[2]

First we shall investigate a common assumption, which cut across the political spectrum, that the rise of mass commercial leisure coincided with a decline of 'good' citizenry. Second, the chapter will assess the role of the music hall and public house within male working-class culture as these key institutions provide a useful test to the hegemonic qualities of mass commercial leisure. The third section will explore how reactions to intemperance in the music hall and public house stimulated both cross-class collaborative and class-specific movements which placed temperance at the heart of their own particular narrative of citizenship. In addition, we shall explore the attempts by both class-collaborative and class-specific movements to forge narratives of 'good' citizenship by attacking mass commercial leisure and adopting the temperance cause. Finally football, one of the most potent forms of mass commercial leisure, provides a case study challenging the notion that mass commercial leisure displaced an authentic working-class culture. Football, rather, provides an example of a more spontaneous and popular form of civic pride and citizenry generated 'from below' in the factories and streets of Britain's growing cities.

Mass commercial leisure and the decline of 'good' citizenship

As we saw in Chapter 1, the rational recreationalists of the middle years of the nineteenth century constantly attacked popular male leisure pursuits for their deficiencies in providing intellectual elevation. During the 1850s and 1860s, whether the entertainment was delivered by working-class organisations, public houses or early forms of commercial entertainment such as Singing Saloons or Penny Gaffs, was not such a concern for social reformers. Instead social commentators focused their criticism on the form of entertainment and less on the body that delivered it. The emergence of mass commercial entertainment, however, transformed contemporary discourse as providers of leisure rapidly came into sharp focus. For liberal social reformers, mass commercial leisure proved, at times, a difficult phenomenon to explain. The growing respectability of working men, symbolised in the extension of the franchise through the Reform Acts of 1867 and 1884, did not square with their increasing fixation with 'low' commercial entertainment. While they attempted to persuade the working class to adopt elevating activities, social reformers appealed both to leisure providers to improve the content of their entertainment and to employers to reduce excessive hours and monotonous forms of work. For liberal reformers, there was a crucial link between the rapid rise of mass commercial leisure and the growth of semi-skilled and monotonous forms of work. According to this scenario, workers were too exhausted after a long day engaged in monotonous work to engage in elevating pastimes and instead resorted to the low and debased entertainment of the music hall. In the 1890s, one social observer warned bicycle manufacturers that the combination of commercial entertainment and long monotonous work schedules would have some chilling consequences:

> So be it. Make your money if you will. It will perish with you, but remember that you are not only making money and securing large dividends, you are making a sickly, thriftless, restless, pitiless, godless people. You are creating a Frankenstein, a monster without a heart, that will turn round and rend you or your children.[3]

The suggestion that new forms of work and entertainment were pushing Britain towards the brink of a social revolution was, of course, everything that contemporary socialists could have wished for. However, many activists who entered working-class neighbourhoods and venues of commercial entertainment experienced anything but a warm welcome and certainly not an atmosphere of revolutionary fervour. The rapid rise of commercial leisure had left socialists grappling for appropriate terminology and doctrine to explain its immense popularity with the working class, a popularity they neither understood nor instinctively approved of. Initially socialists expressed disapproval of commercial leisure on the grounds that it removed social distinctions, creating a mass culture devoid of class consciousness or radical potential.[4] However, as the century progressed, socialist thinkers arrived at the conclusion that mass commercial leisure was intrinsically linked with industrial capitalism, exploiting not only those employed in the industry but also its working-class customers. For socialists like Robert Tressell, the music hall, with its overtly Tory songs, helped engender a fatalism within working-class culture that ultimately benefited their capitalist masters. In Tressell's novel *The Ragged Trousered Philanthropists*, his socialist alter ego, Frank Owen, describes the impact that the music hall had upon its working-class audience:

for the words of the song gave expression to their ideal of what human life should be. That was all they wanted – to be allowed to work like brutes for the benefit of other people. They did not want to be civilized themselves and they intended to take good care that the children they had brought into the world should never enjoy the benefits of civilization either.[5]

These analyses, then, tended to mix a disapproval of commercial leisure based on its close ties to capitalism with a more traditional critique rooted in a desire to explain 'pleasure seeking' through the moral deficiencies of the individual. In 1894, H.W. Hobart typified the socialist response to commercialism when, after warning how commercial leisure was under the grip of big business, he slid back to more familiar ground, declaring that workers should 'educate yourselves for the enjoyment of rational pleasure, agitate for the opportunities of taking pleasure, and organise yourselves for its final realisation'.[6] One should not be too critical of this rather confused response to mass leisure since, after all, contemporary socialists did not operate within a socio-economic vacuum. Victorian discourse on the nature of late-nineteenth-century society was dominated by the belief that the working-class individual lacked moral discipline which, in this case, was demonstrated through their overindulgence in mass commercial leisure activities. Socialists remained fierce critics of popular leisure and, as Robert Roberts remembered, 'mysteriously aloof' from the rest of the community.[7]

Both liberal and socialist critiques of popular culture during the late nineteenth century thus shared similar anxieties about many of the new characteristics of modern society. In short, a mass urban population and mass vulgar entertainment were a dangerous cocktail which might threaten to extinguish both liberal and socialist civilising missions. In 1910 J.A. Sharp, a leading member of Luton's temperance organisation, encapsulated the social reformer's anxiety with modernity when he announced in a public meeting that:

When a great mass of population worked and lived together they had ab-normal desires, abnormal passions, and abnormal feelings developed, these abnormal feelings, desires, and passions craved for satisfaction, and the only place where they could satisfy them was the public house. There was no authority in the country who would deny that drink dragged men down to the deepest poverty.[8]

Echoing the statements of Gustave Le Bon, Sharp contended that the moral responsibilities and self-discipline that the individual had learned from civilised society were in danger of crumbling due to the psychological change that mass living, working and leisure engendered.[9] There was also a widespread perception that the working man had gained more free time from the workplace due to the gradual shortening of the working day. While the Ten Hour Act of 1847 has been seen as a landmark in reducing workers' hours, it was only in the 1880s that large semi-skilled trade unions managed to gain substantial reduction in hours for large numbers of male workers.[10]

The fear that working men were unable to act with restraint away from the workplace, particularly with the emergence of mass commercial leisure, was a constant concern across the political spectrum. This criticism was particularly acute during the late nineteenth century, since social observers claimed to have witnessed very little thrift among workers despite a rise in real wages levels for some workers. Between 1850 to 1900, real wages rose by 80 per cent, a phenomenon which ensured that some workers had become the first proletarian consumers of a mass commercial leisure industry. These figures, of course, mask the regional industrial decline experienced by northern workers in the traditional industries such as the textiles and steel trades. Although unemployment statistics were only collected for skilled workers, they do indicate the scale of the problem, as unemployment among workers rose from less than 1 per cent in 1872, to 11.4 per cent in 1879, and 10.2 per cent in 1886.[11] In addition, the growing consumer power of some sections of the working class were frequently checked by both short- and long-term socio-economic factors such as seasonal employment cycles and illness.[12] However, it has been estimated that, after spending three-quarters of their income on food and rent, workers who benefited from real wage rises during this period devoted the surplus to commercial entertainment.[13] It was working-class males, free from the difficulties of balancing the family budget, who were the true beneficiaries of the economic circumstances of the late nineteenth century.

Despite regional and occupational variations in income, it was usually the woman's sole responsibility to juggle the family's finances to ensure that her husband had sufficient 'spends' for his leisure time.[14] Due to their meagre incomes, working-class women had no option but to rely on their husband's contribution to the household economy, an arrangement which reinforced male authority in the home. The male's position in the household was sometimes further strengthened by wife-beating, which was tolerated within both working-class communities and wider society in general.[15] The rise in real wages also enabled semi-skilled men in the booming 'new' industries of the Midlands to join their skilled counterparts in experiencing the delights of commercial entertainment. Indeed, it was in areas that possessed high concentrations of semi-skilled workers that social observers concentrated their efforts on educating the masses in the merits of thrift and self-discipline. In the 1880s, one social observer, who called himself 'philanthropic', published an open letter to the 'working classes in the bicycle trade':

> We all rejoice that at the present time this trade is exceptionally brisk, and that most of the large firms are, and have for some time past been working overtime … I am afraid a good deal of the money earned is spent, which by a little frugality and forethought might be saved, and that many a workman who does not at the present time think of putting by any portion of his wage, might by a little effort do so without much inconvenience to himself or his family.[16]

As with other groups of workers that experienced real income rises in the late nineteenth century, Coventry bicycle workers were the subject of moral panics relating to their 'new' spending patterns. After visiting the city, one reporter noted that people 'spoke of workmen drinking champagne at their ordinary meals, and Coventry was in a way depicted as "Tom Tiddler's ground" where money was to be had for the mere asking'.[17] Reports such as these emphasised the workers' apparent inability to handle their new-found wealth and often surfaced during local industrial disputes in an attempt to discredit the strikers' cause.[18] Although these stories were clearly exaggerated, it does appear that contemporaries did witness the emergence in Coventry of a semi-skilled worker who earned higher wages than his counterparts in other regions. One contemporary academic study revealed that 'rates and earnings are stated (officially) to be the highest in the Coventry district', while the social conditions:

> especially in Coventry, appear to be very good indeed. It has been stated on excellent authority that, taking wages paid all round, wages in Coventry district are higher than in any other town in Britain, with the exception of London. Housing conditions are excellent. There was in 1901, little overcrowding in the technical sense, namely about 2.6 per cent of the total number of dwellings. A large proportion of the town has been built of recent years, as a consequence of the regular influx of workers into the cycle and motor industry. The increasing demand for labour, and increasing population are creating a strong demand for houses. Yet rents are reasonable; and the prices

of commodities also. As the Report on the Cost of Living of the Working Class shows, Coventry compares very favourably with any town.[19]

Indeed, other indications that Coventry bicycle workers were able to engage in a form of consumerism previously the preserve of the middle class can be found in the numerous advertisements which began to target working men with luxury consumer goods. For example, advertised as 'A Great Luxury', relaxing in the city's first Turkish Bath after a hard day's cycling or footballing was an invitation extended to working men in early Edwardian Coventry.

With the prices of 1s 6d for second class and 2s for first, the baths would have been an occasional treat for working men. In the local press, customers were informed that

> If you're run-down, knocked-up and feel murky,
> And you're pining once more to be perky,
> At once take the path
> that leads to the bath,
> for which we're indebted to Turkey.[20]

This rhyming advert was clearly targeted at working men in an attempt to draw them into the new world of luxury consumerism, though with the differing price scales careful provision was made to ensure that middle-class sensibilities were not offended.

The music hall

In 1886 Rev. Jay, a young and progressive clergyman, was invited by the Bishop of London to become the vicar of the Holy Trinity of Shoreditch, a notoriously poor district of London's East End. Jay accepted the post with some trepidation as, on arrival at the parish, he found that 'there was no Church nor any beginning made for one'. Instead Jay discovered that the 'chief building is a music-hall, the chief centre a boxing saloon in connection with a tavern'.[21] Jay's experience of 1880s' London illustrates the important role the music hall played in even the poorest working-class communities. Although some historians, such as Davies, have warned that prohibitive entrance fees meant that not all members of the working class could regularly participate in commercial leisure, we should not underestimate the cultural impact that the institution had upon even the poorest members of the community.[22] Although the poorest members of the working community could only regard a visit to the music hall as a special occasion, they were more than familiar with the songs and the social etiquette of the music hall through socialisation in the community and the workplace.[23] The next section will explore the growth and development of the music hall, paying particular attention to its relationship with male working-class culture between 1860 and 1914.

The music hall emerged from a diverse range of public-house entertainment from the 1840s. During this period, proto-music hall entertainment emerged in London and across the country in places as varied as Birmingham, Nottingham, Bolton and Newcastle.[24] The public houses that had successfully served food, drink and entertainment extended their premises to create singing saloons, which then developed into an independent institution. By the 1850s the Singing Saloon had grown into the music hall, some of which could boast capacities of 1,500 in the case of Bolton's 'The Star Music Hall' and over 3,500 people in some London music halls. By 1888, music halls had become the most popular leisure institution in London, public houses notwithstanding. It was estimated that by the early 1890s, there were 14 million annual visits to the thirty-five London music halls.[25] In the provinces, early music hall entrepreneurs faced little in the way of competition and were able to dominate the local entertainment scene and also construct impressive buildings in prominent positions in the town centre.[26] The music hall, then, was an institution born from below and subsequently extensively commercialised through the 1850s and 1860s. Although it was an institution which attracted mixed social classes by the turn of the century, the entertainment continued to be working class in character, and still very much embedded in the culture of that class.

The ability, however, to attend music hall performances on a regular basis was often constrained by gendered expectations of work and leisure roles. Whereas men of all ages could be seen in the halls, women's visits were dictated by patterns of life and work. According to Kift few families visited the music hall, and for many working-class wives the shortage of money and the demands of housework and childcare prohibited regular attendance. It was young, single women who, with work friends and neighbours, attended the music hall on a regular basis. For example, one social observer in Bradford commented that he had been surprised at the large number of women that were unaccompanied by husbands or lovers.[27] In addition, there can be little doubt that the extent to which a music hall had a high proportion of young women in the audience was influenced by the industrial context of the region in which it was situated, with the textile industry in particular employing large numbers of young, single female workers. Indeed by 1881, 35 per cent of working women were employed in the textile industry, a figure which almost matched those in domestic service (36 per cent), the largest female employment sector.[28] For men, on the other hand, the music hall appears to have been more of a lifelong recreational activity, starting with adolescence and carrying through into married life. There is also evidence that groups of young men, with more disposable income than ever before, physically forced their way through to the best seats in the house with members of the audience reporting that men with 'heavy boots' walked 'across the heads of the people' from the back of a crowd to the front, knocking off hats and bonnets in the process.[29] It was also reported that both young and older men had a unique method of reserving the best seats at the front of the gallery.

> Oh! The gallery … at the Royal! I remember the tortuous way of the stairs, the twists and turns thereof, the cruel pushes, the stoppage at the pay box and up again … Nor were the habitues of 'high Olympus' particular in those days. A pal in front, if he secured a seat for a chum coming later, would save it till the arrival of the latter, who had no objection to being tossed or rolled over the heads of the audience until he landed in his 'reserved seat'.[30]

Although some of these rougher practices were eliminated in the 1880s, music hall still retained its working-class and masculine identity throughout the many changes and the intensive commercialisation of the nineteenth century. The music hall was a peculiar fusion of what Kift has described as a 'spontaneous and oppositional people's culture from below and commercialised mass culture from above'.[31] Although by 1914 the music hall was still an institution associated with the working class, the question arises of whether the commercial side of the music hall had come to steer working-class culture, at best, down the road of fatalism and conservatism, and at worst down the rocky path of jingoism and xenophobia. Indeed, focusing on the conservative tone of songs and performances, Senelick has argued that since 'the music hall failed to speak for the people, it could be regarded as a pernicious instrument of propaganda'.[32] However, although the textual analysis of music hall songs has exposed the conservatism of the lyricists, it is a giant leap to suppose they were absorbed by a passive and attentive audience.[33] It will be argued here that working-class audience behaviour was less a product of the music hall than rooted in earlier forms of leisure which were less passive and pliable than some historians have suggested.

The rough-and-ready origins of the music hall can be found in the Singing Saloons and Penny Gaffs that were dispersed throughout the poorer areas of London and the provinces in the 1830 and 1840s. One middle-class observer's account of a Singing Saloon in Whitechapel demonstrates how it resembled the masculine bravado of a rowdy public house, particularly since there was a great deal of interaction between performer and audience. The first act was described by the observer as a 'brawny ruffian' who, naked to the waist, was performing a slave song complete with manacles and costume. However, after the fifth verse, the audience became restless and shouted 'cut it short' while at the same time pelting the unfortunate singer with food. It was only when a large fish bone became lodged in his hair, provoking an 'explosion of mirth', that the performer took matters into his own hands:

> He glared to the right and the left of him, and, apparently marking out the delinquent in the pit, jumped off the stage and rushed towards him. What transpired I cannot say, not being in a position to see, but after a minute of uproar, and cursing, and swearing, and yelling laughter, the black man scrambled on to the stage again with a good deal of blacking rubbed off his face, and with his wool wig in his hand, exposing his proper short crop of carroty hair. 'Now looky here!' exclaimed he, with a desperate, but not entirely successful effort to deliver himself in a calm and impassionate manner, 'looky here, if you thinks by a-choking me off to get a new piece a bit sooner you're just wrong...' And having expressed these manly and British sentiments in genuine Whitechapel English, he readjusted his wig and became once more an afflicted African.[34]

This interaction between performer and audience and the general informality of the Singing Saloons and Penny Gaffs were key traits that were transferred to early music halls. These characteristics were embedded within popular forms of entertainment, and a music hall's ability or desire to accommodate a 'free and easy' atmosphere would often determine whether it attracted working-class custom. For example, after a steady decline in attendances during the 1850s, the Theatre Royal in Birmingham altered its entertainment in an attempt to appeal to working-class audiences by cutting admission prices and staging 'low' entertainment. The transformation proved successful in attracting a predominantly working-class audience who brought with them the social etiquette of the Penny Gaffs and

Singing Saloons. The local newspaper reported that 'every corner of the gallery was crammed' and that there were frequent interactions between the performers and the audience.[35] Likewise in Coventry, musical and comic entertainment was clearly advertised and demarcated into higher and lower cultural categories. The Godiva Concert Hall was described by the local press as a 'fashionable' and respectable place of entertainment 'which excludes all bad characters and permits no improper sentiments or indecent allusions to be introduced into the comic singing'. The interior, with its banked seating, was designed like a theatre, which helped to reduce the high degree of audience participation that had been a defining feature of the Singing Saloon style of scattering tables around a large stage.[36] In contrast, the failing Coventry Theatre Royal was transformed into the Theatre Royal Music Hall and designed to attract predominantly a working-class audience. The theatre's conversion into a music hall involved the removal of the partitions from the back of the boxes, and the installation of bars in the pit and gallery. Moreover, the management contracted caterers to provide food 'apartments' within the hall. Waiters would supply customers with pastry, pork pies, ham, cheese, bread, wine and biscuits. The management's decision to redesign the theatre around food and drink outlets certainly marked an attempt to re-create the 'free and easy' ambience of the Singing Saloons in larger and more salubrious surroundings.[37] The extensive changes proved a great success, with the building regularly 'besieged by an immense crowd' long before the doors were open.[38] Not only had the alterations attracted crowded houses, the music hall devotees were clearly of a different social class from the former theatre audience. One observer noted that the reserved quiescence of the theatre was broken by the 'tobacco smoke, varied by the waiter's wandering voice, seeking and delivering orders for drink, which was openly consumed in the auditorium'. He went on to observe:

> the prices of admission had been cheapened, and the additional attraction was offered to some of its patrons of at least one glass of refreshment during the evening at the expense of the bar, or as they tersely put it 'the pit was sixpence, but you got twopence back in beer' ... The call for 'orders' from the waiters and the rise of odours from the pit frightened away the fashionable folk. And on any night of the week it was easy to see that an entirely new audience filled the house.[39]

The contrast between the theatre and music hall during the 1850s and 1860s was particularly stark. The reserved and polite protocol of bourgeois theatre contrasted with the gregarious and noisy atmosphere of the early music halls. The installation of a bar, the placement of tables in the auditorium and a waiter service encouraged the audience to engage in more conversation and greater mobility. The music hall entrepreneurs' success in tapping into male working-class culture was noted in the 1860s by Thomas Wright, who observed that 'the music halls are the most popular places of Saturday night resort with working men, as at them they can combine the drinking of the Saturday night glass, and the smoking of the Saturday night pipe with the seeing and hearing of a variety of entertainments'.[40] Significantly, Wright also made observations on the audiences' conduct, indicating that different social groups engaged with the performances in distinct and diverse ways. According to Wright's observations in the gallery, the cheapest section of the auditorium,

> the roughs are the most numerous division; it consists of those who come to the theatre with unwashed faces and in ragged and dirty attire, who bring bottles of drink with them, who *will* smoke despite of the notice that 'smoking is strictly prohibited', and that 'officers will be in attendance'; who favour the band with a stamping accompaniment, and take the most noisy part in applauding or giving 'the call' to the performers.

In this clear reference to semi-skilled or unskilled workers, Wright indicates that this section of the audience was intent on consuming the entertainment on their own terms and, in doing so, broke the venue's protocols and regularly engaged with the performers. With such gregarious behaviour, it is unlikely that the music hall was an efficient institution in transmitting an imperial culture to the vast majority of the audience. However, Wright does indicate that other sections of the audience behaved rather differently. The 'snobs', as he dubbed them, though less numerous, were 'to be found there two or three nights a week, and are amongst the most deeply attentive portion of the audience'. While it is difficult to identify the social origins of this group, Wright does hint upon their petty-bourgeois pretensions as 'they seem very ill at ease in their place of choice, and shrink from the glances of the occupants of the pit and boxes'.[41] If the music hall was successful in shaping notions of empire and imperialism it would have been with this section of the audience who seemed to have been more attentive and passively engaged with the entertainment.[42] Wright's evidence also questions recent claims by Maloney that the audience participation in the performance of music hall songs helped nurture a 'sense of communal well-being and "oneness" – of an instant community' that was socially inclusive.[43] Thus, although Wright's account of the music hall audience identified a social mix, their behaviour and reaction to the audience participation within the music hall differed significantly.

If the physical environment and audience behaviour of early music halls resembled the structure and atmosphere of traditional singing saloons, it is perhaps no surprise that performers frequently struggled for attention against the clatter of glasses and cutlery and, in worst-case scenarios, a hostile crowd. Indeed, the type of act that was successful in the music hall cultivated a high level of audience participation, an interaction between performer and public that is, for the historian, important in understanding the popularity and significance of music hall to the working-class audience. For example, music hall songs contained lines in which the audience was invited to sing or make a great deal of noise. Songs of this genre were, on the whole, overtly bawdy and masculine in character and were a celebration of drinking to excess and hedonism in a bid to escape the monotony of the day. George Leybourne's 'Champagne Charlie', Vance's 'Slap Bang, Here We Are Again', and J. H. Milburn's 'Come Along My Boys Let's Make a Noise' all fall into this category and epitomise the character of music hall performance from the 1870s onwards.[44] These popular acts relied on a certain interaction and complicity with the audience that baffled those excluded from this hybrid of working-class and commercialised music hall culture. Comedy sketches would invariably draw from familiar incidents in working-class life, interspersed with repetitive catch phrases or songs with which the audience were invited to join.[45] For example, one of Charles Booth's researchers noted in one London music hall that 'the catchwords of the comic characters were well known to the audience. The boys in the pit shouted them out as soon as the actor appeared and were chaffed in return by the actors from the stage.'[46] Indeed, the cultural disparity between a middle-class observer and a predominantly working-class audience was captured when an investigative reporter entered a music hall in the East End during the 1870s. The reporter noted that the 'star' of the show was Fred Molloy, who entered the stage dressed as a Bedlamite sporting a 'set grin':

> All these celebrities have their 'points' of which they are extremely jealous. Freddy's 'point' is contained in a little bit of dirty rag with holes in it, and which he makes believe serves as a pocket-handkerchief, and with-draws from its receptacle with a flourish to blow his nose before he begins to sing. By mistake, however, he thrusts a thumb and fore finger through two holes in

the rag, and applying them to his nose, blows on them – a disgusting trick, and one that would earn him a kick in private society, but which sends the numskulls into hysterical laughter.

The performers' 'points' were clearly anticipated by the audience, as was the expectation that they would interact with the artist at some point during the act. The reporter explained that Molloy then broke into song about how he had fallen in love with a servant girl who chopped mincemeat:

> despite the irresistible way in which Freddy thrusts his tongue out, and bangs his hat about, the song would possibly fall flat were it not for its miraculously funny chorus:
>
> And her mince-meat knife went chop, chop, chop,
>
> Chop, chop, chopetty chop-chop!
>
> In which the audience are invited to join, Freddy, giving them encouragement by a 'Now then-all together' and a stamp of his foot. And they do, the imbeciles … Encore! Encore! encore! Here he is again! This time he wears a white apron and sleeves, and announces in Catnach rhyme that his name is Sam and he keeps a ham and beef shop.[47]

Chorus singing and interactions with the performer were behavioural traits that stretched back to the singing saloons and gave the audience the opportunity to shape the evening's programme.[48] Thus, in total, the audience's use of the encore drew Molloy back to the stage for two further sketches, which squeezed the less popular acts from the schedule. The encore and slow handclap also gave the members of the audience the opportunity to manufacture meanings which related to their own tangible experience. Sometimes the audience would alter verses to their own liking, and more often than not the revised version would supersede the original.[49]

Towards the end of the nineteenth century, however, the design and management of music halls shifted from facilitating interaction between the stage and audience to attempting to limit and contain it. Earl has argued persuasively that changes to the design of music halls helped subtly modify and mould the audience's and performers' behaviour.[50] Thus the informal Singing Saloon ambience was removed in favour of a more regimented seating plan with the removal of tables and the introduction of theatre-style seating. The removal of tables also helped to formalise the starting times of performances as the auditorium had to be cleared after each performance, a requirement that meant the management had to have full control of the hall. The audience was strictly divided within the hall into a hierarchical pricing structure, 'each mingling with its own kind and all confined to seats of varying degrees of comfort'.[51] Although many of these changes were implemented on the grounds of safety, there can be little doubt that they had the effect of reinforcing social divisions, a factor which encouraged a more affluent music hall devotee. These more 'fashionable' customers were also more attractive to the music hall manager since their spending power was greater than the traditional working-class audience.

This was undoubtedly a factor behind the management's attempt to stamp out more 'riotous behaviour' in the halls by drawing up rules and identifying deviant behaviour. However, Bailey has shown that music hall audiences were not becoming more unruly by the end of the nineteenth century. Rather it was managers who became more officious, so from about the 1870s 'what once may have been tolerated as custom was now redefined as delinquency'.[52] The crusade to cleanse the music halls became closely associated with the late-nineteenth-century moral panic over the emergence of the male 'hooligan', who some contemporaries believed was partly a product of low entertainment. During the Boer War, one correspondent to the music hall industry's magazine *Era* claimed that the music hall was responsible for hooliganism 'which perverts a city's tribute to its brave sons into an orgy that would shame even a savage people'. He went on to conclude that music hall songs

> glorify drink, licentiousness, greed, theft, in fact vice in its worse aspects. The patriotic songs are a compact of bombast and bloodthirstiness and are unworthy of an Englishman ... the modern comic song appeals mainly to the basest impulses in the human beast and the songs which strike the lowest depths are the most readily caught up.[53]

Likewise, a concerned correspondent to *The Times* visited a music hall in one of the 'roughest' districts of London 'with a view to ascertaining how far a music hall programme may be held to encourage lawlessness'. He noted that by the early stages of the evening's entertainment the programme had 'passed from idleness to drunkeness, from drunkeness to robbery and from robbery to perjury'. He concluded that it was 'likely to appeal with terrible force to the ill-educated, ill-clothed, ill-fed, and often ill-paid hobbledehoys of the threepenny gallery'. Worse still, he was certain that the millions spent on state education was going to waste since the young male was learning his hooliganism at 'these "night" or "continuing" schools under the name of music hall' which 'propagate the worst forms of immorality'.[54]

In the 1880s and 1890s, along with an increase in newspaper reports criticising rowdy audiences, there were moral panics regarding the plethora of artistes who relied on sexual innuendo for their comic routine. A typical complaint was aired in the magazine *Era*. The correspondent watched with disgust two female comic singers, 'the one singing of the charms and fancies of her "pussy" and the other dilating upon the joys of a certain article described as the "Hokee-Pokee"'.[55] While there was an unsuccessful bid by some particularly zealous social reformers to abolish music halls in Glasgow, music hall managers attempted to stem the flow of criticism by asking performers to adhere to certain codes of conduct. For example, in a discussion on music halls and morals in *Era*, it was suggested that a notice should be placed in performers' dressing rooms to read 'no language in song or speech is permitted on the stage of this hall which the most refined ear may not listen to'.[56] In a moral climate such as this, local councils put pressure on music hall proprietors to ban certain songs or comic skits from the programme. On the whole, managers, keen to usher in a new air of respectability, claimed to follow councillors' advice as a matter of course. In London some music hall managers threatened to fine vulgar acts and deemed that 'coarse jests and rough language' were to be avoided.[57] However, one commentator recalled that 'so little in proportion depended on the words and the tune, so much on the personality and the art of the performer ... this pause, that gesture, the other glance. There, not in words, or tune, lay the song – the work of art.'[58] Thus, moralising initiatives that attempted to cleanse music hall entertainment failed to curb the audiences' appetite for the double entendre and the performers' ability to side-step managers' bids to introduce more respectability.[59]

However, there can be little doubt that by 1914 music halls had undergone a fundamental change from the free and easy atmosphere of the 1850s to the rather regimented and management-controlled event of the early twentieth century. Nevertheless, traditional audience participation did continue to survive in the less heavily policed, smaller halls. One researcher working on Charles Booth's survey observed that in one particularly poor area of London, 'public-houses get up a sing song of an evening but there are no music-halls'.[60] During the Edwardian period, Arthur Harding remembered that the costermongers used to come armed with fruit to his favoured music hall in London 'and directly anybody come on that was no good, they used to pelt the life out of them, you know. Sometimes they didn't give the man a chance; if the first few minutes didn't go off good, whallop!'[61] William Woodruff recalled that unsuccessful performers at his local music hall in Blackburn were still subjected to a flurry of rotten tomatoes from an audience laden with soft-fruit missiles even after the First World War.[62] The larger music hall chains, though, were successful in ridding the entertainment of audience participation, albeit in a more piecemeal manner than some historians have assumed. This transformation of the music hall had not gone unnoticed and had not been welcomed by the working-class audience. One correspondent to the *Daily Mail* describing himself as a 'common man' complained that,

> In the name either of art or public morality they have improved the style of entertainment to a point at which we cannot understand it and cannot afford to pay the price of admission … if you come to look into it you will find that the improvement of the entertainment amounts to no more than the exclusion from the auditorium of the vulgar working class population.[63]

The big music hall chains' attempt to 'purify' the entertainment and the audience 'out of existence' proved to be fairly successful in the short term. However, by the eve of the First World War these changes had ensured that the music hall lost its centrality to working-class culture, as other, newer forms of entertainment took its place. Indeed, the *New Statesmen* recognised that the music hall had fallen out of step with working people when it questioned 'whether the music hall has moved with the times. As the times become more lax, the music hall becomes more strict'.[64] The music halls had become so immensely popular precisely because they had attempted to reflect the demands and character of traditional forms of working-class leisure. Indeed, the success of the Victorian music hall, particularly during the early years, can be explained by its compatibility with drinking and public-house culture, perhaps the most important traditional leisure activity in working-class culture.

Drink and the public house

Despite the availability of consumer luxuries, it was the traditional habit of pub-going which continued to dominate male working-class leisure. Drink was the enduring consumer item that became a central component in the success of the new leisure industries. Be it a post-football-match drink or the conspicuous consumption of the new light ale in the music halls, drink neatly dovetailed into these emerging leisure ventures. However, drinking did more to separate male and female leisure spheres than any other leisure activity, prompting Harrison to stress that the public house was 'primarily a masculine republic'. Since the home, apart from being cold and noisy, was the centre of domestic duties, for working men it was 'oftener a place to fly FROM, than to fly TO'.[65] The public house's masculine culture also ensured that women's participation in pub-going was restricted and largely reflected the surrounding neighbourhood work traditions. In Manchester and Salford, where there was a fairly rigid sexual division of labour, women were largely excluded from pub life, entering the lounge on occasions but preferring to drink at home. Davies has argued that pub life constantly reinforced the sexual division of leisure 'as men sought escapism via "the shortest way out of Manchester": through the door of the pub vault'.[66] While women did drink, it was only males who claimed the 'right' to drink, no matter the financial circumstances of the household. So entrenched was the belief that male drinking took precedence in the household budget, wives rarely questioned the expense and sometimes routinely supported it. During the First World War, one Coventry women recalled that she and her mother would queue every evening for her father's beer at a local public house. Indeed, her mother somewhat resented the large army of women munitions workers who were also queuing for their beer, feeling that working men had a greater right to rationed beer than their female counterparts:

> when he (father) got home at night he used to need a pint of beer and me and mother used to go to queue, queue at the Ball hotel ... for to try and get him a drink and at that time no she couldn't get him one because all the drinks were being served to these girls that were working in the factories that were filling shells and they'd be going with fur coats, 'cos the money they got was tremendous in them days. And she (mother) used to feel very bitter because me Dad needed the sweat he'd lost, he needed a drink like a pint of beer to put it back.[67]

Similarly, commenting on traditional working-class culture, Hoggart observed that 'drinking is accepted as part of the normal life, or at least of the normal man's life, like smoking. "A man needs 'is pint"; it helps to make life worth while; if one can't have a bit of pleasure like that, then what is there to live for? It is "natural" for a man to like his beer.'[68]

As we shall see, although the temperance movement had been largely unsuccessful in attracting working men from the public house, it enjoyed rather more success in influencing government policy towards the end of the nineteenth century. Mounting temperance pressure in the 1860s provided the backdrop to Bruce's 1872 Licensing Act, which restricted drinking in public houses to 11.00 p.m.[69] The social difficulties that the Act would initiate in placing restrictions on an institution at the heart of working-class culture was appreciated by *The Times*, which suggested 'what the Government has to deal with is the public life of the working classes, and at every turn of the debate it has been reminded that the public life is something sacred'.[70] *The Times*'s prediction that the Act would cause social difficulties was confirmed throughout various provincial towns and cities in England on the first night that it was implemented. Indeed, Coventry, Liverpool, Wolverhampton and Exeter all experienced serious disturbances after 11.00 p.m. Significantly, the Act was perceived by the protesters as a class-specific piece of legislation, since they drew parallels with prominent middle-class clubs that were exempt from the Act. In Liverpool broadsheets were distributed claiming that there was 'one law for the rich and another for the poor', while similar scenes occurred in Cheltenham after middle-class clubs were barracked, attacked and forced to close.[71] In Coventry after 11.00 p.m. the crowd began 'hooting and shouting "down to the City Club. They are not closed. They have no business to be open".' After breaking through a police line with sticks and stones the protesters marched to the City Club, the most well-known middle-class club in the city, with cries of 'smash the Club'.[72] Apart from these very direct and physically violent protests, working men developed more subtle strategies for sidestepping the legislation. In Croydon, a railway station waiting room was converted into a makeshift taproom, once the public houses had closed at 11.00 p.m. A passer-by claimed that there was 'dancing, singing and shouting, and accordion-playing, a large trade at the same time being done at the bar'.[73] Since it would have been highly unlikely that all of these people had been waiting for a train, this does give us an indication of the lengths that working people went to in order to keep their entertainments open throughout the night. A more common response by working men to the legislation, however, was the rapid increase in working men's clubs after 1872. Like their middle-class counterparts, working men's clubs were left largely unaffected by the 1872 Licensing Act. Furthermore, evidence suggests that the number of 'unofficial' working-men's clubs ran their societies without outside interference or regulation. According to one disgruntled social observer in Coventry:

> It is surprising how many social clubs have sprung up during the past few years, a large number being known as working men's clubs, and it has often

occurred that where a licence has been refused the premises have been opened as a working men's club, and a great deal more business in the spirit and beer trade has thus been done than would have been – and this without a licence.[74]

Such was the widespread exploitation of this loophole in the licensing legislation, a Select Committee in 1877 identified it as a source of immorality in urban Britain. When asked whether there were many working men's clubs in Birmingham, its Chief Constable, Major Bond, replied:

> There are two clubs of a most objectionable character. I may say two or three perhaps. We have no control what ever over them, and I think that it would be a most advantageous thing that there should be some further legislation upon the subject, because those clubs became simply unlicensed drinking houses; there is one of them in which the subscription is of a most ridiculous amount just to bring it within the law, and the drunken and disgraceful state of that house is something beyond conception. We have no power whatever over it; of course we have over the members when they come into the streets, but then the evil is done.[75]

Thus, unlike the street, which was coming increasingly under the surveillance of the authorities, the club remained free from police interference.[76]

A cursory glance at the steady decline in alcohol consumption in Britain between 1870 and 1914 indicates that the state and employers had successfully eroded the traditional drinking patterns of working-class men. Indeed, as we shall see, the interwar period witnessed a further decline in drinking, with a more pronounced demarcation between work and leisure for working men. This, however, would be to simplify greatly the impact government legislation had upon drinking patterns within working-class culture. The government was successful in helping shape a recognisable working week and define new boundaries for drinking, particularly with the 1872 Licensing Act. However, these new working routines and drink legislation were tempered by circumstance and working men's attempts to circumvent restrictions. The preservation of drinking customs in some trades and the exploitation of more relaxed club licensing laws provided scope for working men to sidestep the restrictive measures found in the 1872 Licensing Act.[77]

As late as 1914, drinking remained very much part of the working day for many men and was not restricted merely to evening leisure time. The publican was also instrumental in sustaining traditional drinking customs in the workplace. One contemporary remembered that, 'before 1914, in many workshops ale was sent for and consumed on the job.'[78] In the 1860s, Thomas Wright, the working-class journeyman engineer, observed that beer breaks were still an important ritual in workshops. In his workplace, Wright noted 'the thirsty souls who towards eleven o'clock in the day find themselves afflicted with a craving for a hair of the dog that bit them last night, and significantly observe in the hearing of an apprentice, that they could do nicely with a pint if they could get it'.[79] Likewise during the Edwardian period, Roberts recalled how, at his father's work, drink was a constant source of disruption to the rhythm of the working day:

> For a long time he worked for an old-fashioned firm where everyone, management included, drank daily to excess. Many a Monday when Father didn't appear on the job the foreman, a notorious 'ale can' himself, arrived at the house in mid-morning and from beyond the shop counter (Mother would not allow him in the kitchen) he would set up loud cajoleries aimed to persuade his henchman, still stupefied on the sofa, back into work. 'We're stuck Bob lad!' he would call. 'Can't get on with that job! Mister Barton', 'Bill Barton (the owner) sent me 'isself!'[80]

The blurred distinctions that drink induced between work and leisure (perhaps literally on some occasions) have prompted some historians to assume that workshop drinking was a relic of the pre-industrial order and was phased out by the regularised week and the new 'scientific' industries of the late nineteenth century.[81] However, drinking breaks were also a feature of the new industries, as one worker of a bicycle component factory recalled just prior to the First World War:

> I had to fetch the beer from the Three Horseshoes. I had two long sticks called 'muggie sticks', and I could carry as many as twenty-four cans on them. A pint of beer cost twopence, and I've known some stampers in hot weather drink as much as sixteen pints in a single shift. Most stampers would have been insulted if you had offered them tea![82]

Significantly, both the management and timekeepers turned a blind eye to these unofficial breaks and in some cases even accepted the legitimacy of employees drinking during working hours. For example, one firm offered a 'beer allowance', all gratis, for any men who worked overtime. Once again, the public house played a central role in awarding men the overtime bonus as a nearby taproom put aside two barrels of beer for the factory timekeeper to dispense to workers in the morning and afternoon. However, on one occasion a worker recalled how a timekeeper abused his position, as although 'the morning allowance – a big one – was served out … when the time came for our afternoon ration, we found the timekeeper flat on the floor lying in a pool of beer that was running from the tap'.[83] The public houses' central role in providing premises for work-based societies was largely due to the high level of trust that the working community placed in the publican. In some cases, Friendly Societies not only used the public house as a meeting place but also entrusted the publican as treasurer for their society.[84]

The First World War certainly brought workshop practices involving drink out into the open, especially with the introduction of new licensing legislation designed to help the war effort.[85] Remarkably in 1917, workers involved in the light engineering industries, which supplied components to the motor trade, convinced a government commission on the necessity of drinking in the workplace. A commission of inquiry on the light metal working industry in the West Midlands reported that restrictions on drinking beer during the First World War had initiated industrial unrest:

> The commission was frankly amazed at the strength of the objections to the liquor restrictions. These come not only from men in the habit of drinking beer, but from those who were life-long teetotallers and yet recognised the need of beer to those working in certain occupations … it must be remembered that we are dealing with men who all their lives have been accustomed to drink beer as and when they want it … it must be recognised it is more than a drink … it is certainly a social habit or a custom of life, as two witnesses expressed it.

The commission's investigation of the shop-floor workers reveals an interesting solidarity between drinkers and teetotallers on the importance of drinking in the workplace. In endorsing the view that beer was 'more than a drink', even teetotallers linked restrictions on drinking in the workplace with a loss of control within the work process. Indeed, faced with the overwhelming hostility of workers to alcohol restrictions, the report recommended that the drink supply 'should be largely increased'.[86] For many workers, then, drink and the public house were not only central to their leisure activities but also an important aspect of their work, a custom that allowed them some autonomy over their working day.

In short, drinking moderately, and on occasions to excess, did not preclude men from taking up their role as respectable citizens, even among the artisanal section of the working community. During the 1860s, when the temperance movement was at its most prominent, one Coventry artisan defended their right to drink in the local press as it livened up potentially dull evenings:

> Drinking, smoking and chatting is what we mostly indulge in. Now I don't say that drinking and smoking are not indulged in to a moderate extent; but the chatting, sir, is without any redeeming; it is insufferably dull, the fact being, sir, that we read nothing excepting the most exciting parts of the newspaper … we have nothing but gossip and scandal to entertain ourselves with; so that we are obliged to drink a little more than we otherwise would in order to make our pleasure palatable.[87]

Furthermore, although most artisans did not approve of drinking to excess, slippage from moderate drinking was not perceived simply as the activities of the morally corrupt, a position at odds with those attempting to reform working-class culture. For example, when a group of artisan weavers organised a day trip from their Coventry 'Kingfields' factory to Southam in the 1860s, onlookers may have mistaken their departure for a teetotal excursion to the Warwickshire countryside. However, as one weaver remembered, the activities of his colleagues were far from temperate:

> Bedecked with button-holes, top hats, velvet waistcoats, they presented a very dignified appearance. So much so that one of their number addressed the company with 'gentleman. I congratulate you on your appearance, it is a credit to Kingfields, I can only say I hope we shall all look as respectable on our return'. It is related that on arriving home the aforesaid speaker was lying at the bottom of the break, lost in oblivion, and had to be carried home.[88]

Respectability and drink among the vast majority of the working community were, then, not mutually exclusive activities. Indeed, this contrasts sharply with both middle- and working-class reforming groups who fused notions of citizenship and temperance in a bid to eliminate drinking from working-class leisure.

Improving the citizen: temperance societies and working-class self-improvement

Although drink, as we have seen, played an important role in many working men's employment and leisure time, the temperance cause also provided a rare platform for both cross-class collaboration and working-class self-improvement. Indeed, the call for temperance found pockets of support across the social spectrum, a factor which ensured that it played an important role in contrasting and sometimes contesting narratives of citizenship throughout most of the nineteenth century.

During the 1830s a number of national temperance societies were established, such as the British Association for the Promotion of Temperance (1833) and the New British and Foreign Temperance Society (1836). Although these middle-class-led movements proclaimed national coverage, membership had clear regional variations, with a high concentration of teetotallers residing in the North West of England.[89] Lancashire was home to approximately one third of the anti-spirit membership in the country, a concentration of teetotallers possibly due to a strong tradition of popular Liberalism in these areas.[90] Furthermore, the stormy industrial and political climate of the 1830s encouraged the formation of societies designed to facilitate a new understanding between masters and workers. According to one temperance activist, questioned during a select committee on drunkeness during the 1830s, intemperance was a chief cause for the poor relations between master and worker: 'I have known men meet at public-houses and get intoxicated with liquor, and if there is any misunderstandings, liquor makes it worse: and if there is none, will very often cause them to create one with their employers.'[91]

The perceived widespread problem of intemperance among the poor was an argument that had been widely deployed to ward off working-class calls for universal manhood suffrage during the 1830s and 1840s. It was in response to this challenge that a number of leading Chartists such as William Lovett attempted to enhance the movement's respectability by encouraging Teetotal Chartism.[92] The diffusion of teetotal ideals within Chartism led Harrison and Hollis to claim that the temperance movement provided a new cause for Chartist leaders and encouraged their integration into an emerging liberal state. They have argued that the leading Chartist Robert Lowery's support for the temperance cause 'provides one instance of the long-standing process of *embourgeoisement* within the working class which characterised several Chartist leaders'.[93] Certainly, there can be no doubt that a number of working men embraced temperance on middle-class terms, enthusiastically joining teetotal organisations and subscribing to their literature. For example, *The British Workman*, established by the middle-class philanthropist Thomas Bywater Smithies in 1854, was a monthly sheet designed to attract working men and women. Lavish pictures would decorate the newspaper, which was preoccupied with religion, temperance and 'other useful information for the working-classes'.

Although the newspaper began as a loss-making venture with a circulation of only 20,000 in 1855, sales increased considerably by the early 1860s, to peak at 250,000 by 1862.[94] However, the number of working men joining the middle-class temperance societies was still relatively small, a pattern acknowledged by Joseph Chamberlain in 1877. When questioned on the success of temperance societies during a Select Committee meeting, Chamberlain replied that 'there are some temperance clubs in Birmingham, but I am afraid that they do not effect much ... I do not think they attract the sort of people we want to save.'[95] In Coventry, a number of coffee taverns were established in 1878 'to counteract the evils of the common public-house system and thus benefit the working classes, for whom they are more especially intended'.[96] The chief backers for the company were leading temperance leaders and key manufacturers in the city's traditional industries of watchmaking and weaving. However, after only eleven years the company reported that it was scaling down its operations as it had only succeeded in attracting middle-class customers.[97]

The failure to attract a large working-class membership led temperance movements to concentrate on conveying their message to opinion-formers in government and members of the community who had contact with the working class through religious or civic duties. John Taylor, chairman of the National Temperance League, explained in 1877 that they had largely abandoned attempts to recruit the poor, and that instead

> the special work of the National Temperance League, especially of late years, has been to influence those classes who influence others. Our objective has been to appeal, for instance, to religious societies ... in the same way we have held conferences with the leading inhabitants of towns – merchant, bankers, manufacturers, and others – and put before them our great principle, that in a movement of this kind, we must work by example as well as by precept.[98]

From the 1850s, movements such as the National Temperance League argued that those in the religious or civic realm could employ temperance ideals as a means of fostering cross-class collaborative ventures, drawing working men into respectable leisure practices which would eventually map out the road to full citizenship. In short, what marked these temperance societies out from others was their desire to locate temperance as a central component in citizenry and encourage a model citizen who would help enhance and sustain existing socio-economic and political institutions.

Middle-class-organised temperance societies were not the sole outlet for those determined to sign the pledge. Since the early nineteenth century, working-class societies had beaten a distinct path towards self-improvement which had embraced issues such as religion, political education and temperance. Although these organisations were less concerned with cross-class collaboration, the moral certainties of their convictions, over the issue of drink, matched that of their middle-class counterparts. Indeed, these working-class organisations, whether temperance, religious or political, often outlined clear guidelines pertaining to the model citizen, guidelines that were often at odds with working-class culture. Working-class temperance societies were particularly striking in their almost religious devotion to the cause, a trend verified by Thomas Wright's account of his visits to such a society in the 1860s. Wright had been persuaded to attend a series of temperance meetings by a number of workmates who had 'become the bane of my existence by their fanatical attempts to induce me to sign the "pledge"'. In total he visited three meetings with between 200 and 300 people in attendance, who, according to Wright were predominantly working class and who previously had been 'slaves to drink'.[99] Although there was no apparent religious affiliation, Wright's observations indicate a 'spiritual' tone to the meetings, with sessions divided between the singing of temperance hymns and speeches updating the members of the movement's activities in the community. The temperance movement had divided the town into districts, each having been appointed a captain and crew to spread the temperance word. During the meeting there was intense competition between captains to claim that they had captured the 'fieriest and the lowest' characters for the cause as this generated the most excitement in the hall. For example, captain twelve announced to an astonished audience that he had persuaded 'Fighting Joe' to sign the pledge, a declaration which was met with a burst of cheers in the hall. However, the uneasy relationship between working-class self-improvement and working-class culture was sometimes exhibited in the most public fashion during temperance meetings. During Wright's third and final visit to the temperance meetings, he noted that all the captains were present with the exception of one:

> The absent captain was number twelve, who was unable to attend, owing to the effects of a severe thrashing he had received from Fighting Joe; Joe, as we learned from the statement of the chairman, having in addition to breaking the pledge, broken the nose of, and otherwise maltreated the unfortunate captain of Number Twelve lifeboat crew. Joe, it appeared, had

> gone to the races, and was returning from them in a state of intoxication, when he was met by the captain, who taunted him with having broken his promise; whereupon Joe instantly assaulted him ... [100]

Wright's account also highlighted the transitory nature of working-class temperance organisations, even among activists. According to Wright, who admittedly was no sympathiser, his once zealous colleagues were to be found in the public house and police courts only a few months later. [101]

Ever since the Chartist movement, working-class proponents of self-improvement had trumpeted causes such as temperance as a qualification for model working-class citizenship. Indeed, in many respects, working-class advocates of self-improvement were pushing against the all-pervading effects of popular culture. Nowhere was this more apparent than in the labour movement during the last quarter of the nineteenth century. Like temperance organisations, socialists projected a quasi-religious feel to their meetings, often advocating strong temperance principles. John Burns, for example, regularly spoke at socialist meetings warning that drink led to industrial bondage and personal depravity. For a significant number of socialist activists, only through total abstinence could the working class claim their rights to full citizenship and social equality. [102] Indeed, by the late nineteenth and early twentieth centuries, there was a concerted effort to remove the socialist and trade-union meeting from the public house. In 1906, two Labour MPs, Arthur Henderson and David Shackleton, worked with the National Temperance League to create the Trade Union and Labour Officials' Temperance Fellowship. Through public appeals, the aim of the organisation was to encourage total abstinence and end the public house as a natural home for the trade-union meeting. They faced, however, a daunting task for it was estimated in 1902 that only 70 out of 2,400 branches of 9 significant trade unions held meetings away from the public house. This meant that over 50,000 members were attending public houses on a regular basis under the auspices of trade-union business. [103]

The significance of temperance within socialism was accentuated by the movement's religious dimension. Although the free Churches, such as Methodists, Congregationalists, Salvation Army and Baptists, were traditionally linked with the Liberal Party, a growing number of evangelicals became attracted to the radicalism of the labour movement during the Victorian and Edwardian periods. Indeed, the movement had its own religious strand after 1891 when John Trevor, a minister who had become disillusioned with Unitarianism, founded the Labour Church movement. Furthermore, a strong religious dimension was also present at the birth of the Parliamentary Labour Party. The conference held in Bradford to establish the Independent Labour Party in 1906 incorporated a Labour Church service that attracted over 5,000 people. Significantly, the evangelical presence in left-wing movements did little to change the social composition of activists, and if anything reinforced the lower-middle- and upper-working-class membership profile of British socialists.[104] Such was the influence of the free churches, the Labour Party Secretary Arthur Henderson was able to conclude in 1929 'that the bulk of the members of the Parliamentary Labour Party at any given time during the last twenty-five years had graduated into their wider sphere of activity via the Sunday School, the Bible Class, the temperance society or the pulpit'.[105] With such an education, then, it is perhaps no surprise that temperance ideals became a mainstay in socialist organisations' battle to reform and improve popular culture.

The linkages between religious bodies and socialism that temperance fostered ensured that their experience and immersion into popular culture reinforced their critique of working-class lifestyles, even if they did not always agree on the solutions to the 'drink problem'. Interestingly, temperance success stories, retold in speeches, memoirs and biographies, followed a familiar narrative whether the teetotaller was a socialist activist or member of a free church. For example, the biographer of Will Crooks, a working-class socialist during the late nineteenth century, described how he had shunned fellow workmates who had urged him to drink in the Railway Tavern after work. As a consequence, Crooks was 'mercilessly "chipped" in the workshop and referred to as the man whose missus was waiting for him'. However, merely through the power of persuasion, Crooks convinced his workmates of the benefits of temperance and 'at the end of six weeks the "Railway" was without a customer from the shop'.[106] The outsider looking into a degenerate culture from a morally superior position was a familiar scenario for the temperance advocate. Although of a different social class and with a different message to tell, a London missioner's engagement with working-class drinkers, as told by the Salvation Army's official historian, adopted this recognisable narrative:

> On one occasion men were given drink and sent, in a half intoxicated condition, to create a disturbance while a missioner was speaking outside the building. Next a policeman was called, who ordered the preacher to desist and threatened him with arrest. All crowded into the little hall, and before the meeting ended the ringleader of the attack had been converted![107]

Whether these incidents actually happened in the fashion stated is perhaps not as important as the message they conveyed. Facing ridicule and against the odds, the lone activist, armed only with the virtues of temperance, successfully won over the 'lowest' and most hardened drinkers. Indeed, for many teetotal socialists, their regular forays into working-class culture were often unrewarding and unhappy affairs, experiences which serve to underline the rather limited impact that both middle- and working-class advocates of temperance had upon popular culture.[108]

However, there is evidence to suggest that working men during the late nineteenth and early twentieth centuries did forge a sense of identity in rapidly growing urban centres through developing notions of local patriotism. This popular notion of citizenship was shorn of the moralising tone of the urban elites' 'social citizenship' and instead placed emphasis on attachments to the working-class's immediate environments. Since these expressions of civic pride were often informal and spontaneous, working-class identification with citizenry caught the authorities by surprise. Indeed in football, working-class males had found a new medium in which to express a civic pride. The emergence of the game will form the final section of the chapter.[109]

Association football:
popular forms of citizenship

By 1914, association football had become the most popular form of male entertainment in Britain. Professionalism within the game had been firmly established and, by the mid-1890s, a league had been founded comprising sixteen clubs and attracting between 300,000 and 400,000 spectators a week. This phenomenal growth continued with over 6 million people paying to watch First Division professional football alone during the Edwardian period.[110] Significantly, it was also relatively cheap, with matches costing only sixpence in the late nineteenth century, a charge that the regularly employed semi-skilled worker could afford.[111] The form and style of association football for those playing and watching in 1914, however, was vastly different to the vision of the game the Football Association (FA) had in mind during the 1860s. Founded in 1863, the FA set about codifying the game's rules, largely as a response to variances that had emerged from public schools that had adopted football as a gentlemanly sport. The public school ethic of amateur athleticism and sportsmanship was perceived as a set of ideal traits that could be introduced into work-ing-class neighbourhoods through the formation of football clubs. In the North and the Midlands in particular, church teams such as Aston Villa, Birmingham, Bolton and Barnsley were initially established to offer lo-cal working men a healthy and civilising alternative to the public house. Football was deemed essentially an athletic activity, and the idea of a partisan and animated crowd watching meaningful and fierce competition between teams was far removed from anything the early football organis-ers envisaged. This was, of course, the path along which both amateur and professional football developed, with the emphasis on winning rather than on the 'technical beauty of the game'. To the horror of the rational recreationalists, the working-class crowds that began flocking to the grounds were taking the 'rational' dimension out of the game, adopting a mindless fanaticism for their team and a loathing towards opposing players, sup-porters and the referee. In response to the crowd's demands, teams began to change their playing style in an all-out bid to win rather than 'play the game'. The public school ethos of individual flair and the cavalier style of attack were dropped for a more measured approach in which players were deployed to defend and prevent the opposition from scoring.[112] Critics of the game came thick and fast, with Herbert Spencer describing football as the 're-barbarisation of society', while A. F. Hills regretted the demise of fairplay since the purpose of sport was not to 'hire a team of gladiators, and bid them fight our football battles for us'.[113]

The socialists were equally unimpressed with this new working-class passion.[114] One activist wrote in 1908 that he did not 'suggest there is anything wrong with football, but there does seem something wrong with the majority of people who habitually attend football matches and fill their minds with things that don't matter', adding that 'difficult though the task may be to push football out of their heads and push socialism in, the task must be undertaken'. Alongside the problem of engendering a passion for socialism rather than football, activists also worried that the game, with its vociferous local patriotism, damaged working-class solidarity. In addition, the professionalism and commercialism of the game suggested to many socialists that football was simply another form of 'opium', dulling the masses into accepting and supporting the status quo.[115] These anxieties have been echoed by neo-Marxist historians who have argued that football helped spawn traits such as competition, nationalism and inter-class rivalry that were deemed natural behaviour in late-nineteenth-century society. In short the rules of society were learnt on the nation's playing fields. By 1914, it is argued, the process was complete in that a genuine working-class culture had been supplanted by a culture of consolation.[116] Those who argue that sport performed a hegemonic role in British society tend to present working-class males as passive actors in the whole process, swept up in a tide of emotion into the arms of leisure entrepreneurs. While rejecting this rather mechanistic approach to class relations, Russell has rightly argued that the working-class's ability to shape key characteristics of football should not be exaggerated. In terms purely of power relations, the working class wielded very little control within the game.[117] In an attempt to understand, then, why so many men were attracted to football, it is perhaps more fruitful to explore how and why they shaped their own identities around the game. It was a process which gave football an added meaning and a focus in the local community and one which the club owners had never anticipated. Indeed, football's popularity during this period was less to do with a manipulative ruling class than due to the process of socialisation and citizenship in the growing cities of the late nineteenth century.[118]

The working-class neighbourhood had become a recognisable characteristic of the large city or town by 1914.[119] These large socially homogeneous communities sprawled out from the city centres, hidden away from the 'civilising' influences of the symbolic architecture and elevating governance of the municipality. For the inhabitants of these neighbourhoods, then, the city centre with its town hall and civic grandeur provoked little in the way of civic pride, since it was far removed from their own neighbourhoods that comprised row after row of terraced housing. This monotonous landscape created new problems of identity for the inhabitants, particularly if they had migrated to an anonymous and often unfriendly city in search of work. Football, though a popular sport to play, became an even more attractive spectacle to watch, as it fostered a sense of place and belonging for working men away from the family home. For boom cities like Coventry, which in the 1870s had few football teams to speak of, the influx of workers entering the bicycle industry transformed the city's footballing culture. A local paper explained:

> thousands of working men have helped to increase the population by coming to Coventry from the large industrial cities in which first class football is provided. Working in the principal factories of the city today are men from London, Newcastle, Woolwich, Birmingham and many other large centres.

After carrying through their week's work they have been used to watching
the crack team of the first league.[120]

By the 1880s, football had surpassed rugby football, its nearest rival,
as the most popular sport in the city, provoking one newspaper editor to
comment on the 'almost incredible' speed at which 'Singer's [Coventry's
premier cycle works' football team] should have so quickly won their way
to popularity'.[121] It was significant that the commentator in his discussion
on the merits of rugby and football continued to link football's success
with the growing bicycle industry. A number of key cycle firms, such as
Singer's, Humber and Rudge, appeared to have provided an outlet for male
workers to express a sense of pride in the products and the place they
were produced, particularly since they were able to afford bicycles after
firms introduced hire purchase schemes.[122] Bicycle firms gave migrant workers an initial sense of identity and a connection with their new city that
eventually expressed itself through supporting works' football teams. The
strong links between the football clubs and the city's principal industries
continued into the twentieth century since, prior to the First World War,
Coventry City football club acquired the nickname the 'Bantams' after a
make of car produced by Singer's.[123]

The bicycle workers' appetite for football was initially satisfied through
the formation of a number of well-supported bicycle factory teams in the
1880s, provoking fierce rivalry that sometimes spilled over into the local
press. After a particularly heated encounter between Great Heath, a works'
team based in the Foleshill area of Coventry, and Rudge, a leading bicycle
works' team, a Great Heath supporter complained to the local press about
the poor conduct and bad language emanating from their opponent's supporters. In reply, a supporter of Rudge wrote that the correspondent and
others in the city were jealous of his team's achievements and that 'he
oughtn't to expect to go to a football match and hear the spectators recit-
ing the parable of the loaves and the fishes', especially since 'the Rudge
earlier in the season had beaten Great Heath by six to none at Foleshill
and he should have heard the language from the Foleshill tribe'.[124] With
a new and growing level of interest in football, it was not long before a
successful team emerged, which went on to represent the city. Prior to
the team becoming Coventry City Football Club, Singer's was a bicycle
works' club that dominated the city's football competitions and, by the early
1890s, amateur football throughout the Midlands. Indeed, 1891 proved a
turning point, since Singer's won the prestigious Birmingham and District

Junior Cup, providing the springboard from which eventually to represent the city.[125] The team's triumphant homecoming after the victory is worthy of closer inspection since it provides an insight into the peculiar fusion of citizenship and masculine identity which working men projected onto their team.

From the moment the news was received by telegram in Coventry that the Singer's team had won the cup in Birmingham, 'there was a spontaneous desire that the victors on coming home, should at least have a cordial reception'. What proceeded resembled a civic procession and reception, except that this was an event that had no municipal planning or involvement. Instead, the demand for the team's recognition had emerged from the working men in the bicycle factories, who for the two weeks preceding the game had talked of little else. The *Coventry Standard* reported the scene when the team arrived at Coventry station:

> The station yard and below was packed with admirers, hundreds of men wearing in their hats either a cardboard bird (symbolic of Singer's) or a card giving the names of the team beneath 'Play Up Singer's' with a portrait of the head of the firm. The Apollo band also came out. The enthusiasm of the people seemed to know no bound, and coloured fires were burnt. The train was pretty punctual in arriving. A way had to be made for the passengers to get out of the station. At last the team appeared – best indicated by the much coveted cup lifted above their heads. Cheer upon cheer was raised, cry upon cry went up. The reception accorded them was such as now-a-days is usually reserved for a great personage, whose reputation has long fascinated the imagination. In ancient Athens at the Isthmian games, there must have been such scenes. For the eleven and a few other men a brake was reserved and a procession was formed. The band started off with 'should auld acquaintance', other well known tunes were played into the centre of the city, popular ditties were sung.[126]

Although the city's council were oblivious to this excitement, the Singer bicycle firm hastily arranged an 'informal' reception at a city-centre hotel, which offered a suitable climax to the procession.[127] Clearly, there are inherent dangers in using the local press as an insight into how civic pride was generated by the homecoming of a triumphant team. As Hill has pointed out, there was often a desire on such occasions for newspapers to present a community free from social division.[128] Nevertheless, the marked absence of civic involvement during Singer's celebratory parade effectively deprived the press of a socially consensual dimension to the story. This spontaneous procession, which had largely been generated by the enthusiasm of the workers themselves, offered male workers a sense of belonging, or a 'symbolic citizenship'.[129]

The celebrations that greeted the victorious Singer's team did not go unnoticed by the city's urban elite, however. In 1905, seven years after changing its name to Coventry City Football Club, the club was taken over by a number of prominent city councillors, including Alderman Fred Lee and Samuel Rollason.[130] This was the start of the process which saw moves to formalise the linkages between local patriotism, good citizenship and support for the city's football team. Moreover, the club's ties to the local community were also strengthened 'from below' as trade unions, particularly during the industrial conflicts during the First World War, used Highfield Road to stage mass union meetings and rallies.[131] After large crowds watched Coventry after the war when competitive football was resumed, the club was allowed to leave the Southern League for Division II. This effective promotion provoked wild celebrations in the factories and streets of the city, a phenomenon that confirmed for many among the urban elite football's potential as a vehicle for civic patriotism. For example, the club's application for Division II was signed by the Mayor and the city's MP, providing a ringing endorsement both of the new found respectability of football and of its power in stimulating a popular civic pride in a city.[132]

After Coventry City had been successful in joining Division II, a meeting on the future of the club and the city was held at St Mary's Hall, significantly the closest venue Coventry had to a town hall. In attendance was the Coventry MP, E. Manville, Charles Sutcliffe of the Football League, and no fewer that ten city councillors. Throughout the meeting it was made clear to the people of Coventry they had almost a civic duty to support the club's momentous step into Division II. Indeed, it was announced that working-class supporters should push aside the political discontent that had surfaced during the war and pull behind the club and the city. During the meeting Sutcliffe warned supporters that

> they [the League] had taken Coventry into the League on faith. Were the citizens of Coventry going to make good? They did not want a bankrupt club; they had enough of them. No matter what they thought of the Capitalist, the club without capital was no good. The citizens had to redeem the promise which was made by Mr Clayton and others [Coventry directors] who were at the special meeting of the Football League. They had to make Coventry City into a club worthy of its name and worthy of the League.[133]

Earlier, a similar theme had been taken up by the club's chairman, David Cooke, who proclaimed 'that there were plenty of working men in Coventry who would be willing to put a few pounds into the club'.[134] Although Coventry City had become a registered limited company in 1907, with capital shares of £2,000, it was only in 1919 that a sustained appeal went out to working-class investors.[135] As Mason and Vamplew have argued, clubs had for some time issued small amounts of shares to their supporters in a bid to strengthen commitment to their team.[136] However, the timing of Coventry's appeal does suggest an attempt to encourage a local patriotism in both the club and the city during a period of demographic uncertainty induced by the end of the war. For the club's directors, who were also city councillors, it was important to extend the peoples' enthusiasm and pride for the club exhibited at the end of the war into the civic domain, a process that they had singularly failed to achieve during the late nineteenth and early twentieth centuries.[137] Yet there lurked a danger that the football craze might desert the city with the munitions workers after the war, a scenario that had troubled the directors of the club. The *Midland Daily Telegraph*, however, noted, with some relief, the good attendances during the start of the 1919 season:

> The hold which football had on the public in pre-war days was a source of wonder to that section of the nation which did not find its recreation and its pleasure on the playing field ... when gates of twelve thousand or so were seen at Coventry City's home matches last season many rubbed their eyes in wonder and explained the phenomenon by the fact that Coventry was living under artificial conditions with an enormously inflated population still with us due to the war, which has just terminated, and that a great percentage of the strangers in our midst being Northerners that patronized the game more heartedly than Coventrians. But the city has lost many thousands of its temporary residents since then, there has been two attractive league games being played in Birmingham last Saturday and yet 16,500 people crowded to the Highfield Road ground.[138]

The civic elites' association with Coventry City continued throughout the interwar period, with councillors occupying prominent roles on the board and linking the team's success with the city's civic development at every opportunity. Given Coventry City's rather chequered history, admittedly opportunities to celebrate the success of the team were few and far between. During their brief stay in Division II, Coventry became something of a music hall joke, constantly avoiding relegation by the skin of their teeth and changing their colours regularly in a bid to change their luck.[139] Nevertheless, the club's promotion to Division II once more in 1936, after ten years in the wilderness, provoked the city's Mayor to announce that 'apart from anything else, a team holding a high position in the football world is an asset to the city and enhances its representation'.[140] Support for the club during the interwar period appeared to track the city's wider demographic and economic fortunes. A fall in population coupled with an economic recession during the 1920s coincided with Coventry City's slide from Division II and a fall in attendances. However, between 1931 and 1939, the population grew rapidly from 167,083 to 224,247. Migrants accounted for over 42,000 of the population rise, most attracted to the city's resurgent motor industry and allied trades. Significantly, the vast majority of migrants were blue-collar workers, a trend which made Coventry one of the few communities in Britain to have an excess of males in the late 1930s.[141] During the 1930s, there was an upturn in Coventry City's fortunes on the pitch, which was matched by large crowds of between 30,000 and 40,000, figures which placed the club as one of the best supported in country.[142] We can only speculate on the correlation between the club and the city's demography but the evidence suggests that for these new migrants, like the bicycle and munitions workers who preceded them, football proved a popular leisure activity as it gave them a sense of place and identity. Although the civic elite attempted to capitalise on football's popularity, at ground level this popular notion of citizenship defined their relationship with the city, not through municipal initiatives or civic architecture but through their support for the football club. This allegiance would be constantly reaffirmed through regular matches with other clubs and supporters from different parts of a city or region. Indeed, similar fierce allegiances to clubs was a marked feature in northern England and Scotland, a late-nineteenth-century phenomenon which indicates that football was the vehicle for the male working class's expression and celebration of town identities.[143] Football, then, conveyed a popular form of citizenship which constructed assumptions about the town or city's achievements and, significantly, developed ideas about the 'otherness' of those from outside the town. In addition, this was both a class-specific and a gendered form of citizenship. Between 1870 and 1914, the football match, along with other key leisure institutions such as the public house, was the preserve of the male; it was his own space outside of the family household and neighbourhood, which was usually the woman's domain.[144]

The public house also reinforced football as primarily a masculine sport since a post-match drink and 'football talk' were almost obligatory for the male supporter.[145] Thus, football enthusiasts generated their own vernacular, which, as Russell has pointed out, 'could be used wittingly or otherwise to exclude women, or indeed men who withstood the game's attractions'.[146] In a sense it bound men who, in rapidly growing cities, would have struggled to forge a shared identity outside of work had it not been for the appeal of football. Inside the ground, the unruliness, gestures, bad language and intimidatory tactics of the crowd were rooted in older forms of male-centred popular culture and were a reminder that the crowd saw themselves as much part of the event as the players themselves. In a place such as Coventry, where an industrial boom had encouraged extensive immigration, supporting a football team fostered an attachment to the city and a popular civic pride, a feat which repeated municipal schemes of social citizenship had singularly failed to achieve.[147]

Conclusion

The landscape of working-class male leisure significantly altered during the last quarter of the nineteenth century. It has been tempting for historians to cite increasing government legislation to curb drinking and the intensive capitalisation of mass leisure institutions as significant agencies in shaping working-class culture. Certainly, groups formed within both middle- and working-class communities to oppose the hedonism of mass commercial leisure, placing sobriety at the heart of their notions of the 'model citizen'. Moreover, while some historians have argued that the process represented the introduction of a mass culture at the expense of an authentic working-class culture, others have maintained that mass commercial leisure merely helped foster an existing conservatism and inward-looking perspective among working-people.[148] These interpretations at first appear quite compelling since skilled and semi-skilled men, particularly in the industrial boom towns of the late nineteenth century, experienced unprecedented levels of consumerism. Indeed, running concurrently, key institutions within male working-class leisure – the public house, music hall or the football match – were all subject to some form of legislation or codified rules. However, these restrictions did not necessarily curtail traditional traits in working-class leisure but instead forged new baselines on which working men would impose their own layer of meaning. Thus drinking continued to feature as the centrepiece of a working man's leisure and work time, proving a barrier to neither respectability nor civic responsibility, while audience participation in the music hall continued into the late nineteenth century. Likewise, the ability of the crowd to take an active role in a match ensured that football had become the most popular male sporting spectacle by 1914. It is perhaps more useful, then, to see mass commercial leisure less as replacing an authentic working-class culture and more as a successful imitator of it. Football, however, also provides a glimpse into how working men perceived their own relationship with the neighbourhood or town they were living in. Supporting the local football team cultivated a symbolic class-specific form of citizenship that differed markedly from the municipal initiative that emphasised class cooperation.

Notes

1 D. Read, *England 1868–1914* (London, Longman, 1979), p. 22; A. Davies, *Leisure, Gender and Poverty. Working-Class Culture in Salford and Manchester 1900–1939* (Buckingham, Open University Press, 1992), p. 73.

2 L. Senelick, 'Politics as entertainment: Victorian music hall songs', *Victorian Studies*, 19 (1975–76); P. Wild, 'Recreation in Rochdale, 1900–1940', in J. Clarke, C. Critcher and R. Johnson (eds), *Working Class Culture. Studies in History and Theory* (London, Hutchinson, 1979), p. 160; H. Cunningham, *Leisure in the Industrial Revolution, 1780–1880* (London, Croom Helm, 1980), p. 187; G. Stedman Jones, *Languages of Class* (Cambridge, Cambridge University Press, 1983), pp. 179–238; P. Johnson, 'Conspicuous consumption and working-class culture in late Victorian and Edwardian Britain', *Transactions of the Royal Historical Society*, 38 (1988), 27, 41; C. Waters, *British Socialists and the Politics of Popular Culture 1884–1914* (Manchester, Manchester University Press, 1990). For a more positive gloss on the formation of class identity and commercial leisure, see E.J. Hobsbawm, 'The making of the working class 1870–1914', in *Worlds of Labour. Further Studies in the History of Labour* (London, Weidenfeld, 1984); P. Bailey, *Leisure and Class in Victorian England. Rational Recreation and the Contest for Control 1830–1885* (London, Methuen, 1978); D. Kift, *The Victorian Music Hall. Culture, Class and Conflict* (Cambridge, Cambridge University Press, 1996).

3 *Coventry Times*, 18 March 1891.

4 Waters, *British Socialists and the Politics of Popular Culture*, p. 38.

5 R. Tressell, *The Ragged Trousered Philanthropists* (1914; London, Flamingo, 1993), p. 451.

6 Cited in Waters, *British Socialists and the Politics of Popular Culture*, p. 42.

7 R. Roberts, *The Classic Slum. Salford Life in the First Quarter of the Century* (Manchester, Manchester University Press, 1971), p. 16.

8 *Luton Reporter*, 3 November 1910.

9 G. Le Bon, *The Crowd. A Study of the Popular Mind* (1897; London, New Brunswick, 1995).

10 M. Savage and A. Miles, *The Remaking of the British Working Class, 1840–1940* (London, Routledge, 1994), ch. 3.

11 D. Read, *England 1868–1914* (1979; London, Longman, 1985), pp. 223–43.

12 J. Benson, *The Working Class in Britain, 1850–1939* (London, Longman, 1989), p. 56.

13 T. Mason, 'Sport and recreation', in P. Johnson (ed.), *Twentieth Century Britain. Economic, Social and Cultural Change* (London, Longman, 1994), p. 112.

14 M. Tebbutt, *Making Ends Meet. Pawnbroking and Working-Class Credit* (Leicester, Leicester University Press, 1983), p. 38; E. Roberts, *A Women's Place. An Oral History of Working-Class Women 1890–1940* (Oxford, Oxford University Press, 1984), p. 110.

15 A. August, 'A Culture of consolation? Rethinking politics in working-class London, 1870–1914', *Institute of Historical Research*, 74 (2001), 199.

16 *Coventry Standard*, 27 June 1884.

17 *Coventry Herald*, 24 March 1899.

18 A. Dingle, 'Drink and working-class living standards in Britain, 1870–1914', *Economic History Review*, 4 (1972), 616.

19 G. R. Carter, 'The cycle industry', in S. Webb and A. Freeman (eds), *Seasonal Trades* (London, Constable, 1912), pp. 129, 142.

20 *Coventry Herald*, 7 December 1906.

21 A. O. Jay, *Life in Darkest London* (London, Webster & Cable, 1891), pp. 12, 30.

22 Davies, *Leisure, Gender and Poverty*, p. 43.

23 Although Tressell in *The Ragged Trousered Philanthropists* does not describe a music hall scene in the novel, he shows that despite the low pay and the constant flirtation with poverty working men were conversant with the latest music hall entertainment. See particularly Tressell, *The Ragged Trousered Philanthropists*, p. 451.

24 J. Crump, 'Provincial music hall: Promoters and public in Leicester, 1863–1929', in P. Bailey (ed.), *Music Hall. The Business of Pleasure* (Milton Keynes, Open University Press, 1986), p. 53.

25 S. D. Pennybacker, *A Vision of London 1889–1914. Labour, Everyday Life and the LCC Experiment* (London, Routledge, 1995), p. 211.

26 Kift, *The Victorian Music Hall*, pp. 2, 26.

27 Kift, *The Victorian Music Hall*, pp. 2, 26.

28 Savage and Miles, *The Remaking of the British Working Class*, p. 25.

29 D. A. Reid, 'Popular theatre in Victorian Birmingham, in D. Bradby, L. James and B. Sherratt (eds), *Performance and Politics in Popular Drama* (Cambridge, Cambridge University Press, 1980), p. 71.

30 Cited in Reid, 'Popular theatre in Victorian Birmingham', p. 71.

31 Kift, *The Victorian Music Hall*, p. 72.

32 Senelick, 'Politics as entertainment: Victorian music hall songs', 150.

33 Stedman Jones, *Languages of Class*, ch. 4.

34 Anon, 'An evening at a Whitechapel "Gaff"', in J. Greenwood (ed.), *The Wilds of London* (London, Chatto & Windus, 1874), p. 15.

35 Reid, 'Popular theatre in Birmingham', p. 68.

36 *Coventry Herald*, 25 November 1864.

37 B. Poole, *Coventry Its History and Antiquities* (Coventry, 1870), p. 337; *Coventry Herald*, 24 November 1865.

38 *Coventry Herald*, 29 December 1865.

39 Coventry Local Studies (hereafter CLS), W. H. Stringer, 'Coventry theatricals half a century ago', in A. Heap, 'Newspaper cuttings', vol. 7, 102.

40 Wright, *Some Habits and Customs of the Working Classes*, p. 198.

41 Wright, *Some Habits and Customs of the Working Classes*, pp. 158–9.

42 This accords with Price's findings on imperialism and the lower middle class. See R. Price, *An Imperial War and the British Working Class. Working-Class Attitudes and Reactions to the Boer War, 1899–1902* (London, Routledge & Kegan Paul, 1972).

43 P. Maloney, *Scotland and the Music Hall* (Manchester, Manchester University Press, 2003), p. 218.

44 P. Bailey, 'Champagne Charlie: Performance and ideology in the music hall swell song', in J. S. Bratton, *Music Hall. Performance and Style* (Milton Keynes, Open University Press, 1986), p. 58

45 For analysis of how the traditional coster character performed by Gus Elen was a combative rather than a submissive depiction of working-class life, see S. Featherstone, 'E dunno where 'e ave: Coster comedy and the politics of music hall', *Nineteenth Century Theatre*, 24:1 (1996).

46 London School of Economics (hereafter LSE), Charles Booth Archive, notebook B371, p. 217.

47 Anon, 'An "anti-idiotic entertainment company"', in Greenwood, *The Wilds of London*, pp. 306–7.

48 P. Bailey, 'Conspiracies of meaning: Music hall and the knowingness of popular culture', *Past and Present*, 144 (August 1994), p. 138.

49 P. Bailey, *Leisure and Class in Victorian England*, p. 160.

50 J. Earl, 'Building the music halls', in P. Bailey (ed.) *Music Hall. The Business of Pleasure* (Milton Keynes, Open University, 1986), p. 2.

51 Earl, 'Building the music halls', p. 31.

52 P. Bailey, 'Custom, capital and culture in the Victorian music hall', in R. Storch (ed.) *Popular Culture and Custom in Nineteenth Century England* (Beckenham, Croom Helm, 1982), p. 193.

53 *Era*, 10 November 1900.

54 *The Times*, 26 September 1898.

55 *Era*, 26 January 1879.

56 *Era*, 7 March 1875. See also Kift, *The Victorian Music Hall*, p. 116.

57 Pennybacker, *A Vision of London*, p. 222.

58 *The Times*, 30 January 1942.

59 *Era*, 28 February 1875.

60 LSE, Charles Booth Archive, notebook B346, p. 21.

61 R. Samuel, *East End Underworld. Chapters in the Life of Arthur Harding* (London, Routledge, 1981), p. 41.

62 W. Woodruff, *The Road to Nab End. An Extraordinary Northern Childhood* (London, Abacus, 2002), p. 113.

63 *Daily Mail*, 25 November 1913.

64 *New Statesmen*, 18 November 1916.

65 B. Harrison, *Drink and the Victorians. The Temperance Question in England 1815–1872* (1971; Keele, Keele University Press, 1994), p. 46.

66 Davies, *Leisure, Gender and Poverty*, p. 61.

67 Coventry Record Office (hereafter CRO), Paul Thompson Oral History Archive, Acc 1647/1/72.

68 R. Hoggart, *The Uses of Literacy* (Harmondsworth, Penguin, 1957), pp. 94–5.

69 Harrison, *Drink and the Victorians*, p. 228. For a contemporary account of the impact of Government legislation on drinking, see W. Lawson, 'The drink difficulty', *Nineteenth Century*, 5 (1879).

70 *The Times*, 9 August 1872.

71 Harrison, *Drink and the Victorians*, p. 255. In many of these demonstrations the crowd subverted a patriotic song, 'Rule Britannia', into an attack on the government with the constant emphasis on 'Rule Britannia, Britons never shall be slaves.'

72 *Coventry Standard*, 30 August 1872.

73 *The Times*, 26 August 1872.

74 CLS, A. Lowe, 'City of Coventry newscuttings, 1899–1900', p. 8.

75 British Parliamentary Papers (hereafter BPP), *First report of the select committee of the House of Lords on Intemperance*, 20 April 1877, p. 204.

76 A. Croll, 'Street disorder, surveillance and shame: Regulating behaviour in the public spaces of the late Victorian town', *Social History*, 24 (1999). For an analysis of how the public house was associated with a criminal underworld, see M. A. Smith, 'Social usages of the public drinking house: Changing aspects of class and leisure, *British Journal of Sociology*, 34:3 (1983).

77 C. Behagg, 'Narratives of control: Informalism and the workplace 1800–1900', in O. Ashton, R. Fyson and S. Roberts (eds), *The Duty of Discontent. Essays for Dorothy Thompson* (London, Mansell, 1995), p. 136.

78 Roberts, *The Classic Slum*, p. 123.

79 Wright, *Some Habits and Customs of the Working Classes*, p. 86.

80 Roberts, *The Classic Slum*, p. 123.

81 Cunningham, *Leisure in the Industrial Revolution*, p. 58.

82 A. Muir, *75 Years of Progress. Smith's Stamping Works* (Tonbridge, Tonbridge Printers, 1958), p. 31.

83 Muir, *75 Years of Progress*, p. 31.

84 P. Weller, 'Self-help and provident societies in Coventry in the nineteenth century', M.Phil. dissertation, University of Warwick, 1990, p. 99.

85 G. Phillips, 'The social impact', in S. Constantine, M.W. Kirby and M.B. Rose (eds), *The First World War in British History* (London, Edward Arnold, 1995), p. 128.

86 University of Warwick, Modern Records Centre, MSS 36/19, 'Industrial Unrest', p. 9.

87 *Coventry Herald*, 24 June 1864.

88 CRO, Acc 562/74, 'Cash Centenary 1846–1946' (unpublished report, 1946), ch. 6, p. 1.

89 BPP, *Social Problems, Drunkeness*, 3, 1877, 220.

90 C. Waters, 'Manchester morality and London capital: The battle over the Palace of Varieties', in P. Bailey (ed.), *Music Hall. The Business of Pleasure* (Milton Keynes, Open University Press, 1986), p. 149; Harrison, *Drink and the Victorians*, p. 132.

91 BPP, *Report on the Select Committee into Drunkeness*, 5 August 1834, p. 90

92 For a fierce condemnation of teetotal Chartism, see Feargus O'Connor's letter in the *Northern Star*, 3 April 1841.

93 B. Harrison and P. Hollis, 'Chartism, Liberalism and the life of Robert Lowery', *English Historical Review*, 82 (1967), p. 534.

94 P.R. Mountjoy, 'Thomas Bywater Smithies, editor of the *British Workman*', *Victorian Periodicals Review*, 18 (1985), 48.

95 BPP, *First Report Select Committee of the House of Lords on Intemperance*, 20 April 1877, p. 230

96 *Stevens' Coventry Leamington, Nuneaton, Kenilworth and Warwickshire Directory 1880*, p. 33; for list of shareholders, see CRO, Acc 91/1, 'Coventry Coffee Tavern Minute Book', 27 February 1878.

97 *Coventry Times*, 30 January 1889. The company was fairly successful in procuring a middle-class custom and only folded in 1905 after the secretary 'disappeared' with the profits. See CRO, Acc 91/1, 'Coventry Coffee Tavern Minute Book', 4 September 1905; *Coventry Herald*, 8 September 1905.

98 BPP, *First Report Select Committee of the House of Lords on Intemperance*, 20 April 1877, p. 220

99 Wright, *Some Habits and Customs of the Working Classes*, pp. 134, 139.

100 Wright, *Some Habits and Customs of the Working Classes*, p. 146.

101 Wright, *Some Habits and Customs of the Working Classes*, p. 151.

102 Waters, *British Socialists and the Politics of Popular Culture*, p. 33.

103 D.W. Gutzke, *Protecting the Pub. Brewers and Publicans against Temperance* (London, Boydell Press, 1989), pp. 222–3.

104 M. Bevir, 'The Labour Church Movement', *Journal of British Studies*, 38 (1999), 217, 229.

105 P. Catterall, 'Morality and politics: The free churches and the Labour Party between the wars', *The Historical Journal*, 36 (1993), 668.

106 G. Haw, *The Life Story of Will Crooks M.P.* (1907; Cassell, London, 1917), p. 54.

107 R. Sandall, *The History of the Salvation Army, vol. 1, 1865–1878* (London, Thomas Nelson & Sons, 1947), p. 58.

108 Gutzke, *Protecting the Pub*, p. 233.

109 Pennybacker, *A Vision of London 1889–1914*, p. 211.

110 R. Holt, *Sport and the British. A Modern History* (Oxford, Clarendon Press, 1990), p. 135. For forthcoming books on the rise of football, see M. Taylor, *The Leaguers. The Making of Professional Football in England 1900–1939* (Liverpool, Liverpool University Press, forthcoming 2005); M. Taylor, *The Association Game. The History of British Football 1863–2000* (London, Longman, forthcoming 2005).

111 T. Mason, *Association Football and English Society* (Brighton, Harvester, 1980), p. 148.

112 Mason, *Association Football*, ch. 7.

113 Quoted in P. Bailey, *Leisure and Class*, p. 152; Holt, *Sport and the British*, p. 144.

114 For an analysis of sport and politics, see S. G. Jones, *Sport, Politics and the Working Class. Organised Labour and Sport in Interwar Britain* (Manchester, Manchester University Press, 1992).

115 Quoted in Waters, *British Socialists and Popular Culture*, p. 35.

116 W. J. Barker, 'The making of a working-class football culture', *Journal of Social History*, 13 (1979); S. Wagg, *The Football World* (Brighton, Harvester, 1984); J. Hargreaves, *Sport, Power and Culture* (Cambridge, Polity Press, 1987).

117 D. Russell, *Football and the English. A Social History of Association Football in England 1863–1995* (Preston, Carnegie Publishing, 1997), p. 70.

118 R. J. Holt, 'Football and the urban way of life in nineteenth-century Britain', in J. A. Mangan (ed.) *Pleasure, Profit, Proselytism. British Culture and Sport at Home and Abroad, 1700–1914* (London, Frank Cass, 1988), p. 68.

119 Savage and Miles, *The Remaking of the British Working Class*, pp. 62–8.

120 *Midland Daily Telegraph*, 1 September 1906.

121 *Coventry Times*, 2 January 1889.

122 See Chapter 3 for the 'pay as you ride' schemes.

123 N. Foulger, *Coventry. The Complete History of the Club* (Wensum Books, Norwich, 1979), p. 16.

124 *Midland Daily Telegraph*, 8 July 1897.

125 Foulger, *Coventry. The Complete History of the Club*, p. 13.

126 *Coventry Standard*, 24 April 1891.

127 *Coventry Standard*, 24 April 1891.

128 J. Hill, 'Cup finals and community in the North of England', in J. Williams and S. Wagg (eds), *British Football and Social Change* (Leicester, University of Leicester Press, 1991), p. 135.

129 Holt, *Sport and the British*, p. 172.

130 Foulger, *Coventry. The Complete History of the Club*, p. 14.

131 *Midland Daily Telegraph*, 1 May 1919.
132 J. Crump, 'Recreation in Coventry between the wars', in B. Lancaster and T. Mason (eds), *Life and Labour in a 20th Century City. The Experience of Coventry* (Coventry, Cryfield Press, 1986), p. 265.
133 *Midland Daily Telegraph*, 3 May 1919.
134 *Midland Daily Telegraph*, 13 March 1919.
135 Foulger, *Coventry. The Complete History of the Club*, p. 14.
136 Mason, *Association Football and English Society*, p. 35; W. Vamplew, *Pay Up and Play the Game. Professional Sport in Britain, 1875–1914* (Cambridge, Cambridge University Press, 1988), p. 166.
137 B. Beaven and J. Griffiths, 'Urban elites, socialists and notions of citizenship in an industrial boomtown: Coventry 1870–1914', *Labour History Review*, 69:1 (2004).
138 *Midland Daily Telegraph*, 6 September 1919.
139 Foulger, *Coventry. The Complete History of the Club*, p. 21.
140 *Midland Daily Telegraph*, 4 May 1936.
141 B. Lancaster, 'Who's a real Coventry kid? Migration into twentieth century Coventry', in B. Lancaster and T. Mason, *Life and Labour in a Twentieth Century City* (Coventry, Cryfield Press, 1986), p. 66.
142 J. Crump, 'Recreation in Coventry between the wars', in Lancaster and Mason, *Life and Labour in Twentieth Century Coventry*, p. 265.
143 J. Williams, '"One could literally have walked on the heads of the people congregated there": Sport, the town and identity', in K. Laybourn (ed.), *Social Conditions, Status and Community, 1860–1920* (Stroud, Sutton Publishing, 1997), p. 125.
144 Holt, *Sport and the British*, p. 173.
145 Holt, 'Football and the urban way of life in nineteenth-century Britain', p. 77.
146 Russell, *Football and the English*, p. 64.
147 Williams, '"One could literally have walked on the heads of the people congregated there"', p. 138.
148 For the impact of consumption, see Johnson, 'Conspicuous consumption and working-class culture, pp. 27, 41. For the idea that commercial leisure shaped an inward-looking working class, see Senelick, 'Politics as entertainment', p. 150; Stedman Jones, *Languages of Class*, ch. 4.

3

Fearing for the Empire: male youth, work and leisure, 1870–1914

The behaviour of male youths in both work and leisure has troubled the minds of social observers from time immemorial.[1] From the high-spirited misdemeanours of the early modern apprentices to the low cunning of the Artful Dodger in early Victorian England, male youth behaviour has always been cited as a cause for concern. By the late eighteenth and early nineteenth centuries, the juvenile criminal had become central to the growing discussion on the nature of crime and punishment in this period.[2] However, during the late nineteenth century, youth delinquency became associated with wider anxieties related to increased urbanisation, changes in work and leisure patterns, and fears of imperial decline.[3] The youth 'problem' was perceived as the downside of rapid urbanisation that saw the formation of large distinct and 'culturally deprived' working-class neighbourhoods. This degenerate city was compounded by a significant increase in semi-skilled youth employment, largely initiated by the 'new' consumer industries and service sectors. From these freshly formed work-ing-class neighbourhoods emerged a new type of youth, free from the social controls of traditional forms of employment and keen to spend his relatively good wages in the mass leisure industries. This chapter will explore contemporary anxieties that revolved around the youth and citi-zenry in modern society and the key youth movements formed to alleviate the 'crisis'. Finally, the chapter will investigate whether these new working and leisure conditions, particularly prominent in the Midlands, encouraged a culture of consolation among male youths, replacing a more authentic and less compliant working-class culture.[4]

Contemporary discourse: the moral panic over the 'boy problem'

Between 1890 and 1914, the British male youth came under intensive scrutiny from social scientists and observers. Inspired by Charles Booth's survey on the London poor, a whole host of reports focused on the development of the male youth's work and leisure activities.[5] Academic interest in the male youth was stimulated, first and foremost, by the rapid growth of cities in the late nineteenth century. Although contemporaries acknowledged that throughout the nineteenth century Britain was becoming more urbanised, there was a consensus that the city was entering a new and dangerous epoch. Social division was now enshrined in the physical structures of the city, with the affluent middle-class suburbs segregated from the large tracts of working-class neighbourhoods that remained at the heart of many cities. These large working-class disticts had formed in a rather haphazard and unregulated manner, a phenomenon which initiated attempts by the middle class to catalogue and observe the social character of these large urban developments.[6] Moreover, the working class was forging a culture which, despite the overcrowded and poor sanitary conditions, utilised the benefits of living in close proximity to one another. Thus a culture of self-reliance developed in which elaborate social support networks were established internally between members of a neighbourhood.[7] Significantly, along with the local public house and corner shop, the street became an important crucible for sociability and recreation, a factor which ensured that working-class culture, particularly among the young, became increasing visible to the social observer. The social observer claimed the right to survey the dense pockets of working-class housing in the name of health, education and, more significantly, the desire to maintain the 'civilising ethics' which would preserve the Anglo-Saxon race in the enduring imperial struggle. The feelings of uncertainty that the city engendered were encapsulated by liberal social observer C. F. G. Masterman, whose research directly tapped into middle-class fears. Writing on the back of the Boer War, which had uncovered fears that the British city was harboring 'unfit stock', he wrote that Britain was faced with a phenomenon unique in world history:

Turbulent rioting over military successes, Hooliganism, and a certain temper of fickle excitability has revealed to observers during the past few months that a new race, hitherto unreckoned and of incalculable action, is entering the sphere of practical importance – the 'City type' of the coming years; the 'street-bred' people of the twentieth century; the 'new generation knocking at our doors'.[8]

According to Masterman, this new type of worker was very different from the polite, reserved and silent man of the small towns and villages. The very epitome of Englishness and all of its civilising values were at risk from aspects of the city, which, through its cramped and squalid material conditions, was 'rearing' a working-class that would endanger the very future of the civilisation. Thus this new 'City-type' was 'stunted, narrow chested, easily wearied; yet voluble, excitable with little ballast, stamina, or endurance – seeking stimulus in drink, in betting, in any unaccustomed conflicts at home or abroad'.[9] In fact, Masterman was one of many influential observers and social scientists who were increasingly attracted to the assumption that urban culture was failing the nation.[10] Contrasts were constantly made between squalid cramped cities and the open countryside and the impact this must have had upon both the physical and the moral make-up of the individual. Pethick Lawrence, contributing to Masterman's collection of essays on the domestic turmoil at the heart of the British Empire, was in no doubt that the modern city was 'an evil' due to sheer overcrowding and the denial of the countryside, which fostered a 'moral, physical, and aesthetic degradation'.[11] Likewise, T. H. Manners Howe argued that migration from country to town had produced a 'shorter and lighter race, but, to an even more serious extent, a narrower-chested one as well, for the decrease in chest measurement has been proportionately greater than stature'.[12] According to one social worker, the labyrinth of rookeries and backstreets of Britain's inner cities hid different 'types' of working class, whose physical and moral variation depended on the degree to which they had broadened their horizons to the countryside. Thus, while boys attached to youth organisations were able to embark on countryside activities which regenerated both mind and body, others would only have been exposed to the degenerative slum. Consequently, as one volunteer worker noted on a visit to the slums, 'the animal type, or rather the low moral type, will also be discovered, and, try as we will to reform, our efforts often seem to end in failure'.[13]

Encouraged by the urban studies of Charles Booth, Rowntree and Masterman, contemporaries became drawn to investigating the impact that the modern city had upon Edwardian youth and the future of the British citizen.[14] Moreover, the 'poor quality' of young recruits for the Boer War had forced the 'youth and city' question onto the national agenda, ensuring that research on adolescent boys became enmeshed with studies on the condition and future of the British Empire. The serious research on youth began with Professor E. J. Urwick's *Studies of Boy Life in Our Cities* (1904) in which a series of contributors, many of whom had lived among the poor in Toynbee Hall, gave first-hand experiences of the adolescent boy in his 'natural' environment.[15] This seminal book was followed by numerous investigations, including R. A. Bray's *The Town Child* (1907), Frank Hayward's *Wasted Lives* (1910) and Arnold Freeman's, *Boy Life and Labour. The Manufacture of Inefficiency* (1914). Freeman's study, like many investigations at this time, was permeated with eugenic notions of national efficiency and its implications for the future of empire. In concluding his study, Freeman noted that in modern industry there was a 'weeding out of less efficient youths' whose common feature was their 'unemployableness':

> There is, of course, no rigid selection, but it seems certain that in the competition for places, the least efficient tend to get rejected. These take to the streets and to casual labour; they provide much of the material for the problems that concern the various agencies connected with relief, crime, disease and metal deficiency.

Clearly, there was widespread concern that, left to their own devices, some of the 'lowest' youths may never aspire to gaining full citizenship due to their inherent inability to rise beyond the 'residuum class'. Thus, in this internationally competitive era, it was perceived that Britain's industrial strength was becoming undermined by an urban generation of inefficient stock whose only contribution to society was 'crime, disease and mental deficiency'.[16]

The assumption that the city was rearing a new race of degenerate workers placed the male youth and his work and leisure activities at the centre of the debate on the future of the nation. Contemporaries believed that the city's degenerate influences had most impact on the impressionable youth, which might eventually result in the creation of a new and more hostile working class.[17] Indeed, in a bid to address the manifestation of this physically and socially disfigured youth, contemporaries made a more concerted effort to instil the values of 'good citizenship' through organised youth activities.

Organised youth: the Boy's Club and Boy Scout movement

During the 1870s, a number of clubs were formed in Britain devoted to the education and cultural elevation of working-class boys. These clubs, with their emphasis on the instruction of religious or 'useful' knowledge, were modelled on the adult male societies that had been at the heart of the rational recreation movement. Until 1925, these Boy's Clubs operated on an independent and localised level with only limited coordination between clubs or regions. However, the values that governed the 'Club movement' were outlined in C. E. B. Russell's *Working Lad's Clubs* (1908), which had long been regarded by Club organisers as the 'classic text-book of the Boy's Club Movement'.[18] Russell, a businessman and philanthropist, had risen to national prominence through his extensive involvement in the organisation of Manchester Boy's Clubs during the 1880s. Russell declared that Boy's Clubs had three definite objectives, comprising recreation, education and religion; ideals which had descended from Henry Solly's mid-nineteenth-century vision of Working Men's Clubs. Russell's textbook was also a hostile response to new forms of youth organisation such as the Scouts, declaring that their movement was 'showy' and unable to train youths for good citizenship.[19] The 'citizenship' that Russell envisaged had its roots in the late nineteenth century and centred on the notion that the 'club' could culturally elevate its members to a higher plane where the full rights of citizenship were within their grasp. Essentially, this was a more optimistic philosophy of youth and citizenship that contrasted with the bleak imperial anxieties expressed by commentators during the early twentieth century. Indeed, when Russell established his Manchester clubs he intended to attract 'these hordes of young blackguards who showed little promise of growing into anything better than vagabonds and criminals'. There is evidence to suggest that, unlike subsequent youth organisations which had more disciplined and regimented activities, Boy's Clubs were successful in attracting the 'delinquent' boy.[20] The Boy's Clubs most effective in attracting the 'lowest' type of boys were located in the heart of working-class communities and placed a greater emphasis on leisure activities. Significantly, Clubs were keen to gain the confidence of their working-class neighbours, which inevitably meant that organisers were forced to compromise over their principles. Knowing that Club organisers would risk local hostility and a rapid fall in membership if they cooperated with the police, youths engaging in illegal activities usually found the Club a safe haven. This obviously posed an unenviable ethical dilemma for Club organisers, who, on the whole, attempted to maintain an independence from the law-enforcing authorities. Rev. Robert Hyde, a Club organiser in Hoxton, London noted that

> There are times when the police seek assistance in the connection with some prevailing epidemic of petty crime. It may be that a club member is using his membership as a means of disposing of pilfered property; the members may be known as leaders of a street gambling set; they may have been involved in a street fight. In any case, if the matter is brought to the notice of the club manager, he himself should see it through without seeking in any way the cooperation of the police. As an instance of this particular point, the street at the back of the Hoxton club building was a *cul-de-sac*, and it was the happy gambling ground of many of the residents. By using this door of the premises the police could have secured quite easily many of the indulgers in illicit games. Requests were made for the use of this door, but they were always refused. Had they been granted, the whole of the workers connected with the club would have been regarded as 'Narks' and the confidence of the neighbourhood absolutely lost.[21]

Youth organisers also became drawn into disputes and criminal cases outside of the Club's premises. They represented youths in a whole range of neighbourhood disputes and criminal proceedings and only drew the line at interventions in the boys' home lives. McG. Eagar, a youth worker in London, recalled that Club men regularly intervened on behalf of youths in disputes with angry residents and the police over the playing of football in some 'deserted street'. In addition he had represented club members in court, supporting the boy's case by vouching for his 'general good character', which unfortunately, according to McG. Eagar, was often 'shattered by the [police] officer's evidence or even more surely by some witness for the defence who attempted some fantastic alibi'. However, there were many examples where Club men succeeded in halting the police harassment of youths. Paul Schill noted that during the late nineteenth century Manchester Club men, through an appeal to the Bench of Magistrates, were successful in ending the practice of police arresting lads for loitering on street corners near to the Club. The Club men claimed that the band of lads regularly gathered on the street corner before attending the Club's religious services, a plea which was sufficient to convince the Manchester magistrates that the youths had no case to answer.[22]

To recap, then, there appears to be a dichotomy between the ideals of the Boy's Club, as outlined in Russell's textbook, and the actual activities many Club organisers found themselves enmeshed in. Far from elevating the 'lowest' boys, the Boy's Clubs were accommodating and, at times, defending the very activities that they had vowed to stamp out. In this light, it is perhaps not hard to see why many youths were attracted to Club life, as it both engaged and sanctioned their own youth culture. This did not go unnoticed by those working in the Club movement as some organisers began to become disillusioned with the failure to elevate the delinquent youth. The Church of England's support for Boy's Clubs, for example, began to fade during the early twentieth century as they concluded that the movement had done little to improve Church attendances. In addition, a more widespread criticism questioned whether the Club movement, and sufficiently equipped to deal with modern youth and the new demands that urbanisation and imperial rivalry had ushered in. Writing in 1914, Freeman reviewed the recent history of the Boy's Club, noting that the Club,

> while in so far as it provides amusement, it is not assisting, except incidently, the moral and mental unfoldment of the boy. Most Clubs make amusements and sports the main concern of their organisation. This is right because otherwise, the boy who is tired after his work will not attend … But it would seem as if, in many Clubs, the positive educational influences were exceedingly small. The Boy Scout Movement, combining physical, mental, and moral training all in one, seems to be an almost perfect escape from this dilemma. The organisation, and those like it, are successful because they are based on sound psychology. 'Call these boys "boys", which they are, and ask them to sit up in a Sunday class, and no power on earth will make them do it; but put a fivepenny cap on them and call them soldiers, which they are not, and you can order them about till midnight.'[23]

The Scouts were a new and altogether more dynamic youth organisation which embraced contemporary imperial anxieties and helped to recast notions of youth citizenship. Rejecting the Club movement's aim of simply providing 'cultural and religious elevation', the Scouts, in the face of a perceived increased threat to national security, aimed to disseminate a notion of youth citizenship that was imbued with patriotic duty. It is the Boy Scout movement to which we now turn.

Within the historiography of youth movements, there can be little doubt that Scouting has generated the greatest controversy among historians.

Since the 1970s, debate has run along two distinct and opposing camps. The first contend that the Scout movement was a reflection of Baden-Powell's militaristic ambitions. In leading this interpretation of the Scouts, Springhall has argued that Baden-Powell organised his movement with 'one primary motive – to prepare the next generation of British soldiers for war and the defence of the Empire'.[24] Likewise, Rosenthal demonstrates that Baden-Powell made 'usefulness in times of war' a central theme in early Scouting, adding that 'the notion of the Scout as a serviceable citizen trained to follow orders in wartime is at the heart of Scouting'.[25] Revisionist challenges to this perspective have alternatively pointed to Baden-Powell's emphasis on improving youths as citizens, rather than soldiers, carving out a niche in the youth movement which cast it apart from more overtly militaristic organisations. Indeed, Warren has argued that a sharp distinction should be drawn between the Scouts and contemporary organisations like the Boy's Brigade, with their dummy rifles, drills and parades, or Lord Roberts's National Service League, which demanded conscription and military training for the young.[26] Recently, both Dedman and Pyke have refuted claims of Scout militarism, pointing to the Baden-Powell's own careful rejection of such allegations and his insistence that they were in fact 'Peace Scouts'.[27]

The debate, then, has stalled upon Baden-Powell's motivation for establishing the Scouts and definitions of militarism. In effect, historians have taken their cue from contemporary Edwardian debates, since the Scout movement itself emerged at the time when sections of society were beginning to question whether training youths in military activities was appropriate in a burgeoning liberal democracy. Indeed, Baden-Powell was keen to avoid courting controversy with the anti-militarisation lobby as he feared this would have a damaging affect on Scout recruitment.[28] Thus, Baden-Powell's anti-military rhetoric, read particularly closely by the revisionists, should be treated with caution. Moreover, historians have tended to present a false dichotomy, projecting the Scouts as a movement of either 'citizenship or militarism'.[29] It is argued here that the principles which lay behind the Scout movement were instead part of a broader shift in ideals of citizenship that emerged during the late nineteenth and early twentieth centuries. Differing from the mid-nineteenth-century 'rational recreation' ethos that epitomised Boy's Club activities, the citizenship that the Scouts embraced tapped into a number of significant Edwardian undercurrents which, if appropriately harnessed, would prepare the boy and the nation for the twentieth century. It was against the backdrop of Lord Meath's attempt to make youths aware of their responsibilities as 'citizens of the greatest Empire the world had ever seen' that Baden-Powell formulated the Scouting ideal. To achieve this aim, Meath initiated Empire Day in 1903, which was designed to 'arouse interest in the need for promoting imperial education and knowledge, particularly through schools'.[30] In a revealing letter to *The Times*, Meath contended that citizenship was inseparable from duty, discipline, patriotism and national defence. He put the current ills in society down to an increase in luxuries 'amongst all classes, and with it a desire to lead an easy life', adding that discipline has been relaxed and 'sentimentality and humanitarianism have had their say'. Contrasting the courageous imperial pioneers that left Britain to start new lives in Canada, Australia and New Zealand, Meath believed that the current exodus of people from the country to the town constituted a very different stock of humanity. He wrote that 'now our emigrants in large measure avoid the land, settle in towns, and hasten to get rich by methods which may be softer and easier, but are less calculated to produce a moral, hardy, and un-conquerable race of men such as were their forefathers'. The cure for this 'softer' and unmasculine way of life was, according to Meath, a course of citizenship training for the young:

> In the nursery and the school, the cry has been raised that no child is to be compelled to do that which it dislikes – that its natural inclinations are to be consulted, and that age is to yield to the caprice of youth. Hence, the loosening of the sense of duty, of respect for years and authority, and a weakening of the moral fibre through the avoidance of struggle with self ... [I] desire to see every lad between the ages of 14 and 18 trained in arms, but I foresee dangers not only in regard to the military defence of the country, but also to its social and moral condition, unless serious steps are taken in the nursery, and in the schools, in society, and in the State to inculcate on the rising generation the virtues of self-sacrifice, a greater respect for authority, and a deeper sense of personal duty and responsibility towards society and the State.[31]

Elsewhere, Meath argued that 'sentimentality', a doctrine which he noted had been imported from the continent, had damaged the 'moral fibre' of men, encouraging effeminacy at the expense of traditional masculine traits.[32] The belief that the modern city, and its associated leisure activities, were promoting a weak and effeminate class of working men gained widespread currency prior to the First World War. Bishop Welldon argued that in citizenship training of the young 'it is desirable to cultivate a certain hardness of character', since 'men and women, boys and girls, are becoming soft ... the age, I'm afraid, is self-pleasing, self-indulgent'. He added that 'To-day they suffer too little. Their lives are so easy, they live so well, they spend so much money, that it is difficult to sympathise with human suffering.'[33] For Welldon, and many social commentators, the city and the new commercial leisure pursuits of the modern age had created a new breed of young pleasure-seekers who had no grasp of hardship, which in times past had bound the nation together forging a patriotic duty. The solution was to train youth in an early-twentieth-century form of citizenship which would instil patriotic duty, encourage masculine traits and bring discipline to their work routines and leisure pursuits.

This crusade to cure the nation and Empire's ills through a dynamic form of youth citizenship appealed to Baden-Powell. In his original text of *Scouting for Boys*, published in 1907, Baden-Powell claimed that 'the main cause for the downfall of Rome is similar to that which resulted in the downfall of other great empires and that cause may be summed up in each case as the decline of good citizenship and the want of energetic patriotism.'[34] During this period of imperial anxiety, Baden-Powell placed duty to the nation and Empire at the heart of Scouting. Moreover, it was a duty grounded in the Edwardian obsession with Arthurian legend as, according to Baden-Powell, King Arthur was 'the founder of British Scouts, since he first started the "Knights of England"'.[35] The Edwardian search for a society free from industrial conflict or physical degeneration led them to look to a mythical society governed by heroism embodied in the 'Knights' Code' and where race and manhood were uncorrupted by modernity. Thus Baden-Powell envisaged the Scouts as an antidote to the eugenicists' conviction that modern industrialisation and urbanisation were essentially decaying the Anglo-Saxon stock. Through Scouting, sickly, weak and barrel-chested boys would be trained in the traits of manhood such as courage, patriotism, strength, chivalry and, where needs be, conflict.

The Boy Scout movement was established by Baden-Powell in 1908 and quicky caught the imagination of large sections of the population. By 1910, almost 4,000 Scoutmaster warrants were issued and membership stood at over 100,000 Scouts attending 3,898 troops in Britain.[36] Although revisionist historians, through a close reading of Baden-Powell's thoughts and memoirs, deny the militaristic nature of Scouting, the movement from its inception was regarded by many as a paramilitary organisation. Even if it was not Baden-Powell's intention, the high concentration of ex-military men involved with the movement on a national and regional level gave rise to the suspicion that the Scouts were linked to the armed forces. As Wilkinson has pointed out, 'Baden-Powell's inspections of Scouts in his General's uniform, the large number of ex-military scout-masters sporting spurs, sword belts, and swagger canes, and the use of carbines for drill, created, understandably enough, a wide spread impression that the scouts were a paramilitary organisation.'[37] For example in Birmingham, where the first Scout troop was established, the President, Vice-Presidents and Secretary of the city's Scout Association were all leading members of the local National Service League. Indeed, the high concentration of ex-military personnel in the organisation led to local divisions when its Honorary secretary, F. C. Bennet, took the official Scout line and turned down an opportunity to join a military parade organised by the Territorial Force. A number of Birmingham Scoutmasters vigorously protested against this decision, claiming that 'the Boy Scouts are no more a peace organisation than the Boy's Brigade or the Church Lad's Brigade'.[38] In neighbouring Coventry, the early Scouting organisation mirrored Birmingham's military bias, with Col. Bleech leading the Association alongside four others with military backgrounds.[39] Significantly, after the First World War, the city's Scout organisation appears to have taken on a more civilian outlook, as those with a military background gravitated towards the Church Lad's Brigade. They were replaced by local aldermen and prominent city businessmen, who also allowed their work premises to be used as troop headquarters.[40] Thus, although by the interwar period Scouting had assumed a more civilian perspective, prior to the First World War many observers and participants acknowledged undercurrents of a militarist culture, particularly at a local level.

Proctor has recently demonstrated that the perceived link between the Scouts and militarism was sufficient to dissuade many working-class families from encouraging their sons to join the movement.[41] Indeed, the Scout uniform seemed to have symbolised for some poorer working-class families both inaccessibility and a suspicion of the Scout agenda. Unlike the Boy's Brigade, which supplied free uniforms to their members, Scouts were required to purchase uniforms, a cost which a significant number of working-class boys could ill afford. Moreover, the distinctive Scout attire, which Baden-Powell had adapted from his South African uniform, ensured that the Scout was easily identified and set apart from his local community.

The Scout uniform, a large brimmed hat, neck scarf, shorts, long socks and patrol ribbons made the young Scout easy prey for hostile youths in 'rough' neighbourhoods.[42] Indeed, one East End social worker noted that 'there is the dislike to the use of shorts, and to a uniform which does not altogether appeal to the older adolescent'.[43] One prewar Scout remembered that 'courage was needed to face the ridicule (and the brickbats too at times) to wear Scout Kit in the rougher streets. Staves then were a necessary and useful part of the outfit.'[44] It is perhaps not surprising that the inhabitants of solidly working-class neighbourhoods were generally belligerent towards the movement and drew clear parallels between the Scouts and paramilitary organisations. For those witnessing troops of Scouts parading through their streets, it would have been difficult not to forge strong associations with other 'outside' organisations such as the Boy's Brigade, the Church Lad's Brigade and the Salvation Army. Evidence suggests that, certainly prior to 1914, the Scout movement recruited broadly upper-working-class and lower-middle-class boys, a membership which set it apart from the Boy's Club organisation.[45] Indeed, although Baden-Powell had originally set himself the task of civilising the 'hooligan' and 'street-boy', Scouting rarely recruited in the poorest areas. The Club movement proved more successful in this respect as they were prepared to bend rules and base their premises in the heart of working-class communities, a difference in strategy recognised by one former youth worker:

> whereas Brigades and Scouting attracted boys who were in the comity of the nation, who attended church or chapel, had decent and orderly homes and, as a rule, accepted the usages of society, Clubs, if not intended for the outcasts, were, generally speaking, for boys who were not fully included in society, partly because they had reached the neglected age of adolescence, partly because they did not attend a place of worship, had unhelpful homes, and so were in danger of coming into conflict, if they were not actually in conflict, with society.[46]

Scouting did, however, become a more socially heterogeneous organisation after the First World War. Free from the anxiety-laden prewar era encapsulated by Meath's patriotic citizenship, the Scouting movement began to adapt, allowing more space for Scouts to carve out their own meanings in Scouting and subsequently doing much to attract working-class membership.[47] Although historians have debated the nature of youth movements, there is little disagreement that they had emerged to counter the 'damaging influences' of modern society. The following sections will investigate the two modern developments deemed the most pervasive and corrupting to youth: the emergence of new work routines and leisure experiences.

Youth culture: work and the 'blind alley jobs'

The era of mass production and consumption had arrived and male youths were at the forefront of this new productive process. However, this new vision of a mass society caused many to question whether it would ultimately undermine 'traditional values and dissolve the individual's moral strength and the community's social purpose'.[48] The period 1870–1914 has often been regarded as the 'second industrial revolution' as 'new' consumer-based industries such as light engineering, chemical, electrical and mass-produced food sectors began to make a significant impact on British employment structures. Indeed, a significant sector of the British economy shifted from fairly small units of production employing artisanal workforces to large-scale factories producing mass-produced goods.[49] Moreover, the seasonal nature of a great many of the goods produced, such as bicycles and later motor cars ensured that cyclical unemployment also became a feature of the 'new' industries.[50] Since northern textile firms had been employing large pools of semi-skilled labour from the 1850s, it was the Midlands and Southeast which appeared to be most affected by these economic shifts.[51] The expansion of the 'new' industries and service sector, which provided relatively well-paid semi-skilled jobs, was a source of concern for reformers, since male youths seemed to have gained an unprecedented financial and moral independence. Thus youths were free to enter 'blind alley' monotonous jobs, which, with no training or moral guidance, would further encourage the unrestrained consumption of unsuitable leisure activities. These combined influences would lead to a degenerate youth not only incapable of making rational political judgements in this era of mass democracy but also unfit to engage in the nation's future battle for imperial supremacy.[52]

It is perhaps worth identifying the key characteristics associated with semi-skilled work that purportedly shaped the youth's leisure choices and opportunities. For example, it is no coincidence that Birmingham, with its combination of small-scale workshops, increasing mechanisation and growth of large new industries, became the focal point for a number of sociological studies on the 'boy' and commercial leisure problem. Commenting on the rapid increase in 'blind alley' jobs in Birmingham, Norman Chamberlain argued that the disastrous conditions of boy labour 'are affecting both individual lives and the national well-being'.[53] Chamberlain summarised contemporary views on youth employment, characterising three responses to the phenomenon. 'One bewails the disappearance of apprenticeship and the growth of unskilled or semi-skilled boy labour; another the restlessness of the modern boy with his ever-changing jobs; to a third, boys' work means a reservoir of cheap labour.'[54] Chamberlain saw the root cause of the youth's apparent descent into indiscipline and restlessness in the relative freedom that boys enjoyed when leaving school and obtaining work. The expansion of semi-skilled work allowed boys a mobility between jobs impossible under the older schemes of apprenticeship, with their emphasis on the acquisition of skill and loyalty to the employer.[55] One social reformer reporting for the Poor Law Commission noted his concern that boys 'light heartedly throw up job after job'.[56] Another witness for a Royal Commission on Technical Instruction observed that the apprenticeship promoted social harmony in the workplace. Mr G. Shipton, a representative from the London Trades Council, noted that the relations of masters and workmen or apprentices were 'closer and more intimate and friendly … under this new system "masters" no longer cared to be bothered to take apprentices to teach them their trade'.[57] Indeed, one of the defining characteristics of the 'new' industries was the systematic abandonment of the apprenticeship system in favour of monotonous work routines, a factor which concerned contemporary reformers, who held the notion that work shaped a youth's moral character. There can be little doubt that apprenticeships were in decline, a trend perhaps more apparent in the light industries in the Midlands, which had long been associated with the apprenticeship system. The emergence of the bicycle and car industries brought to the Midlands many of the hallmarks of twentieth-century manufacture: large-scale production, use of power machinery and the division of labour. Such was the influence of this form of manufacture that more traditional industries such as gun, jewellery and watchmaking began to adopt similar work practices.[58] Nevertheless, historians have continually overestimated the importance of skilled labour in the British economy between 1870 and 1914. While Childs has assumed that the new industries were reliant on a higher level of technical expertise, thereby creating a 'new body of skilled workers', Sandler's research on Birmingham has shown that the proportion of skilled workers in the new industries between 1900 and 1914 was relatively small.[59] Indeed, Arnold Freeman's investigation into the 'problem' of boy labour in Edwardian Birmingham provides an insight into the shift from apprenticed to semi-skilled work during this period. One employer reported that,

> In a few trades only is it possible to take apprentices now; owing to the large scale of production, the subdivision of labour has been carried to a minute degree and automatic and semi-automatic machines installed in most industries; the worker being now a specialist in the reproduction of a few articles on machines devised for their rapid and economical production.[60]

A similar story unfolded in Coventry, which had been a magnet for the youth worker. The bicycle and motor industries had been founded in the city in the late nineteenth century and became increasingly important to Coventry's economy. In 1891, there were over 100 bicycle firms in the city of varying size, employing between 15 and 500 each.[61] By 1901 there were 6,001 cycle and motor workers in Coventry, rising to 13,000 in 1911. Of these 13,000 workers, 10,188 were under thirty-five, while over 5,000 were under twenty-five. The vast majority were semi-skilled.[62] Coventry apprentices were entered into the 'Coventry Freeman Admissions Journals' after completing a seven-year apprenticeship and consequently the first motor car apprentices would have emerged during the early years of the twentieth century. The journals reveal that very few apprentices completed their indentures at motor car firms during a period traditionally characterised as the 'craft production' era. On average, fewer than three apprentices qualified from motor car firms each year between 1905 and 1921.[63] Without an established apprenticeship system, there appears to have been no uniform demarcation between types of bicycle work. Indeed, unlike the 'blind alley' jobs in the service sector, which drew exclusively from a pool of youth labour, bicycle firms made few distinctions between their semi-skilled youth and adult male employees. The job title of 'cycle hand' or 'machinist' could cover a multitude of tasks that included operating machinery, assembling, packing, warehouse work and the transportation of goods.[64] The 'problem' of employing large numbers of youths in semi-skilled tasks was, however, not lost on even the bicycle employers themselves. E. W. Cooper, a bicycle manufacturer during the 1880s, commented that it was 'more difficult every day for a youth to thoroughly learn a trade, especially in a large works. Without doubt the modern system of working, especially in the cycle trade, is answerable for the ruin of many a promising youth'.[65] Bicycle work was also seasonal, with employees working long hours and earning relatively good money during eight months of the year before being released by the firm when the four-month 'slack period' commenced.[66] Indeed, one observer of the new industries noted that youths and boys 'readily return to the cycle factories when work revives, since they can earn more money there'.[67] Although evidence on the average rates of pay for bicycle workers is rather sketchy, it has been estimated that youths entering the industry in 1900 would earn approximately 32s 6d per week, a considerable sum for a youth with few household responsibilities.[68]

Contemporary reformers' concern over apprenticeships was based on the desire to see not simply a more technically educated workforce but also a well-disciplined and harmonious youth both in and outside the workforce. Indeed, Childs has argued that middle-class observers believed that working-class families could offer little in the way of moral guidance, and consequently they became convinced that 'the breakdown of the apprenticeship and its replacement by the various types of exploitative boy labour were potent factors in the creation of a lawless and asocial youth'.[69] It was the belief of many social reformers that the experience of the workplace defined the moral character of the individual. For example, in regions that had witnessed the rapid movement from traditional apprenticed labour to the semi-skilled youth of the new industries, social commentators harked back to a mythical golden age. The work that this imagined skilled artisan was engaged in was one which required education, skill and intelligence – a craft that would result in an individual and unique product. Moreover, the long training under the watchful eye of a master was thought to have instilled discipline into the artisan's life and respect for his employer. One Midlands newspaper noted that 'masters were strict with apprentices. Employers would think nothing of boxing their [young apprentices] ears if they did not behave properly.'[70] In other words, this was a form of work which brought discipline, contentment and fulfilment both in and outside the workplace. This analysis was extended to the new worker who was largely engaged in monotonous semi-skilled mass production, a work process which was thought to lead to unhealthy and irrational leisure pursuits. Perhaps this view is best demonstrated with the following observation from a correspondent to the *Coventry Herald* who called himself a 'Peaceful Citizen':

> We are really in Coventry at the mercy of the machinist. The weaver and the watchmaker in the height of the prosperity were not so rowdy. The cause is doubtless to be found in the fact that the peaceful art and craft

of the weaver and the watchmaker have a more civilising effect upon the youth and allow him more opportunities for thought than does the fire of the forge and the clanging and hanging of the hammers in the cycle factory. The human product of a cycle works is a more boisterous creature than the human product of a weaver's or watchmakers shop. Is there no hope of civilising the machinist?[71]

It is perhaps now appropriate to investigate further the relationship between the 'new' semi-skilled machinist and 'uncivilised' commercial leisure that emerged in the cities from the 1870s.

The male youth and mass commercial leisure

As we have seen in the previous chapter, the music hall dominated commercial popular entertainment, provoking contemporary anxieties over its impact on the 'pleasure seeking' masses. These concerns were accentuated when the youth 'problem' was added to the equation. In addition, in regions where large numbers of youths worked in the 'new' industries, social observers identified their monotonous and well-paid labour as the principal reason for the popularity of music hall among the young. Certainly, there can be little doubt that youths in the Midlands could afford to visit the music hall more often than their counterparts in the North, a relative affluence which caused further concerns for social reformers.[72] This mounting unease prompted the contemporary sociologist Freeman to conduct extensive research into the leisure time of Birmingham youths. Adopting a fairly progressive research methodology, Freeman gave diaries to a number of semi-skilled male youths to describe their work and leisure activities during a nominated week. He discovered that lads would often visit the music hall as much as four times a week.[73] The frequent attendance by some youths confirmed for many the belief that music halls encouraged a culture of deprivation. One commentator, writing about excessive hours in the bicycle industry, complained that

> A man is hard at work all week upon a purely mechanical and monotonous task. He leaves off late at night or Saturday afternoon, wearied out. He has no time to read, or think or pray. His mind is not equal to anything that makes a demand on his intellect. He must enjoy himself, but it must be in an easy way, something that will cause no strain on his understanding. And we know what effects such amusements have. The music-hall with its meaningless ditties or *double entendres* and pipes and drink, is more appreciated than the theatre, and a rowdy sing-song than a decent concert.[74]

Thus, unlike the apprenticed youth, the semi-skilled worker in the 'new' industries was not challenged by his employment. Instead he was caught in a cycle of deprivation in which his daily monotonous labour stimulated an unquenchable thirst for the low and vulgar entertainment of the music hall.[75] However, a new form of leisure had, by the late Edwardian period, begun to challenge the music hall as the working-class's premier entertainment institution.

In February 1896, the first film was shown to the British public when the Lumière cinematograph was presented in the Regent Street Polytechnic in London.[76] After appearing as 'turns' in music halls and palaces of variety, cinemas were built in or near working-class neighbourhoods to cater for popular demand. By 1914, the cinema has been described as 'the most universally accepted modern amusements', a claim supported by 364 million admissions in that year and the rapid infrastructure that accompanied the craze.[77] In 1914, Birmingham had forty-seven cinemas providing seating for 32,836 customers, while thirteen cinemas had been built in Salford to rival its four music halls.[78] The close proximity to working-class districts and the low entrance price made the cinema the chief attraction to the youth on both weekdays and weekends. During the week, the male youth could visit the cinema after work in his informal clothes with his friends primarily to view the picture, while the weekend visit to a cinema or music hall would be more of an 'event' when he might have opportunity to 'click' with his female counterparts.[79] Thus during the Edwardian period, youths tended to mix most of their commercial leisure time between the music hall and cinema, particularly since, as Freeman discovered, youths would often go a couple of times a week to each institution.[80]

However, like many new and rapidly popular inventions or recreational activities, social reformers were concerned that the cinema was leading youths to a life of crime. Although the music hall was perceived as 'silly' and at its worst culturally degrading, there was a widespread fear that youths might imitate the worst excesses displayed on the screen and confuse fact with fiction. In 1913, one commentator condemned the cinema as an 'incentive' for crime by filling young minds with 'terrific massacres, horrible catastrophes, motor-car smashes, public hangings, [and] lynchings'.[81] Given that many social reformers shared Freeman's belief that the male youth's 'mind is sponge-like in its nature, in which it will drink greedily ideas from all the things which it comes in contact', it is perhaps no surprise that the cinema was seen as a poisoned chalice. Furthermore, magistrates became convinced that petty larceny and housebreaking were on the increase due to youths stealing to generate money for the cinema.[82] The first attempt by the government to address the expansion of the cinema came as early as 1909 with the Cinematograph Act, which was designed to secure safety at cinemas. By 1917, though not a government-inspired body, the National Council for Public Morals had formed to monitor the content and effects of films.[83] Notwithstanding the moral panic that accompanied the cinema craze, some researchers were hard-pressed to make tangible connections between cinema and crime. Despite his negative disposition towards the cinema, Freeman was forced to concede, through examining the type of films popular among the youth, that the 'boy is amused, and is, on the whole, innocently amused'. Indeed, even the chief constables, presenting evidence to the National Council for Public Morals, concluded that the cinema was unlikely to lead to a life of crime.[84]

The debate on whether commercial entertainment led juveniles into criminal activities was reflected in the criticism of mass commercial boy's literature, which began in the 1860s. Labelled 'penny dreadfuls', these melodramatic novels about villains, pirates, highwaymen and thieves sold in weekly parts for one penny. The largest sales were in London and the large manufacturing cities such as Birmingham, Manchester and Liverpool. One of the most successful serials was *Black Bess* or *The Knight of the Road* (1863–68), which consistently sold between 30,000 and 40,000 copies per week, though like most working-class literature it was almost certainly borrowed by thousands more.[85] The social reformers' chief concern with cheap literature was, once again, rooted in the perceived inadequacies of the monotonous job which led the youth to crave excitement in far-fetched penny comics. The type of excitement contained within the mass cheap literature centred around crime, and in some cases sexual innuendo, which would awaken 'low passions' and set youths an immoral framework. J. B. Paton, in his investigations into youth literature during the Edwardian period, complained that 'anything more vulgar and low in taste than the letterpress and most pictorial illustrations cannot be perceived' and that the literature did nothing to elevate and 'everything to degrade'.[86] Although Freeman concluded that the cheap press's influence had been exaggerated, he viewed comics as a cause for concern since their degenerate content would make an impression on the 'blank sheet of the boy's mind'. Thus, ultimately, elevating influences such as religion would die through a lack of nourishment and be replaced by an altogether more unpleasant low culture.[87]

The publishers, like their counterparts in the music hall, were committed capitalists, who had no desire to undermine the status quo and imbued their literature with conservative values. Thus manliness, as defined through the swashbuckling stories in the Victorian and Edwardian comic, entailed hard work, class loyalty and patriotism.[88] Either way, the common contemporary assumption that male youths simply consumed the material they read in a passive and uncritical manner is, however, somewhat misleading. Although youth literature was written for and not by working-class youths, according to Springhall, the penny dreadfuls were customer-led, 'with readers exercising positive choice over the wide range of material which they were being offered'.[89] Certainly, the impact that conservative comics had upon youths is a vexing question since, unlike the behaviour of music hall audiences, readers' responses to literature is difficult to gauge. However, in their purchase and shared consumption of the literature, youths were drawing from working-class traditions that were far removed from the exaggerated fiction of the penny dreadfuls. In a form of cooperation similar to the working-class neighbourhood burial, savings or holiday clubs, groups of lads would regularly pool their money to purchase as many papers as possible. Paton appeared genuinely surprised when he found that boys could afford to form 'libraries' complete with their own set of rules and contributions:

> A half penny amongst the very poor has to go a long way, and half-penny among the hooligan class are none too plentiful. So the boys pool their money. A group of six lads agree to purchase six different periodicals which when read are passed around, so that for one-half penny each boy may read half a dozen sensational papers.[90]

The cheap press provided escapist entertainment which, like the music hall and cinema, did not so much replace earlier forms of youth activities but instead sat easily alongside traditional working-class culture.

The rise of football as a professional game, though, undoubtedly had a major impact on youth's commercial leisure expenditure and made inroads into their informal leisure pursuits in working-class neighbourhoods. Not only did youths have yet another form of mass commercial leisure to spend their money on, but working-class streets also became impromptu football pitches. As we have seen, in towns or cities which grew rapidly during the last quarter of the nineteenth century there was a strong demand from workers that their district should be represented by a successful football team.[91] Indeed, in many areas, football became a spectator sport when successful works teams became identified with a particular district of a town or city. However, like street gangs that emerged, football loyalties could bring out intra-district competition – much to the disapproval of social reformers, who attempted to shape football into a rational recreation.[92] The more successful clubs eventually came to represent their district or city on a professional basis, which inevitably increased the support base and fanaticism for football. Certainly, the entries made in the diaries which Freeman gleaned from the semi-skilled youths demonstrate how football dominated many of their lives. Although male youths did not attend professional football matches as regularly as the cinema or music hall, Freeman found that 'football is the greatest single interest in the life of the ordinary working boy ... most of them spend Saturday afternoon in watching "Birmingham" or "the Villa". No subject arouses their enthusiasm like football.'[93] Moreover, football was the sport which many male youths played almost every day. A common routine for a weekday was to play a game of football with work colleagues at lunch time followed by a game in the evening during the summer. The week-ends would be dominated by football, usually watching it on Saturdays and playing marathon games in their local neighbourhoods on Sundays. One respondent wrote how on a typical Sunday he called for his friends at 9.50 a.m. and played football until 2.00 p.m. In the afternoon they met up with 'some lads who live at the other end of our street' and played football until late afternoon.[94]

The football craze and its subsequent commercialisation in the late nine-teenth century had a significant impact on informal leisure patterns. Male youths added football to their street activities, a sport which, according to many outside working-class culture, was undergoing a downward transition from its purist and rational origins. To social observers who witnessed street football, rules and fair play had been replaced by noisy enthusiasm and a boy's desire to win at all costs. In other words, left to their own devices, working-class lads had shaped the game they had adopted into an unrecognisable one which, without middle-class guidance, had descended into a primitive and uncivilised activity. In 1914, Rev. Pelham, the Bishop of Birmingham, concerned about the 'boy's recreations', ventured into a working-class neighbourhood and reported that football was the dominant activity. 'The street is the only available pitch, and though the gutter and a passing cart are a bit of a nuisance, quite a thrilling game can be enjoyed, so long as no policeman appears.' Pelham, though, was quite puzzled when it came to interpreting the rules:

> It would seem as if the main features of the game were to run across the streets as often as you can without being run over, or caught by your opponent, to give as many nervous shocks as possible to grave businessmen and old ladies, and then, if your opponent catches you, to say he cheated and to back up your argument to this effect with muscular force. All very splendid, but hardly educative for the boy or conducive of peace of mind to the passer by.[95]

Football lent itself ideally to street gang activities since it could provide a group of lads with a local identity, offered group participation and the opportunity to assert their masculinity within the neighbourhood. However, the 'threat' to passers-by made street football a constant cause of friction between youths and the police. Throughout Britain, police attempted to enforce local by-laws that were designed prevent 'dangerous' play in the streets and to protect life and property. This effort grew more vigorous during the 'football' craze of the 1890s, in the attempt to eliminate at least one new and disruptive street activity.[96] In Coventry during the 1890s the Watch Committee issued repeated warnings to youths playing football in the streets, while the *Coventry Herald* complained that,

> in Coventry the young man who wants to kick a football or see it kicked is very much in evidence. He is not always a well behaved young man, and there are grown up people who find him under certain circumstances rather trying, and who would like to kick *him*. However, he is in the ascendant.[97]

As in many towns and cities, the upsurge of interest in football in Coventry was linked to the introduction of the new industries and the numerous works' teams they spawned. Moreover, the impact of the new industries had a further impact on working-class male leisure with the mass production of the bicycle in the 1890s.

One of the leisure pursuits which became most identified with the youth employed in the new industries was the bicycle. By the 1890s, this was no longer simply a means of transport or recreational pleasure; it had become the symbol of a widespread sense of modernity. The bicycle prompted mixed responses and anxieties within all levels of society, though according to one historian it 'became a sign of distinction, which in certain milieus discriminated traditionalists from innovators, conservatives from modernists'.[98] For those conscious of living in the *fin de siècle* the bicycle became a powerful symbol of emancipation, since greater personal mobility was no longer restricted to the few.[99] Certainly, sections of the late-nineteenth- and early-twentieth-century male youth became closely identified with the bicycle, particularly those in the West Midlands who were employed in bicycle production. Midlands cycle workers assumed a unique position in working-class history for they were the first group of workers to be at the centre at of the mass productive and consumer axis.[100] Freeman's research on boy labour in Edwardian Birmingham suggests that bicycles were affordable for many young cycle workers, especially as firms pay 'very high wages for their busy season'.[101] Moreover, in Coventry astonished journalists reported that during the high season, cycle workers could afford lavish food and drink which were beyond reach for the vast majority of the working class.[102] Even as early as the 1880s, the purchase of cycles was within the reach of the semi-skilled youth employed in the new industries. For example, in 1889 it was estimated that over 100 Singer employees who had joined the firm's annual bicycle parade had purchased their own bicycle, many of them through a hire-purchase scheme arranged by the bicycle manufacturer.[103] Indeed, a number of bicycle firms such as Swift Cycles targeted working men with hire-purchase offers advertised as 'pay as you ride' schemes.[104]

The close relationship between young males working in the bicycle industry and their new spending power was not lost on advertisers, who framed the production and consumption of cycles in overtly masculine terms. In 1906, the Triumph Cycle was advertised under the heading 'male or female labour', with the explanation that

> The male mechanic in the workshop has proved himself infinitely superior to the female – he is capable of doing better, more exact, more reliable work. Morally, mixed labour does not raise the standard of either worker, and considerably lowers the standard of the work produced. *Triumph cycles* are made in a factory where no female labour whatever is employed. Female labour and best work do not go together therefore let your machine be a *Triumph*. 'The Best Bicycle British Workmanship can produce' and made by skilled male mechanics only. The *Triumph* is the only Coventry cycle factory not employing female labour.[105]

Thus, despite the large cohort of semi-skilled male and female labour in the Midlands bicycle industry, the 'ideal' bicycle was projected on both moral and technical grounds as the product of skilled male engineers for an essentially masculine market.

The male youth's first steps into the consumer society raised concerns that young workers could not be trusted to spend their money on wholesome recreation. Even cycling, which for all intents and purposes seems a rational and healthy form of exercise from a twenty-first-century perspective, was at the centre of a number of social panics during and after the cycle craze in the 1890s. At the start of 'cyclemania' there were some initial worries that prolonged use of the cycle would result in 'bicycle face', 'bicycle hand', 'bicycle foot' or 'bicycle hump', a painful condition which was allegedly caused by low handlebars.[106] One satirical forecast suggested that a combination of these afflictions could see the formation of *cyclo-anthropos*, a twentieth-century being that had 'a doubled-up hunchback with atrophic arms'.[107] However, despite these concerns, rational recreationists were quick to see the advantages that cycling could bring the male youth. Cycling could not only distract working-class youths from the evils of drink and gambling but also encourage them to leave city vices and embrace the purity of rural England. During this era of expanding democracy, the socialists were particularly keen to elevate young males away from what they perceived as a degenerate popular culture to civilised and rational recreation.[108] For example, Tom Groom, a socialist cycle club organiser in Birmingham, optimistically claimed in 1895 that 'the frequent contrasts the cyclist gets of the beauties of nature and the dirty squalor of the towns makes him more anxious than ever to abolish the present system'.[109] The largest socialist club was the Clarion Cyclists, an offshoot of the *Clarion* newspaper, which had seventy-six clubs and approximately 2,000 members by 1897. However, most young male workers did not enjoy their cycling within the confines of a club. Although no records survive of the social composition of the Clarion cycling clubs, it has been estimated that like the political organisation itself, they largely comprised well-paid artisans and those from the lower middle class.[110] Indeed, since the bicycle had provided unprecedented personal mobility and freedom, lads were reluctant to use their bicycles within the confines of club rules or etiquette. In the eyes of contemporary observers at the end of the 1890s, male youth had transformed a rational form of recreation into another urban vice which threatened to bring further danger to the streets. In an article in *Pall Mall Magazine*, the respected Italian criminologist Professor Lombroso was left in no doubt that in 1900 'no modern mechanism has assumed the extraordinary importance of the bicycle, either as a cause or instrument of crime'. He continued that he was certain that many muscular young men are

> longing to surpass others without possessing any special mental qualification
> for so doing is one of the strongest tendencies of our times; and it is most
> marked amongst youths … [he] is a *neophile* – a lover of the new, an anti-
> conservative. He has therefore a predilection for this new machine, and knows
> better than others how to derive advantage from it. For him it has special
> sources of pride; for being by nature an idler, an enemy to labour he is free
> from the class-scruples of clergymen, magistrates, or doctors, for whom the
> bicycle is a source of possible public contempt and professional damage.[111]

What is revealing here is the implication that the bicycle was enabling
working-class youths to move above their station without any 'mental
qualification' or merit, and to disregard the traditional moral standards
and codes of conduct set by the professional classes. In other words,
the novelty of the bicycle had created a moral vacuum in terms of its
application and etiquette, providing youths with an opportunity to carve
out their own uses for the bicycle, which upset and sometimes physically
threatened their social superiors.

Perhaps the most widespread complaint levelled at the young male cyclist
was his tendency to 'scorch' or ride too fast through the streets and thoroughfares of urban areas. The bicycle 'scorcher' became identified as a new
menace, particularly in the areas which had a strong association with the
cycle industry. An editorial in the *Coventry Herald* complained that inconsid-
erate cycle riding was 'common everywhere, but there are in proportion to
population, probably more cycle riders in Coventry than in other places'.[112]
This view was confirmed by another concerned citizen, who observed that
Coventry is 'called the home of the cycle and certainly the cyclist seems
very much at home here he does what he likes'.[113] Correspondents to the
local press described the 'cycle fiends' who would break up Sunday con-
gregations by rushing among them at between 13 and 15 miles an hour,
while others claimed that the streets were at the mercy of the cycle-riding
'hobble-de-hoy mechanic with his coarse manners, foul language and reckless disregard for the rights of others'.[114] These moral panics were perhaps
more acute in cities of cycle production since the bicycle had brought both
disorder to the streets and a new young 'uncivilised' worker.

The bicycle, however, should be regarded as an additional leisure pursuit
for the working-class male youth rather than a replacement for traditional
recreations. The social reformers' hope that the bicycle would enable young
males to visit the rural idyll and liberate themselves from the urban squalor
was partially fulfilled. Day trips to the countryside became a regular feature
for some youths, with one observer in the 1890s reporting seeing over

25,000 cycles crossing the Thames one Sunday, while Booth noted a 'stream of cyclists' heading out of the city.[115] However, the social reformers had not considered that by encouraging the youths to embark on the bicycling craze, they might continue to do what they did in the city but in a more green and pleasant setting. In 1898, *The Times* raged about the 'East-End or suburban "scorcher", dashing along quiet country roads and through peaceful villages with loud shouts and sulphurous language, and reckless of life and limb'.[116] The reckless use of the bicycle was perceived in both class and gender specific terms. While the editor of *The Times* admired cycling as 'one of the manliest and most healthful of outdoor recreations', he despaired at the male youths' abuse of such a rational recreation:

> To see a pleasant country road or village in the neighbourhood of the metropolis invaded by a troop of cockneys, clothed some-what like seaside bandsman in knee-breeches, each doing his utmost, with the most painful result to make himself seen and heard, is a hardship none the less real because no spectator takes physical harm thereby. Grotesqueness of outfit and loudness of manner are perhaps superficial matters enough; but they not unnaturally prejudice homely people against the gregarious bicyclist.[117]

To the social reformers' horror, far from elevating the uncivilised youth, the bicycle was helping to transport the 'city-boy' problem to previously unpolluted areas. One observer fumed that the cyclist can 'drive to a country village, where as a *bona fide* traveller, he can drink to his heart's content, and carry his town vices into village homes'.[118] Indeed, Warwickshire publicans were not slow to exploit the cycle craze, advertising in the Coventry press that they had a range of ales for the cycle enthusiast. Around Coventry's rural hinterland, a number of publicans announced that they catered for both large and small cycle parties and that their establishments were in the circuit of a 'Capital cycle run'.[119] The youths' own peculiar use of the bicycle, one that contravened bourgeois convention and mores, was drawn from a culture that evolved from the informal leisure activities of the street. It is to the characteristics of male youths' informal leisure activities that we now turn.

Youth culture: informal leisure activities

The most common complaint against the activities of male youth was their behaviour on the streets. It was no coincidence that the grievances expressed in the press and social surveys on street rowdyness were at their height during the period in which urbanisation was perceived to be at the centre of the nation's degeneration. For example J. B. Paton, a London social reformer, remarked in 1908 that working-class youths 'are now to be found in the congested streets ... they are no longer widely scattered in the open country engaged in healthy industries on the land'.[120] For many social observers, the streets were no longer neutral functional thorough-fares but dangerous arenas in which working-class youths openly flouted their degenerate culture. Furthermore, in their infrequent explorations into working-class neighbourhoods, social reformers were horrified that male youths appeared actually to 'possess' the streets, making 'outsiders' distinctly unwelcome. Many contemporaries noted that young males were prone to 'hanging' around the corners engaging in loud vulgar language, smoking and gambling and generally acting in a mischievous manner. One Chris-tian missionary who ventured out into the working-class neighbourhoods observed that there were gangs of 'big rough lads' who, when work was over, were to be found 'lolling in an archway, smoking bad cigarettes, and jawing and chaffing in their vernacular'. Their activities would generally consist of 'cuffing and quarrelling with one another, and shouting low jokes and giving rude shoves to groups of girls'.[121] Middle-class passers-by were not exempt from the practical jokes of the street-corner gangs. Easily identifiable with their top hats, middle-class males were subjected to spates of 'hat tipping' in the late nineteenth century where gangs would throw rotten fruit or fish in a bid to 'tip' the hat.[122] Perhaps, though, a more serious concern for the social reformer was the type of culture they were uncovering. Gambling was considered to be on the increase among male youths as the street provided an environment free from parents and employers.[123] Beatrice Webb, on a visit to the East End, noted that

> Gambling was the amusement of the street. Sentries would be posted, and if the Police made a rush the offenders would slip into the open houses and hide until the danger was past. Sunday afternoon and evening was the heyday time of the street. Every doorstep would be crowded by those who sat or stood with pipe and jug of beer, while lads lounged about, and the gutters would find amusement for not a few children with bare feet, their faces and hands besmeared, while the mud oozed through between their toes. Add to this a group of fifteen or twenty young men gambling in the middle of the street and you complete the general picture.[124]

The 'evil' of gambling was prioritised along with drinking as the worst characteristic of youth culture, since youths effectively openly flouted the law and developed 'low and cunning' strategies to avoid police detection.[125]

Male youth street gangs also forged strong identities with their immediate local areas, often naming the gang after their street or district.[126]
Competition among gangs inevitably led to street fighting; this had its
roots in attempts by gangs to establish their 'territory' or street, which they
regarded as their personal property. Robert Roberts recalled that in Salford
'all the warring gangs were known by a street name and fought, usually
by appointment – Next Friday, 8 p.m.: Hope Street *v* Adelphi!'[127] Gang
fighting was not restricted to the older industrial areas but also became a
feature of urban life in cities that had experienced rapid expansion due
to the growth of the new industries. One former gang member in 1880s'
Coventry recalled:

> There used to be a practice of a gang from one district suddenly descending
> on another district, armed with sticks and belts and such like. The Spon End
> gang would pay a visit to the Dog Lane area, and vice-versa, while Hillfields
> and Gosford Street would do the same. Miniature battles would be fought,
> and there was usually a return visit on a subsequent occasion.[128]

The level of organisation, which in the Coventry case involved arranging
'home and away' battles, was perhaps the new development in street fighting and something which continually shocked contemporaries. In Glasgow
one notorious gang, the 'Penny Mob', took their name from the custom
of each member contributing one penny into a communal fund for the
payment of fines, an effective response to those nineteenth-century social
commentators who maintained that the youths were incapable of thrift.[129]
By the late nineteenth century the press had coined a name for the violent
gang or youth: 'hooligan'. It is not clear where the word originally came
from. From the late 1890s it crops up in music hall songs and contemporary reminiscences of street life; it has sometimes been attributed to a
notorious public house bouncer, Patrick Hooligan, who was famed for his
lawlessness.[130] However, the most important aspect about the 'hooligan'
phenomenon was the speed it was adopted throughout Britain by social
commentators and by both the local and the national press. For social
observers, the hooligan was the culmination of twenty or thirty years of
city life, a symbol of the growing lawlessness that seemed endemic to
urban living. The term 'hooligan', with its overtly Irish connotation, was
adopted enthusiastically, as it seemed to represent the spread of a foreign
and unwelcome influence. According to the press, the quiet and reserved
Englishman was being usurped by the hot-headed foreigner who was bring-
ing mayhem to the once peaceful streets of Britain.[131] Pinning the blame

on 'the other' was given more credence when social observers noted that these new gangs of youths could be distinguished from the 'law abiding English citizen' through the dress they wore. Remarkably, despite regional variations in income, male gangs tended to dress in a similar and distinctive manner. Robert Roberts remembered the northern gang member as having 'his own style of dress – the union shirt, bell-bottomed trousers, the heavy leather belt, pricked out in fancy designs with the large steel buckle and the thick, iron-shod clogs'.[132] Similar descriptions of 'hooligans' can be found in the Midlands and the Southeast as the press took a great deal of interest in this new style of dress. W. McG. Eagar, noted during the late nineteenth century that hooligan gangs were easily identified by their names and dress throughout Britain, commenting that

> the Scuttlers and Ikes of Manchester; the Peaky-Blinders of Birmingham; the Forty Gang, the Bengal Tigers, the Dockhead Slashers and the Bermondsey Street Yoboes, all the racily local gangs of roughs and toughs with studded belts and bell-bottomed trousers and possibly razors of definitely non-safety type up their sleeves, who plagued the police, took toll of small shopkeepers and drivers of vans and made the areas they dominated singularly uninviting to strangers.[133]

Earlier on in the nineteenth century, the 'rough' wore clothes appropriate to his description – ragged and unclean. What surprised contemporaries was the 'uniform', almost smart, quality of the hooligan's dress with the mandatory bell-bottomed trousers and large and decorated buckled belt, which was thought to double up as an effective weapon.[134]

By 1914, then, social investigators no longer held the view that youths were without a culture, but perceived rather that theirs was a degenerate one which was threatening the future of English civilisation. This concern was heightened when male youths began to move their recreational activities beyond their territory of working-class neighbourhoods to the city centres. Thus this youth culture was not inward-looking and self-contained but was perceived to be spreading and polluting other parts of the city. For example, Davies has shown that the most ubiquitous street custom in Manchester and Salford was the 'monkey parade' where on Sunday nights youths would 'take over many of the main streets across the two cities' by walking in large groups with the aim of pairing off with members of the opposite sex.[135] This custom was not unique to the Northwest but had been common in the Midlands since the late nineteenth century.[136]

The increase in 'rowdy parades' in Coventry were deemed such a threat to public order that it was raised at the local council, and by-laws 'regulating the streets' were mooted. One councillor reported that,

> In passing along Cross-Cheaping and some other principal thoroughfares about eight o'clock, he found the rough element very much on the increase. There was need of the streets being kept in better order at night. He had had many complaints. Mr Hill said he, too, had had several complaints. Bands of lads patrolled the streets arm-in-arm, and it seemed to be their habit to force people off the pavement.[137]

Actively possessing the streets in their own neighbourhood was one thing, but invading middle-class spheres in the city was an entirely different matter. Cheaper and more efficient transport was, for many contemporaries, accentuating the problem by transporting the 'roughs from the remote part of the parish' into the city centre. One Coventry tramway was so notorious that conductors refused to work on the Bell Green route since 'there seemed to be a class of roughs in that neighbourhood who lost entire control of themselves'.[138] Across urbanised Britain there were contestations over pockets of public space which usually centred on the city's principal streets and public amenities. Councillors in growing towns such as Luton, who had successfully attracted new industries and a young workforce during the Edwardian period, began to experience problems when they opened public parks as a form of rational recreation. In April 1906, councillors proudly opened Wardown Park, the town's largest public park. Within two months the town's youth had colonised the Sunday musical evenings that had been arranged for the 'respectable people of the town'. The *Luton Reporter* noted:

> Wardown Park, as we have observed before, presents many problems to the Town Council, chief of these is the management of the public who frequent the place ... the behaviour of one section of the community; young hooligans of a growing type, is openly acknowledged as being disgraceful, and to such an extent has it grown on the occasion of the Sunday evening concerts, that the Park Committee have actually recommended the prohibition of the Sunday Band Concerts altogether.[139]

During the late Victorian and early Edwardian period, then, an identifiable male youth sub-culture developed which was markedly different from adult working-class culture. The neighbourhood and the street provided the forum, free from parents and employers, for their informal leisure activities. Given this freedom, male youths showed a remarkable propensity to manipulate and customise their immediate surroundings for their own use. Thus, at certain times of the week, the street, city centre or municipal park were colonised by youths intent on flouting the moral codes set by their social superiors.

Conclusion

By 1914, contemporaries had little doubt that male youths possessed their own peculiar lifestyles, which they were convinced had been generated by a combination of the degenerate city, new work conditions and the spread of mass commercial leisure. The boy's mind, 'blank and sponge-like', had been imprinted with the worst excesses that modern society could muster. Initiatives to civilise youths by offering 'elevating' leisure clubs soon gave way to more disciplined and military-inspired youth movements. These movements were intent on instilling a sense of duty, patriotism and masculinity into youths which would help save the British Empire from impending doom. However, despite these initiatives, citizenship ideals were largely unsuccessful in penetrating a youth culture which drew on both commercial and informal leisure activities. Indeed, this chapter has sought to show that the youth's informal leisure patterns in his neighbourhood and his enthusiastic participation in the new world of commercial leisure were not diametrically opposed activities. Male youths' enjoyment of comic literature and of the music hall did not successfully neuter an authentic working-class culture, but lived alongside it, often adding variety to street life in the city. In the regions where youth participation in commercial leisure was most prolific, lads continued with their informal leisure activities around visits to the football match or music hall. In addition, male youths' desire to carve out meanings and identities in their local community saw the colonisation of public spaces such as streets and parks, a trait that continued with their consumption of new leisure activities. The integration of bicycling, initially a 'rational recreation', into a street-based culture of 'scorching' suggests that new working-class consumption patterns had not blunted a rather gregarious youth culture. Indeed, in a wider context male youths belonged to a subculture of traditional working-class culture which, between 1850 and 1914, exhibited the same combative and manipulative qualities that have been described in Chapters 1 and 2. However, historians have questioned whether theses traits in working-class culture continued into the interwar period – a theme that will be explored in the next section of the book.

Notes

1 P. Griffiths, 'Juvenile delinquency in time', in P. Cox and H. Shore (eds), *Becoming Delinquent. British and European Youth, 1650–1950* (Aldershot, Ashgate, 2002), p. 33.

2 H. Shore, *Artful Dodgers. Youth and Crime in Early Nineteenth-Century London* (London, Boydell Press, 2002), p. 2.

3 J. R. Gillis, *Youth and History. Tradition and Change in European Age Relations, 1770–Present* (New York, Academic Press, 1974); J. Springhall, *Youth, Empire and Society. British Youth Movements, 1883–1940* (Beckenham, Croom Helm, 1977); S. Humphries, *Hooligans or Rebels? An Oral History of Working-Class Childhood and Youth 1889–1939* (Oxford, Blackwell, 1981); G. Pearson, *Hooligan. A History of Respectable Fears* (London, Macmillan, 1983); C. Sandler, 'Working-Class Adolescents in Birmingham: A Study of Social Reform, 1900–14', D.Phil. thesis, University of Oxford, 1987, p. 28; H. Hendrick, *Images of Youth. Age, Class and the Male Youth Problem, 1880–1920* (Oxford, Clarendon Press, 1990); M. J. Childs, *Labour's Apprentices. Working-Class Lads in Late Victorian and Edwardian England* (London, Hambledon, 1992); J. Springhall, *Youth, Popular Culture and Moral Panics. Penny Gaffs to Gangster-Rap 1830–1996* (London, Macmillan, 1998); K. Boyd, *Manliness and the Boys' Story Paper in Britain. A Cultural History, 1855–1940* (London, Palgrave, 2003).

4 H. Cunningham, *Leisure in the Industrial Revolution, 1780–1880* (London, Croom Helm, 1980), p. 187.

5 D. Rubinstein, 'Sport and the sociologist, 1880–1914', *British Journal of Sports History*, 4 (1987), 14.

6 M. Savage and A. Miles, *The Remaking of the British Working Class, 1840–1940* (London, Routledge, 1994), p. 58.

7 M. Tebbutt, *Making Ends Meet. Pawnbroking and Working-Class Credit* (Leicester, Leicester University Press, 1983); E. Ross, 'Survival networks: Womens' neighbourhood sharing before the World War I', *History Workshop Journal*, 15 (1983); C. Chinn, *They Worked All Their Lives. Women of the Urban Poor in England, 1880–1939* (Manchester, Manchester University Press, 1988).

8 C. F. G. Masterman (ed.), *The Heart of the Empire* (London, Fisher Unwin, 1901), pp. 7–8.

9 Masterman (ed.), *The Heart of the Empire*, pp. 7–8.

10 D. Pick, *Faces of Degeneration. A European Disorder c. 1848–1918* (Cambridge, Cambridge University Press, 1989), p. 189.

11 F. W. Lawrence 'The housing problem', in Masterman (ed.), *The Heart of the Empire*, p. 56.

12 T. H. Manners Howe, 'Save the boys', in I. Maris (ed.) *Essays on Duty and Discipline. A Series of Papers on the Training of Children in Relation to Social and National Welfare* (London, Cassell, 1910), p. 103.

13 R. R. Hyde, *The Boy in Industry and Leisure* (London, G. Bell, 1921), p. xvii.

14 C. Booth, *Life and Labour of the People in London* (1 vol. 1889; 2 vols 1891; 9 vols 1892–97; 17 vols 1902–03, London, Macmillan); B. S. Rowntree, *Poverty. A Study of Town Life* (London, Macmillan, 1903).

15 W. McG. Eagar, *Making Men. The History of Boys' Clubs and Related Movements in Great Britain* (London, University of London Press, 1953), p. 380.

16 A. Freeman, *Boy Life and Labour. The Manufacture of Inefficiency* (London, King & Son, 1914), p. 205.

17 Childs, *Labour's Apprentices*, p. 71.

18 McG. Eagar, *Making Men*, p. 355.

19 C. E. B. Russell and L. M. Rigby, *Working Lad's Clubs* (1908; London, A. C. Black, 1932), p. 4.

20 McG. Eagar, *Making Men*, pp. 338, 344.

21 Hyde, *The Boy in Industry and Leisure*, p. 6.

22 McG. Eagar, *Making Men*, p. 351.

23 Freeman, *Boy Life and Labour*, p. 129.

24 J. Springhall, 'Baden-Powell and the Scout movement before 1920: Citizenship training or soldiers of the future?', *English Historical Review*, 101 (1986), 935.

25 M. Rosenthal, *The Character Factory. Baden-Powell and the Origins of the Boy Scout Movement* (Pantheon Books, New York, 1986), p. 162.

26 A. Warren, 'Sir Robert Baden-Powell, the Scout movement and citizen training in Great Britain 1900–1920', *English Historical Review*, 101 (1986), 379, 382; A. Warren, 'Citizens of the Empire: Baden-Powell, Scouts and Guides, and an imperial idea', in J. M. Mackenzie, *Imperialism and Popular Culture* (Manchester, Manchester University Press, 1986), p. 235.

27 M. Dedman, 'Baden-Powell, militarism, and the "invisible contributors" to the Boy Scout scheme, 1904–1920', *Twentieth Century British History*, 4:3 (1993); S. Pyke, 'The popularity of nationalism in the early British Boy Scout movement', *Social History*, 23:3 (1998).

28 Rosenthal, *The Character Factory*, p. 191.

29 Pryke, 'The popularity of nationalism in the early British Boy Scout movement', p. 310.

30 J. O. Springhall, 'Lord Meath, Youth and Empire', *Journal of Contemporary History*, 5:4 (1970), 105.

31 *The Times*, 14 December 1903. Meath's letter is written in support of Sir W. B. Richmond, a member of the Army League, who in a previous letter called for conscription to rid the streets of 'loafers'. See *The Times*, 4 December 1903.

32 Lord Meath, 'Duty and discipline in the training of children', pp. 53–9, and R. Blathwayt, 'Sentimental England', pp. 33–8, both in Marris (ed.), *Essays on Duty and Discipline*.

33 D. D. Welldon, 'The early training of boys in citizenship', in Marris (ed.), *Essays on Duty and Discipline*, pp. 45–8.

34 R. Baden-Powell, *Scouting for Boys* (London, C. Arthur Pearson, 1907), p. 18.

35 R. Baden-Powell, *Yarns for Boy Scouts* (London, C. Arthur Pearson, 1909), p. 117. The Edwardian obsession with Arthurian legend can be found in the pageant craze of the early twentieth century. See P.J. Waller, *Town, City and Nation. England 1850–1914* (Oxford, Clarendon Press, 1983), p. 314.

36 P. Wilkinson, 'English youth movements, 1908–1930', *Journal of Contemporary History*, 4:2 (1969), 14.

37 Wilkinson, 'English youth movements, 1908–1930', 14.

38 M. Blanch, 'Imperialism, nationalism and organized youth', in J. Clarke, C. Critcher and R. Johnson (eds), *Working Class Culture. Studies in History and Theory* (London, Hutchinson, 1979), pp. 111–12.

39 *Spinnel's Annual Directory, Coventry and District* (Robert Spinnel Press London, 1912), p. 39.

40 *Spinnel's Annual Directory, Coventry and District* (1912 and 1920); *Coventry Directory* (Coombelands, Addlestone, 1938).

41 T. A Proctor, '(Uni)Forming youth: Girl Guides and Boy Scouts in Britain, 1908–39', *History Workshop Journal*, 45 (1998), 117.

42 Proctor, '(Uni)Forming youth', 108; Wilkinson, 'English youth movements 1908–1930', 13.

43 Hyde, *The Boy in Industry and Leisure*, p. 116.

44 Cited in Proctor, '(Uni)Forming youth', 118.

45 Rosenthal, *The Character Factory*, p. 181.

46 McG. Eager, *Making Men*, pp. 343–4.

47 Proctor, '(Uni)Forming youth', 130.

48 Humphries, *Hooligan or Rebels?*, p. 4.

49 G. Stedman Jones, 'Working-class culture and working-class politics in London, 1870–1900', *Journal of Social History*, 7:4 (1974).

50 Freeman, *Boy Life and Labour*, p. 191.

51 J. Stevenson and C. Cook, *Britain in the Depression. Society and Politics 1929–39* (London, Longman, 1994), ch. 2.

52 Hendrick, *Images of Youth*, p. 52.

53 N. G. Chamberlain, 'Labour exchanges and boy labour', *Economic Review* (1909), 409.

54 Chamberlain, 'Labour exchanges and boy labour', 401.

55 Childs, *Labour's Apprentices*, p. 62.

56 Quoted in Hendrick, *Images of Youth*, p. 56.

57 Royal Commission on Education, *Reports from the Commissioners, Inspectors and Others.* Thirty Volumes, *Technical Instruction*, sess. 5 February–14 August 1884, Vol XXXI, p. 442.

58 Sandler, 'Working-class adolescents in Birmingham', p. 28.

59 Sandler, 'Working-class adolescents in Birmingham', p. 30. Childs has tended to overestimate the skill levels within the 'new' industries; Childs, *Labour's Apprentices*, p. 71.

60 Freeman, *Boy Life and Labour*, p. 179.

61 W. B. Stephens, 'Crafts and industries', *A History of the County of Warwick*, vol. 8 (London, Victoria Country History, 1969), pp. 177–83.

62 B. Beaven, 'Shop floor culture in the Coventry motor industry, *c.* 1896–1920', in D. Thoms, L. Holden and T. Claydon (eds), *The Motor Car and Popular Culture in the 20th Century* (Aldershot, Ashgate, 1998), p. 197.

63 Coventry Record Office (hereafter CRO), Acc BA/C/Q/20/12, Freemen's Admissions, 1905–39.

64 G. R. Carter, 'The cycle industry', in S. Webb and A. Freeman (eds), *Season Trades* (London, LSE, 1912), p. 128.

65 E. W. Cooper, 'Fifty Years of Reminiscences, unpublished scrapbook, 1928), p. 7.

66 *Coventry Times*, 10 July 1889.

67 Carter, 'Paper on the bicycle industry', in Webb and Freeman, *Seasonal Trades*, p. 138.

68 *Coventry Herald*, 24 August 1900.

69 Childs, *Labour's Apprentices*, p. 63.

70 *Coventry Herald*, 30 April 1915. For more on the bicycle worker and citizenship, see B. Beaven and J. Griffiths, 'Urban elites, socialists and notions of citizenship in an industrial boomtown: Coventry 1870–1914', *Labour History Review*, 69:1 (2004), 3–18.

71 Coventry Local Studies (hereafter CLS), 'Coventry Herald Leading Articles', 1889–92.

72 Davies, *Leisure, Gender and Poverty*, p. 74.

73 Freeman, *Boy Life and Labour*, p. 113.

74 *Coventry Times*, 18 March 1891.

75 National Social Purity Crusade (ed.), *The Cleansing of a City* (London, Greening, 1908), pp. 9–10.

76 A. Kuhn, *Cinema, Censorship and Sexuality, 1909–1925* (London, Routledge, 1988), p. 13.

77 *Harper's Magazine*, September 1912; Kuhn, *Cinema, Censorship and Sexuality*, p. 13.

78 Freeman, *Boy Life and Labour*, p. 133; Roberts, *The Classic Slum*, p. 176.

79 Childs, *Labour's Apprentices*, p. 132.

80 Freeman, *Boy Life and Labour*, p. 112.

81 Cited in Pearson, *Hooligan*, pp. 64–5.

82 Freeman, *Boy Life and Labour*, p. 151, 134; Childs, *Labour's Apprentices*, p. 133.

83 Kuhn, *Cinema, Censorship and Sexuality*, p. 13; Hendrick, *Images of Youth*, p. 133.

84 Freeman, *Boy Life and Labour*, p. 140; Hendrick, *Images of Youth*, p. 133.

85 Springhall, *Youth, Popular Culture and Moral Panics*, p. 43.

86 National Social Purity League (ed.), *The Cleansing of a City*, p. 64.

87 Freeman, *Boy Life and Labour*, p. 151.

88 Boyd, *Manliness and the Boys' Story Paper*, p. 179.

89 Springhall, *Youth, Popular Culture and Moral Panics*, p. 44.

90 National Social Purity League (ed.), *The Cleansing of a City*, p. 66.

91 See football section in Chapter 2.

92 *Midland Daily Telegraph*, 6 July 1897.

93 Freeman, *Boy Life and Labour*, pp. 151–2, 110–19.

94 Freeman, *Boy Life and Labour*, pp. 151–2, 110–19.

95 H. S. Pelham, *The Training of a Working Boy* (London, Macmillan, 1914), pp. 43–4.

96 Humphries, *Hooligan or Rebels?*, p. 203.

97 *Coventry Herald*, 29 April 1892.

98 S. Pivato. 'The bicycle as a political symbol: Italy, 1885–1955', *International Journal of the History of Sport*, 3:1 (1990), 174.

99 D. Rubinstein, 'Cycling in the 1890s', *Victorian Studies*, 21 (1977), 47.

100 For how women assumed this role during the interwar period, see M. Glucksmann, *Women Assemble. Women Workers and the New Industries in Interwar Britain* (London, Routledge, 1990).

101 Freeman, *Boy Life and Labour*, p. 191.

102 *Coventry Herald*, 24 March 1899.

103 *Coventry Times*, 10 July 1889.

104 CRO, Box C4 (c), *Lady Godiva Procession. Official Programme* (Coventry, anon, 1907); Rubinstein, 'Cycling in the 1890s', 51–7.

105 *The Graphic* 2 June 1906.

106 G. Pearson, *Hooligan*, p. 66.

107 *Coventry Herald*, 2 March 1900.

108 C. Waters, *British Socialists and the Politics of Popular Culture, 1884–1914* (Manchester, Manchester University Press, 1990), p. 157.

109 Rubinstein, 'Cycling in the 1890s', 69.

110 Rubinstein, 'Cycling in the 1890s', 69.

111 *Pall Mall Magazine*, March 1900.

112 *Coventry Herald*, 14 August 1891.

113 *Midland Daily Telegraph*, 24 June 1891.

114 *Coventry Herald*, 21 August 1891.

115 D. Rubinstein, 'Sport and the sociologist, 1890–1914', *British Journal of Sports History*, 4 (1984), 19.

116 *The Times*, 6 August 1898.

117 *The Times*, 31 May 1882.

118 *Coventry Times*, 18 March 1891.

119 *Midland Daily Telegraphy*, 22 January, 10 April, 3 May 1895.

120 National Social Purity Crusade (ed.), *The Cleansing of a City*, p. 4.

121 M. A. Lewis, *A Club for the Boys. Why Not Open One?* (London, Christian Knowledge Society, 1905), p. 4.

122 *Coventry Standard*, 13 March 1891.

123 A. Davies, 'Police and the people: Gambling in Salford, 1900–39', *Historical Journal*, 34 (1991).

124 B. Webb, *My Apprenticeship*, vol. II (Harmondsworth, Penguin, 1938), p. 286.

125 Hendrick, *Images of Youth*, p. 134.

126 R. Holt, *Sport and the British. A Modern History* (Oxford, Clarendon Press, 1993), p. 150.

127 R. Roberts, *The Classic Slum. Salford Life in the First Quarter of the Century* (Manchester, Manchester University Press, 1971), p. 156; see also Davies, *Leisure, Gender and Poverty*, pp. 97–100; Childs, *Labour Apprentices*, pp. 107–9; A. August, 'A culture of consolation? Rethinking politics in working-class London, 1870–1914', *Institute of Historical Research*, 74 (2001), 201.

128 *Coventry Standard*, 25 April 1942.

129 Humphries, *Hooligans or Rebels?*, p. 205.

130 Pearson, *Hooligan*, p. 255.

131 *The Times*, 17 August 1898. Foreigners were also blamed for the perceived increase in city vice; see National Social Purity Crusade (ed.), *The Cleansing of a City*, p. 116.

132 Roberts, *The Classic Slum*, p. 155.

133 McG. Eagar, *Making Men*, p. 340.

134 *Daily Graphic*, 16 November 1900.

135 Davies, *Leisure, Gender and Poverty*, p. 107.

136 For accounts of monkey parades in Birmingham, see Sandler, 'Working-class adolescents in Birmingham', p. 174; for London, see Pearson, *Hooligan*, p. 101.

137 *Coventry Standard*, 6 January 1888.

138 *Coventry Standard*, 3 August 1900.

139 *Luton Reporter*, 1 June 1906.

4

Male leisure in the industrial suburb, 1918–39: the rise of 'suburban neurosis'?

In 1919 a number of cities and towns across Britain were shaken by outbreaks of fierce civil unrest.[1] Although the immediate causes for the disturbances varied, it had become abundantly clear to the local civic elite that the nineteenth-century vision of social citizenship lay in ruins. This failure was most apparent in the expanding cities in the Midlands and Southeast, which had witnessed some of the most vigorous attempts to implement schemes of social citizenship between 1870 and 1914. With the postwar industrial expansion and the allied suburbanisation of working-class communities situated at some distance from the traditional civic amenities, the notion that a socially integrated city could be forged around civic pride and elevating leisure pursuits began to fade. The spectacular failure of the Peace Celebrations convinced many among the interwar urban elite to abandon large-scale civic celebrations, particularly since large numbers of workers had begun moving to new housing and industrial estates situated on the outskirts of cities. This chapter will examine how male leisure developed in these new housing estates during a period in which the civic elite retreated from taking an active role in shaping 'civilising' recreation. Indeed, the new estate's isolation from traditional working-class leisure institutions has led a number of historians to insist that males began to suffer from a 'suburban neurosis'. In this scenario, working males' leisure became 'privatised' and removed from the public sphere of the city centre to the private realm of home life. However, while interwar leisure may well have become more home-oriented, it will be argued that through the proliferation of works' clubs males continued to exercise a considerable autonomy over their recreation.

The decline of Victorian social citizenship

After the First World War, most towns and cities in England planned 'Peace Day Celebrations' that were to be held nationally on 19 July 1919. *The Times* described the public holiday as 'the greatest ritual day in our history', and for some towns and cities worried about the significant social changes that war-time conditions had brought to their area, it provided an ideal opportunity to restate ideals of social citizenship.[2] Each town or city developed its own series of events, which for some comprised a war veterans' parade, while others emphasised a children's carnival, and a number led the Peace Celebrations with a religious service, while some local authorities ensured that the civic elite were the central focus of the parade. Table 4.1 indicates the type of event organised to celebrate Peace Day for 42 towns and cities in Britain. By far the most popular form of celebration was the military or war veteran parade, followed by events that were organised primarily for children. There were surprisingly few religious activities, while the civic procession accounted for only four events. Notably, in a bid to convey a sense of social stability in regions that had rapidly expanded between 1870 and 1918, cities such as Coventry, Wolverhampton and Luton placed the civic elite and the city or town's heritage at the centre of the celebrations.[3] The Peace Day events led to mass disturbances in these three areas, which appeared to reflect a growing disillusionment with Victorian schemes of social citizenship.

The uneasy relationship between the workers in the new industries and the civic elite was pushed to breaking point during the First World War. For a town like Luton, the war had accelerated the social and economic change that had begun in the early part of the twentieth century when new industries from sectors such as engineering and food processing were established to replace the declining hat trade. Between 1901 and 1921, the town's population grew by over 20,000, boosting the presence of the new young semi-skilled worker. By 1919, trade unions, the shop stewards' movement and the Labour Party had, for the first time, become a significant force in Luton, prompting the Deputy Mayor to note that 'with the influx of the working classes, Luton had become a working-class constituency'.[4]

Table 4.1 Core events organised for the Peace Day Celebrations, July 1919

Military parade	War veteran parade	Children's events	Religious service	Civic parade
10	14	10	4	4

Sources: The Times, July 1919; *Municipal Journal,* January–July 1919.

Notwithstanding the Deputy Mayor's acknowledgement of Luton's social change, Orr has rightly argued that the Luton councillors 'believed it would be possible to return to a pre-war style of rule in which they did not feel obliged to consult with or accommodate those outside their narrow social circle'.[5] Indeed, they were keen to stabilise the town socially through civic ceremony, a form of social citizenship that had survived the nineteenth century. Thus, through the creation of a public spectacle comprising a well-ordered procession representing Luton's harmonious past, local pride and patriotism would be instilled into the more disparate members of Luton's new working class. Dissatisfaction with the town's arrangements had been widespread for some weeks, with local labour leaders complaining that proper housing for the recently arrived munition workers ought to have been the councillors' priority. Indeed, in the days leading up to the Peace Day Celebrations, one complainant at a public meeting claimed that 'those in authority over the town do not care for the working man'.[6] The disturbance in Luton occurred after the civic procession when the Mayor attempted to read out the King's Peace Day Proclamation. The *Luton News* reported that the Mayor's appearance 'was the signal for a hostile demonstration on the part of the crowd, cheering turned into jeering. The attitude of the crowd a little later assumed a distinctly ugly character.' This was perhaps a slight understatement since the crowd eventually stormed the town hall, burning the building to the ground, and causing in total over £200,000 worth of damage to the hall and the surrounding shopping area.[7] Significantly, the crowd's response to the Luton authorities' attempt to instil local patriotism was a symbolic attack on the town hall, a building that represented an old civic elite unable to engage with their new working-class constituency. Moreover, events in Luton cannot be written off as a local aberration. There were striking similarities with how the urban elite in Coventry attempted to use the public holiday to further the cause of social citizenship.

Table 4.2 Composition of Coventry City Council, selected years 1892–1918

	Building	Trad. industries	New industries	Professional	Retail	Gentlemen	Misc.
1892	2	14	2	2	12	5	3
1900	2	12	2	6	13	5	8
1910	2	13	3	6	11	7	6
1918	3	9	6	10	7	3	10

Sources: *Coventry Municipal Handbooks* (Coventry, Coventry Corporation 1892, 1900, 1910, 1918); Coventry Record Office, Acc CCA/1/4/13/8, 'Coventry Watch Committee Minute Book, 1914-1921'; Insurance Claims by city centre businesses; *Kellys' Warwickshire Trade Directories* (London, Kelly's Directory, 1890–1920); K. Richardson, *Twentieth Century Coventry* (Suffolk, Coventry Council, 1972).

Although the introduction of the new industries into Coventry during the last third of the nineteenth century altered substantially the social composition of the city, Coventry's political institutions continued to operate along familiar lines. Table 4.2 demonstrates that in selected years between 1892 and 1918, councillors were consistently drawn from three main areas: industry, the professions and the retail sector. Significantly, while employers from the new industries seem to have made little impact on council affairs prior to the First World War, employers within the traditional industries of watchmaking and weaving continued to have a strong presence.

With the new industrial capital largely disengaged from local affairs, Coventry's civic elite formulated a distinctly nineteenth-century solution to the postwar unrest that had gripped the city. During the First World War, Coventry's key munitions factories had experienced turbulent industrial relations that had culminated in a damaging strike in which 50,000 workers withdrew their labour, paralysing munitions production for a solid ten days in late 1917.[8] Although the strike centred on the role of the shop steward in industrial bargaining, the press portrayed the strikers as unpatriotic, money-grabbing engineers with no loyalty to their city or nation. Indeed, one magazine columnist raged that 'if shooting was good enough for the Irish rebels, why is it not good enough for English traitors?'[9] It was precisely because of this social unrest that the city councillors attempted to organise the public holiday celebrations with the hope that this would at last draw to a close the workplace antagonisms of war-time Coventry. However, the council's proposed Peace Celebrations and their clumsy communication of the project to a sceptical public only served to intensify the atmosphere of distrust with the civic elite. Without consultation and without any press present to record the discussion, a subcommittee of the council announced that the city would celebrate peace by creating a 'memorial park' and holding a traditional pageant on 'Peace Day'.[10] The proposals were met with a general hostility, though working people were particularly vocal and vented their anger through the local press, the trades council and the Coventry branch of the National Federation of Discharged and Demobilised Soldiers and Sailors.[11] The local press was inundated with letters of protest demanding that the £31,000 allocated for the purchase of the park be directed to new and urgently required housing schemes. One war widow wrote, 'surely no more appropriate memorial to our fallen men could be than to build modern homes with every convenience', while another correspondent complained that the purchase of the park would 'not benefit a soul except the owner'.[12] The decision to stage a 'historic pageant also received widespread criticism. For a city that had undergone rapid socio-economic change, the civic elite envisaged that a pageant would remind the population of the city's heritage and civic tradition. The parade celebrated the notion of 'work', though not the type engaged in by munitions workers. Instead, the parade's focus centred on forms of work associated with the ancient guilds that spawned the artisanal crafts of silk weaving and watchmaking, two industries in Coventry which had lost their skilled status and relevance to the city's economy by the mid-nineteenth century.[13] In short, the civic leaders' pageant attempted to project an image of Coventry and the nation that harked back to less complicated times, an imagined medieval chivalry and social stability. The Coventry Peace Celebrations centred on the Godiva Pageant, which was to be of 'a highly educational value as regards costume, armour and heraldry'.[14] The lead figures in the procession were the city's Mayor, aldermen and senior councillors, along with their relatives, donning costumes to portray 'national and civic history'.[15] The civic elite faced a difficult task in persuading Coventry workers to endorse a parade that celebrated local and national patriotism, particularly since these issues had not featured strongly in their community during the war. Social commentators complained that Coventry was 'a long time behind many other parts of England' in forming a Volunteer Corps, while the local press often headlined with beer price rises rather than the latest information from the front. In one instance an observer noted that 'the local public were seemingly inclined to regard the announcement that on Monday beer was to be increased by half-penny a glass as one of the most striking illustrations of the horrors of war.'[16]

The parade organisers did not help their cause by the failure to recognise the 'new' workers' contribution to the war effort, something that was not lost on observers at the time. After the parade had occurred one disgruntled correspondent to the local paper complained that 'I believe that 99 out of every 100 [Coventry people] were disappointed with Saturday's show. They live for what is happening at the present time; think of what happened yesterday, and hope for what to-morrow has in store.' The correspondent added that the people who had worked to 'help Old England' during the past four years had not received the recognition they deserved.[17] Criticism of the parade had started almost as soon as the events were announced. A series of letters in the local press argued that workers in the motor and bicycle industries should be celebrated in the pageant, while one condemned the whole event as 'backward looking'. He argued that 'we are not catering for the middle ages, but for the pressing needs of modern times. Public money spent on pageants could be put to better use', concluding that what was needed was 'more and better dwellings'.[18] Such was the public outcry over the peace celebrations, the city council were forced into publishing a lengthy explanation defending their projects and apologising for the lack of consultation.[19] The criticism of the proposed celebrations, however, continued and, if anything, began to take on more sinister undertones. One correspondent, prior to the disturbances, warned the civic elite that if they did not make housing a priority, then there was no guarantee that the city's citizens would remain law abiding:

> When the Huns were threatening the property of the wealthy classes in Britain it didn't take years to prepare plans and build homes to accommodate workers to produce munitions of war ... The wealthy classes were scared then and matters moved quickly. What was done then can just as easily – in fact, more easily – be done now. However, the owners of slum and brick boxes with slate roofs who, unfortunately, form our local governing body, now imagine the danger to themselves is over now that the Huns are beaten. Therefore they are quite indifferent and do not intend to move in the matter of providing homes, unless compelled to do so. Let them take warning. We homeless ones are a law-abiding class of citizens, but even the worm will turn when trodden upon. We have been trodden upon and slighted in every way by the class who have comfortable villas to live in. We are turning ... I advise the municipal authorities to get to work, if only for their own sakes, without delay.[20]

The volatile situation in Coventry was also monitored nationally, since the government was increasingly concerned about the prospect of Soviet-style political agitation after the 1917 strike. Despite the civic elites' optimism that the parade would help ease social tensions, undercover intelligence officers reported 'that there is not popular enthusiasm for the Peace Celebrations on the 19 July', adding that there was outright 'disapproval' of the events.[21] It had been rumoured in Coventry factories for almost a week that there would be a backlash against the Peace Celebrations, which duly occurred in the form of three nights of serious disturbances. The *Coventry Standard* reported that national peace celebrations had been marked by a 'local war' which had left Coventry as if it 'had been subjected to the outrageous doings of a victorious German Army'. Significantly, among the shops repeatedly targeted was that of Alderman Snape, who, as a prominent organiser of the parade, had fronted the advertisement bills for the event. The press and authorities consistently blamed the 'new' semi-skilled Coventry factory worker, a perceived recent migrant who had brought with him undesirable demands alien to a city that had prided itself on respectable craft traditions. Thus the Bishop of Coventry blamed the disturbances on 'non-local' workers, whereas the *Coventry Standard* pointed the finger at the 'Bolshevik spirit' imported into the factories during the war.[22] The *Coventry Graphic* had no doubts about the identity of the instigators: 'the damage has been caused by the men who hid themselves in a munition factory during the war, drawing big money, and are now discontent because they have lost their positions.'[23]

Civic attempts to shape popular leisure patterns or stage mass events which were designed to forge local patriotism were greatly damaged by the industrial conflict and postwar social disturbances. This demise was also hastened by change in the urban landscape in regions that nurtured the new housing estates and industries.[24] The large light engineering and electrical factories that were built in the suburbs of towns and cities during the interwar period encouraged the growth of working-class housing estates, which further strained the links between workers and municipal institutions. The following section will investigate the impact that these new estates and factories had upon male leisure patterns and examine the perceived new problems that these developments brought to the interwar authorities.

Structural changes in the British economy and urban environment convinced contemporary researchers that, by the end of the interwar period, there had been significant shifts in patterns of work and leisure. Updating Charles Booth's pioneering study on London's life and labour in the 1890s, a team of sociologists led by Hubert Llewellyn Smith attempted to contrast the labour and leisure patterns of 1930s' London with his Victorian counterpart. Llewellyn Smith concluded that widespread mechanisation in the engineering trades had tended to make employment 'more steady' and 'enabled hours of work to be reduced'.[25] However, the downside of mechanisation was that, although widespread casualisation had been reduced since the Victorian era, unemployment had become a more important factor as the scope for manual labour had narrowed. Moreover, although workers laboured for a shorter duration and often obtained more purchasing power than their Victorian counterparts, mechanisation had ensured that their work was more repetitive. According to Llewellyn Smith, these developments had important implications for leisure:

> Thus all the forces of work are combining to shift the main centre of interest of a worker's life more and more from his daily work to his daily leisure, whether that leisure be the margin of time available for rest and recreation after the day's work is done, or the compulsory leisure imposed by the total or partial failure of his means of livelihood. Hence the great and growing interest to London life and labour of the problems relating to the use of leisure.[26]

Ironically, despite Llewellyn Smith's argument that economic change and mechanisation had produced a very different work environment, his focus on workers' leisure reflected the intelligentsia's long-standing anxiety over the relationship between citizenship and leisure that stretched back to Booth's Victorian world. According to Llewellyn Smith, male leisure time was spent less in the public sphere of a city centre concert or music hall and more in the private sphere of the home or the local club.[27] This shift in male leisure patterns was acknowledged by a variety of social observers from across the political spectrum who continued to perceive working-class leisure as a significant problem in the development of urban society. The intelligentsia on the left consistently worried about the 'use of leisure' or the 'leisure problem', an anxiety heightened by shifts in urban landscapes and the political context of the 1930s. The dispersal of working-class families to remote suburban estates, with limited contact with the civic authorities, raised concerns that a working class without civic leadership could be susceptible to the influences of fascism. Consequently, working-class leisure patterns were studied closely for signs of apathy for existing political institutions which could be exploited by fascist agitation.[28]

On the other hand, more conservative observers believed that the new large estates heralded the dawning of a new mass society with working families 'herded' together in monotonous housing to form single-class dormitories. It was argued that the poor leisure facilities the new estates had to offer created the potential for greater social unrest and the formation of 'little Moscows'. These concerns were voiced by one sociologist who ventured that, 'In modern times the vast aggregations of people, mainly segregated into suburbs of housing estates, occupied by people of one grade or condition, and one set of educational backgrounds and outlook, have become little more than disorganised crowds.'[29] Social scientists, from both the left and right, were keen to establish how suburbanisation of working-class families had affected community relations and leisure patterns. The new socialisation and alienation of working-class families in the new estates, combined with the emergence of extreme political movements was, for many researchers, a potentially dangerous cocktail. The implicit assumption running throughout the political spectrum was that without appropriate leadership in homogeneous working-class suburbs, Britain's liberal democracy was under threat.

From 1919, working-class housing was substantially transformed with a number of housing acts which stimulated residential growth on the outskirts of expanding cities and towns. Accordingly, historical geographers have contended that in this period 'the most urbanised country in the world at the end of World War One had by the beginning of World War Two become one of the most suburbanised'.[30] Although for the first time in two hundred years the overall population growth declined in the interwar period, there was a definite shift in population trends from the declining industrial centres of the North to the Midlands and Southeast. Indeed, the Midlands and the Southeast, with their associated new industries, absorbed 60 per cent of the total population growth between 1918 and 1939.[31] This urban dispersal was further enhanced by government subsidies that funded the large council estates which emerged during the interwar period, usually near large out-of-town industrial developments.[32] Between 1919 and 1939, local authorities built 1.1 million houses, 90 per cent of which were located in suburban areas. In addition, local authorities were, through government subsidies, able to charge uneconomic council house rents affordable to the manual working class.[33] A striking feature of these new housing developments was their low density, since houses were either semi-detached or built in small terraced blocks. Moreover, most publicly built houses had relatively large gardens.[34]

The Midlands and the Southeast in particular saw the development of large council estates which on their completion resembled miniature towns. Longbridge near Birmingham and Becontree near London developed in this manner, while industrial centres like Coventry extended their boundaries, relocating industry from the centre to the city's outskirts.[35] For Coventry, the First World War not only enlarged the existing 'new' industrial base of the city, but also provided the economic base and labour supply to take advantage of the demand for mass-produced consumer goods in the interwar period. One correspondent for the *Daily Express* reported that 'Coventry has done extremely well in peace as well as war ... all England wants new cars. Coventry intends to supply a good proportion of them and swell its millions of profitable trade.'[36] Thus, although approximately 15,000 left the city to serve in the army during the war, the population had risen from 114,000 in 1914 to 142,000 by 1918. After the war, the corporation embarked on a house-building scheme, particularly for workers in factories situated on the outskirts of the city such as Peel Connor Telephone works, Standard Motor Company and Morris Motors. Such was the high density of people per acre that employers had no option but to move from the centre, prompting one commentator to note that new industries 'are distributed pretty well all around Coventry'.[37] Thus, until the Standard Motor Company opened a modern factory on the eastern outskirts of Coventry, the local areas such as Canley and Earlsdon had been little more than small semi-rural suburbs. By the 1920s, Earlsdon was described as a 'new town', complete with its public library, schools, cinema, industries and municipal services, while a large housing estate was built in Canley with the specific purpose to house the employees of Standard Motors and allied trades.[38] It was estimated in 1936 that in the Bablake ward of the city the large motor firms of Coventry Chain, Carbodies, Maudslay and Alvis had attracted an additional 20,000 people to the area, living in over a hundred new streets and crescents.[39] While other areas such as Walsgrave, Wyken and Stoke experienced similar growths, the suburb of Cheylesmore underwent a period of spectacular growth in which the developers had 'difficulty in completing the new houses in sufficient time to meet the demand'.[40] One of the chief attractions of Cheylesmore was that it was close to a number of major engineering firms, which saved employees bus fares and enabled workers to get home for a midday meal.[41]

The housing developments in Coventry represented a microcosm of the housing estates that burgeoned in new industrial areas during the interwar period. However, the continual immigration of workers, which in some cases had begun in the late nineteenth century, increasingly concerned the civic authorities. The 1931 Census revealed that over 60 per cent of people in outer London were found to have been born outside it, while in the Midlands and Southeast towns were 'springing up over night'. In Oxford, for example, it was discovered that in July 1936 12,000 of the 30,000 insured workers were found originally to have exchanged their books at other employment exchanges. This led *The Times* to comment that in Oxford 'the make-up of the working population has been radically changed within the space of a few years'.[42] Moreover, a correspondent for *The Times* added an ominous note to his commentary on industrial migration when he warned that 'a too sudden and violent impact of alien traditions must imperil social values, and the growth of a new community with common civic and social ideals, out of a diverse multitude of uprooted immigrants is attended by difficulties'.[43] In Coventry, which had seen a much larger growth during the interwar period, the local press warned readers of the consequences of working-class suburbanisation:

> As the Coventry of the future rises and spreads itself further afield, more and more people arrive from all parts of the country to make their homes here. Are they going to accept their responsibilities of citizenship with the numerically small number of Coventrians left? They are welcomed by the latter, who take pride in the development of their city. Will the new-comers respond and make Coventry their city also? That seems to be the biggest problem of the future.[44]

Similarly in 1937, a study on the social consequences of industrial transference warned that transferees were often isolated in 'depersonalised suburban areas' and 'lost and unhappy in spite of themselves'.[45] A recurrent assumption expressed by social commentators and civic elite, then, constructed a contrast between the civically aware indigenous population and the alienated 'new-comers' who cared little for the town's heritage or civic development.

Since the late nineteenth century, then, social commentators and civic authorities had constantly worried about the large influx of working-class labour into the urban centres in the Midlands and the Southeast. In addition, these migrant workers were settling into new housing estates free from the guidance and watch of the civic authorities. The young male worker caused particular anxiety, since 'they are left to find their feet in London or a Midlands town. Often they have no religious attachment and no social introductions.' Consequently, without civic or religious guidance they could become

> absorbed in the least socially desirable strata of the population, and add materially to the social problems of their new communities. Even the older men, too often entering an atmosphere of suspicion and prejudice, are bewildered and disheartened by differences of local psychology, temperament custom and modes of speech.[46]

The formation of homogeneous working-class suburbs raised doubts among civic leaders about the wisdom of 'herding' together one class of the population. Without a strong enclave of middle-class residents, the estates would lack the social leadership required to enthuse local patriotism and civic pride'.[47]

The linkages between citizenship and leisure were apparent from the proceedings of an academic conference in 1936 devoted to 'the challenge of leisure'. Despite its wide-ranging title, the conference focused specifically on working-class leisure, particularly in relation to the growing new suburbs. One delegate, Charles Cameron, worried about the 'great gulf of unguided activity' that occurred after school and proposed that each town or suburb should have a community centre 'where all voluntary efforts for cultural and social betterment can be coordinated with each other and with organised efforts of central government'. Cameron believed that such a centre would stimulate the development of civic life through the introduction of a 'Certificate of Good Citizenship', an initiative that would improve the working-class's participation in municipal life and end the isolation of many in suburban communities.[48] In the eyes of contemporaries the community centre had the potential to re-energise democracy, a belief endorsed by Wyndham Deedes of the National Council of Social Welfare. In 1937, Deedes wrote that community centres could become the 'elementary schools of democracy', adding that the linkages between the citizen and the state began at a local level, since 'we shall never know how to be one of a nation until we are one of a neighbourhood'.[49] Likewise, political scientists such as Ernest Barker argued that community centres could help foster a new 'folk culture' in which garden gilds, dramatic, choral and physical training societies could flourish and ultimately make for an improved and more informed popular culture.[50] The community centre, then, was envisaged by urban planners as essentially an educational institution which would provide a solution to the 'problem' of male leisure and improve civic responsibility and pride. In Slough, which had attracted a range of new industries through the trading estate on the town's outskirts, the town council, in partnership with local firms, built a community centre in 1936 to serve the neighbouring housing estate. In many respects, the centre resembled a traditional working men's club with the bar, darts room and billiards room the focal point of the mens' activities.[51] Similar anxieties were expressed in Coventry, as the local council, which was 'deeply concerned' with the alienation problem, funded a scheme similar to the one in Slough for the new estate of Keresley. A local reporter noted that new housing estates were all well and good but 'you cannot plant a few thousand people on a new estate and leave it at that ... the residents are faced with loneliness, no place to meet, nowhere for children to play, no churches, no schools, no library, no swimming pools, no parks.' Significantly, the residents themselves, who were consulted on the construction of the new community centre, did not request any of these educational or recreational activities. Instead, like the residents in Slough, they desired a community centre fully equipped with a bar and games room.[52] There can be little doubt, then, that the new housing estates shifted the focal point for male leisure from city centre institutions towards the home and the immediate locality. Indeed, one commentator noted, 'for the first time in his life' the male worker 'has two living rooms now and a garden and a wireless, there is so much more interest in life, and literally so much more room for interests'.[53] The more spacious living quarters that the new houses had to offer ensured that the house became a more attractive place to relax than the cramped and often noisy environment of the small Victorian terraced family house.[54]

Social observers visiting the new working-class housing estates were struck by the clear demarcation between work and the home that males appeared to adopt. Within minutes of arriving home, males dispensed with their work clothes, remaining in a state of undress, unwilling to smarten themselves even for visitors. Moreover, social observers also noticed that the often regimented factory discipline of a working day contrasted sharply with the male's home life which seemed purposefully slipshod. Visitors to working-class homes in Oxford noted that most clocks had stopped or were set to the wrong time and there was a significant absence of calendars. Male leisure also became more domesticated, with spare time being consumed with household chores, odd jobs and gardening. Indeed, during the interwar period 4 million new gardens were established, the majority situated in the homes of the manual working class. The interest in gardening was reflected in the membership of gardening societies, which were consistently the most popular recreational club on the new estates.[55] Gardening, however, was not a new hobby adopted by the suburban working-class. Llewellyn Smith, in his study of London life, found that despite the many logistical drawbacks facing Londoners, such as the lack of space for gardens and atmospheric impurity, many working-class men had an intimate knowledge of gardening. He reported that local gardening societies flourished in London, with over seventy clubs affiliated to the London Gardens Guild, and significantly many were found 'in some of the poorest and most congested areas in London, such as Bethnal Green, Bermondsey, Finsbury Park and Canning Town'.[56]

Even within the home, however, the dichotomy between male and female activities was accentuated, with women finding it impractical to balance domestic duties with waged labour, while for men home-centred activities were increasingly confined to the garden, the garden shed or the allotment.[57] One sociological study in the 1930s found that this was particularly pronounced in relocated families, as 'gardening was mainly carried on by the few married men who had been fortunate in securing a house with a small garden attached, on one of the New Housing Estates'.[58] Thus, Hughes and Hunt have persuasively argued that the new estates of the 1930s helped to cement gender differences within working-class families, since without the plethora of social institutions that characterised traditional working-class neighbourhoods, such as the corner shop or pawnbroker, women stayed at home and focused their attention on ensuring their new house was 'spic and span'.[59] Furthermore, while Hughes and Hunt have uncovered a degree of isolation for women in new 1930s' estates, males maintained the recreational outlet that work offered through the variety of clubs and societies that flourished after the First World War. A post-Second World War study of working-class families who had moved into housing estates in Coventry during the 1930s noted that 'men don't bother with neighbours as women do', as there was less sociability among men in the neighbourhood. Unlike women, men were particularly sceptical of neighbours who borrowed their tools or garden equipment, fearing that 'once it gets inside their house you forget it' and 'no matter how generous you are, after a while you start totting things up'. Revealingly, men regarded an ideal neighbour as 'a bloke who likes to get together with you

– at games, or any social activities – in your house or the club'. Indeed, the report noted that

> It is possible that the needs of men for companionship are satisfied at work, in clubs and public houses, and that they do not therefore require active social relations with neighbours. Mr Douglas, comparing Coventry with Scotland, finds people more at work in Coventry, and more sociable in the pubs, 'but neighbours don't bother you much'.[60]

Indeed, the public house continued to perform an important role in the suburb, often at the expense of the traditional city centre drinking establishments. One suburban Coventry car worker recalled that he and his workmates would visit the city centre pub about once every two weeks as they mainly spent time in their local, which had a piano.

> Half of them could all sing a good song, you know, and on a Saturday night … you'd always finish up at somebody's house, you know, just have what they called a kitty and put two bob in each and buy some bottled beer and take it back to somebody's house and you may continue having a sing song or you might have a game of cards, you know just for pennies or something like that. You used to carry on 'till about 3 or 4 in the morning, go home and sleep it off 'till dinner.[61]

The shift in working-class male leisure from the inner city to the suburbs had important implications for the municipal elites' involvement in working-class leisure patterns. According to Fred Lee, an alderman on Coventry City Council, new leisure pursuits and modern housing estates had diminished the need for a town hall and were responsible for a decline in 'local patriotism'.

> People no longer attend public meetings and concerts to anything like the same extent that they did two decades ago. The introduction of broadcasting provides thousands of people with evening amusement in their own homes, in the comfort of an armchair by the fireside where they can listen to music and other forms of entertainment without paying an admission ticket. The cinemas, which have become an enormous counter-attraction to thousands of those who might have attended town hall functions before this new form of competition provided them with other interests.[62]

Such was the concern that new forms of leisure enjoyed in the home or within an isolated local community were destroying local pride that in 1935 the local council established a committee to promote civic patriotism. Although the committee came up with a definition of civic patriotism as 'an honest pride in the town of one's birth or adoption' and 'a determination to speak well of it'[63], the committee was unable to generate any great enthusiasm for the project among the vast majority of Coventry's population.[64] Similarly, social commentators such as Robert Sinclair argued that new work regimes and new standardised housing estates had what he termed 'robotized man'. Writing in 1937, he claimed that English society was producing 'the mass produced man' adding that 'the moment that he enters what he called without irony a "hall", he does almost exactly what the man in the next house is doing'.[65]

Historians and sociologists of the pre- and post-Second World War working class have seized upon statements such as these to argue that the 1930s saw the emergence of the apathetic and privatised male worker.[66] Working-class male recreation had traditionally been an exclusively male affair away from the home in the local working men's club, works club or public house. Moreover, unlike those of women, male friendships were usually forged at work rather than in the neighbourhood. However, according to some historians, the isolation of the new estates fundamentally changed male leisure patterns. McKibbin argues that the sociability of traditional communities was broken by the spacial layout of the new estates, which helped to promote a family- rather than neighbourhood-centred community after 1918. In addition, the lack of amenities, the energy expended on longer commuting times to work, and the popularity of the wireless and garden all contributed to shape a more domesticated male leisure experience. Thus, according to McKibbin, 'the sociability of the estates – the caution, the suspicion, the domesticity, and the feeling that social withdrawal was safest – was simply a traditional sociability adapted to new physical circumstances'.[67] Likewise, Scannell and Cardiff have suggested working men were being drawn into the home due to

> a more comfortable house, in which people were becoming more home-centred and 'privatized'. Though these trends were in motion well before the inter-war period, they became achievable realities for millions in this period. The clearest sign of this process was in the newly growing culture of suburbia: in sectors of the working class relocated in newly built council estates on the outskirts of towns; in the private housing that stretched out along, and branched off from, the arterial roads leading into the towns and cities of southern and central England.[68]

In this scenario, the community declined with urban dispersal, since the effortless sociability of the traditional residential areas had been replaced by the distant cordiality of the new estates. The implication here is that working-class culture became more inward-looking during the interwar period. Thus historians have argued that the new estates broke the traditional links between work and leisure that had helped import class antagonism from the workplace into the recreational arena. Men, it is argued, began to suffer a 'suburban neurosis', abandoning the local public house and spending more time in their domestic environment. Although focusing on bourgeois neighbourhoods, North has challenged these assumptions that underpinned perceptions of the new suburb, arguing that 'middle class suburban recreation reveals a wealth of both family centred and communal activities, defying the pessimistic image of a demoralised and isolated people forced exclusively into solitary and mechanised amusements'.[69] Certainly within a working-class context, male leisure may have became more home-centred as new large estates often had fewer public houses than traditional working-class areas, with some local authorities refusing to allow them at all.[70] However, it is argued here that a significant portion of male leisure continued outside of the home, often in the new work-based clubs that mushroomed most notably in suburbs which supported large engineering factories. Historians who have embraced the 'suburban neurosis' theory have neglected this important continuity in working-class leisure. The following section will investigate how, with the increase in urban dispersal, initiatives designed to facilitate male leisure passed from the civic authorities to large employers.

With the civic elites' retreat from ambitious schemes of social citizenship, the role of moral guardian of popular leisure pursuits was taken up by modern paternalist employers. Employers justified their involvement in their employees' leisure time on a number of levels which set them apart from the traditional nineteenth-century paternalist master. Certainly it was recognised that a physically and mentally fit workforce would help labour productivity in a period of economic uncertainty. Increasingly, however, modern industrialists began to lose their close involvement with the local community, and ambitious schemes of social citizenship gave way to more pressing concerns revolving around workplace social relations.[71] Thus 'progressive' employers were keen to justify industrial capitalism within a moral as well as an economic framework during an era in which the fundamentals of capitalism were being questioned by the new emergent ideologies of communism and fascism. Jones has noted that during the 1930s 'captains of industry moved in a highly complex ethical and cultural world where religion and humanistic ideas played ... a complicated role, and where morality and capitalism could be conflated.'[72] The First World War had drawn employers into workers' welfare issues to an unprecedented degree. The hastily built munitions factories on the outskirts of major industrial cities often required dormitories and recreational centres, as most of the labour had been specifically brought in from other regions. Thus, by the end of the war, a great many large engineering firms in the Midlands had both a social club and an associated company magazine.[73] Car firms, in particular, dominated the areas in which they were situated. Utilising non-unionised labour, car firms implemented a form of 'welfare capitalism', initiating company magazines and clubs and building extensive leisure and sports facilities for their relatively well-paid workers.[74] With industrialists dominating leisure initiatives in places like Coventry, municipal intervention in working men's leisure activities was minimal.[75] While most firms gained a degree of civic approval by inviting local councillors to club prize-giving events, some company founders, such as Sir Alfred Herbert, dispensed with municipal involvement altogether and acted as local dignitaries themselves.[76] Thus, whereas the nineteenth-century paternalist attempted to project civic ideals from a municipal platform, the twentieth-century paternalist had more limited horizons that did not extend beyond his own workforce. For example, during the Second World War, Coventry councillors encouraged firms to open their leisure facilities to local residents in the hope that they could become community centres in the postwar period. However, the firms were generally hostile to the idea, with the secretary of Alfred Herbert's club responding that 'we cannot agree to any non-employee becoming a member of our club, or to use our sports ground'.[77]

Both the company magazine and works' social club can provide insights into the direction male leisure pursuits evolved during the interwar period. For many male workers in these new housing estates, the local firm represented one of the main recreational institutions for evening entertainment. The Mass-Observer Tom Harrisson noted in the late 1930s that the private club or works' club on the new estates had begun to marginalise the public house, traditionally the cornerstone in every working-class community.[78] The company magazine could also provide a point of contact with employees that could develop an educative dimension. Readers, for example, could be informed on the benefits of industrial capitalism and the principles of good citizenry. One social worker in 1921 noted that there was a 'growing tendency throughout the country on the part of firms to produce a "house" magazine', adding that reports on social gatherings and sporting events helps to capture the readers' attention. After this the magazine could introduce him to the 'study of economics, social and industrial history, or citizenship, [and thereby] he can be given knowledge in "tabloid" form'.[79] The employers' sustained interest in workers' leisure also stemmed from the stormy industrial relations that prevailed in the major engineering centres towards the end of the war.[80] For example, the engineering firm White & Poppe founded a company magazine in 1918 with the express inten- tion that it would 'tighten bonds of friendship' and 'provide a common ground on which Director and apprentice, tool room and tetryl workers may fraternise, and with fuller knowledge realize their oneness'. In addition, the magazine had the objective of 'stimulating interest in the recreational side of factory and colony life'.[81] The employers' notion that their workers were living in 'colonies' away from their traditional environment reinforced their belief that they had a responsibility to provide some wholesome recreation for their employees. Thus, using the vast profits accumulated during the war, White & Poppe founded a social club that included a cinema and games rooms, catering for over 350 people.[82] White & Poppe were typical of large engineering firms in the period immediately after the First World War, in effecting a rapid progression from magazines to social clubs. By the 1920s, the vast majority of the major engineering firms in Coventry, Birmingham and Luton, the three key areas associated with the light industries, had invested in leisure facilities and associated clubs and societies for their employees.[83]

The analysis of company magazines and associated social clubs in order to provide an insight into workers' leisure patterns has attracted widespread interest from historians investigating the social relations of worker and employer beyond the point of production. Recently, historians such as Delheim and Griffiths have argued that employers were largely successful in shaping workers' leisure patterns around an inclusive set of assumptions and activities that reduced the traditional social tensions between capital and labour.[84] Indeed, taken at face value, this historiographical strand would lend support to the view that employers helped contribute towards the concept of the privatised new worker, who had lost the sense of solidarity that had been engendered in the traditional neighbourhoods and leisure of the inner city. However, as we shall see, a closer investigation of the company magazine and the activities in the social clubs reveals a stronger continuity of male leisure and contestation over forms of leisure than some historians have allowed for.

Despite the rhetoric of the company magazine, the early organisational structures of the firm's provision of entertainment resembled the hierarchy of management and labour relations of the factory shop floor. The editorial committees of company magazines and the position of club organiser were initially composed wholly of management and directors. In 1918, the motor car firm Siddeley–Deasy proudly announced the appointment of a 'social worker', a role later to become known as the 'social secretary'. Siddeley–Deasy appointed a former headmaster for the role, which would bring a 'closer understanding and sympathy among employer and employed'.[85] Acknowledging that this was a new but general trend in engineering firms, a newspaper correspondent reported that the: 'social worker is everywhere, even now, still in the evolutionary stage. As far as the factories are concerned, it would almost appear that to build up a scheme sufficiently complete the establishment of clubs was necessary. They would be the centre, the common ground, the meeting place for all.'[86] Clearly, it was significant that a former headmaster was chosen to organise the workers' social activities as it indicated the educational nature of the entertainment that the management was hoping to instil into the leisure activities programme. Indeed, the social secretary envisaged both the magazine and the social club as vehicles for recreational improvement. In a magazine editorial he complained that workers had little option but to indulge in unsuitable recreation, since 'many of our present day forms of amusement are extraordinary and crudely artificial'.[87] In addition, there would be no room in the magazine for discussion on what constituted poor forms of entertainment since, although he explained that he welcomed ideas on out-of-work activities, 'there would be no room for the grouser, the growler, the man with a grievance or the man with an axe to grind. He must find another outlet for his grousing, growling, grieving and axe-grinding.'[88]

The tight control that management attempted to exert on the company's provision of workers' leisure was largely met with indifference from the shop floor and in some cases outright hostility. Within the first few months of the launch of White and Poppe's magazine, *The Limit*, the editor received complaints that the editorial committee had no representatives from the shop floor. This led to workers boycotting the magazine, a situation which resulted in the editor complaining that 'we have had nothing from the shops or office staff. There is nothing to be afraid of.'[89] Alongside technical information on engineering practices, the magazine seemed content to run articles by foremen or managers on their day trips to various Warwick-shire villages or biographies on long-serving members of the management team. It was the exclusion of any input from the 'ordinary worker' which prompted one employee to write at length explaining why the magazine had been boycotted by the shop floor:

> I was one who believed that its [*The Limit's*] specific object was to serve the master class and after reading this month's, I am of the opinion that there is a little Boss Bumming going on, or should I say, that there is no mention of the ordinary worker, but a continual running of different chargehands ... It is not my intention to be unkind to anyone but I contend the articles about Mr. Hedger and 'Foreman's' experiences are mere piffle. We don't want to know who walked into a bakers shop to buy young onions for his tea, or whose motor bike bumped into a pig.[90]

Repeated invitations for dissatisfied anonymous correspondents from the shop floor to meet the editor in his office were consistently ignored, illustrating the level of mistrust that pervaded, from the workplace to recreational activities.[91] Similar failures to integrate management and shop-floor staff in club activities became apparent in most works' social clubs by the 1920s. Perhaps this was best demonstrated in the annual works' outing, often organised by the club's social secretary, and designed to foster a collegiate atmosphere for at least one day of the year.

Traditional works' outings, which had become widespread during the mid-nineteenth century, were fairly regimented affairs, usually comprising a trip to a local rural village, followed by a meal and speeches by the chairman or works manager.[92] There is evidence that some smaller firms attempted to continue with this programme of events immediately after the Great War. However, a more fragmented leisure experience became the norm in the large engineering firms in the Midlands, due to the sheer size of the workforce and the increasing influence that workers began to assert over the management of social clubs. For example, although the Coventry-based Armstrong Siddeley closed the works down for one day in September, the social club organised seven different day trips. Significantly, these day trips reflected the social divides in the workplace: management and office staff took a river trip in Oxford, the Inspection Department visited local Warwickshire villages, while a 'considerable number' of the shop floor took a train journey to Lancashire to watch Coventry City play Blackpool, returning to the Midlands via the Pleasure Beach. The exclusion of a managerial influence prompted some editors of company magazines to offer advice to workers on how to enjoy their day out. Optimistically, in the 1920s one editor for the *Loudspeaker*, the company magazine for GEC, advised his readers that a visit to Blackpool should consist of a 'brisk walk, swim and a visit to the theatre'. Clearly writing for the uninitiated, the author conceded that those familiar to the town 'will have their own ideas on spending a day in Blackpool. For such as these, this article will probably be of no interest.'[93] Although evidence is sketchy, it would be safe to conclude that the editor's ideal programme of activities for a day trip did not correspond to that of the shop-floor. Given that day-trips were not only class-specific but often section- or departmentally specific, this led inevitably to them being sex-specific. The male works' outing tended to be less about sightseeing and more about drinking. One Coventry car worker recalled that the works' day trip was 'a booze-up you know; the outings. They went for a spree and a drink. They carried drink with them and they'd have a drink at the end.'[94] An account of a typical day trip was reported in the *Rudge Record*, the company magazine of Rudge, a cycle and motorcycle manufacturer in Coventry. In 1919, an all-male party went for a day trip to Bidford-upon-Avon, stopping off a few miles outside Coventry for 'very light refreshment'. Once they finally had arrived in Bidford the party split up 'to select their particular mode of pleasure, such as boat-ing, swings, tea parties and not forgetting "clicking"'. This was, however, a brief respite from drinking, for after dinner the party:

> found out why Shakespeare dubbed this pretty spot 'drunken Bidford', the return journey was commenced, stops being made at Stratford upon Avon and Kenilworth for more historical sight seeing and, at the end of a perfect day Coventry was reached about 10.15 pm. It was interesting to note that many of the party were 'dropped' in Styvichale Common, to enable them to take a short route to their homes, one or two 'fell out' on the road, and the remainder alighted as gently as possible in Broadgate.[95]

The gendered and class specific nature of the day trip was, in many ways, only a reflection of the social committee. In 1925, the *The Loudspeaker* proudly announced that the social committee entirely comprised working men, which ensured that 'any task they set themselves is crowned by success'.[96] In the hands of working men, the company magazine became less of a moralising organ and more a results service for the firm's sports club's results, fixtures and announcements of forthcoming social evenings. In effect, by the interwar period firms such as GEC had developed two distinct and separate clubs for workers and staff. The staff club enabled managers to sidestep the works' crowded leisure facilities and enjoy company dinners and a range of exclusive sports and societies. Indeed, GEC provided its managers with a 40-acre golf course where they played both with staff and external golf tournaments with managers from other leading firms.[97]

Although there existed in most firms very distinct staff and worker leisure activities, the absence of women members was a common feature in works' club life.[98] Most engineering firms in the Midlands ran a 'Women's League of Health and Beauty', but in practice women were, for the most part, not welcomed in the social club and had very little influence on the social committee. The one day of the week in which women were invited in large numbers was Saturday, since these early social clubs took advantage of the dance hall craze which swept Britain after the First World War.[99] Llewellyn Smith's report on London life and labour noted that, although there were twenty-three specially designed *palais de danse* halls in London by 1933, the vast majority of working-class people danced in 'mission halls, assembly baths, club-rooms, municipal halls, swimming baths, hotels and restaurants, to all of which music and dancing licences are frequently granted'.[100] Thus the craze for dancing seemed to have been embraced by a surprising range of institutions keen to hire out their premises in both the city centres and the suburbs. Robert Roberts offered an insight into the 'mania' when he remembered that 'in the explosive dancing boom after the war, the young from sixteen to twenty five flocked into the dance halls by the hundred thousand: some went "jigging" as often as six times a week.' Despite the influx of women into the clubs on Saturday nights, the evening would often begin with a male-only 'whist drive' in the bar, leaving the women in the dance hall. Only after the 24-hand whist was complete would the men enter the dance hall, 'lined one side of the hall, women the other. A male made his choice, crossed over, took a girl with the minimum of ceremony from in among and slid into rhythm.'[101]

In attempting to organise and offer advice on workers' leisure time through the magazine or the social club, management were effectively replicating the uneasy social relations of the workplace in the arena of leisure. However, workers did have the advantage, denied them in the workplace, of boycotting events and magazines. Like the evolution of the nineteenth-century working men's clubs, it soon became apparent that control of work-based leisure institutions would have to pass into the hands of the employees if they were going to survive. By 1933 *The Times*, commenting on the German state's desire to create and run working men's clubs, perceptively noted that 'Englishmen would not be grateful to the statesmen who set out to organize their pleasure for them. They prefer to enjoy themselves in their own way.'[102] Whether to statesmen or employer, the working-men's response was similar: unless they had some autonomy over the direction and nature of company-sponsored leisure schemes, the works' institutions had little chance of survival. The transformation of 'club life' from the original purpose as an institution of rational recreation was noted by Llewellyn Smith in his research on London in the 1930s. Llewellyn Smith lamented that the lectures and debates that had been a regular feature of early clubs had been discontinued 'owing to poor attendance and lack of interest'. Instead clubs had turned into entertainment centres featuring 'light variety' and weekly sing-songs or free-and-easys organised by the members themselves. However, the day-to-day experiences for club members were fairly uniform since they observed that 'every club, even the humblest and poorest, provides facilities for many kinds of indoor games – billiards, bagatelle, darts, cards – and it is with these pursuits that the members occupy themselves for the greater part of the time'[103] Nevertheless, the participation of firms in the sporting activities of the workers' choosing should not be underestimated. Such was the demand for sporting fixtures between firms in Coventry that during the mid-1930s the Coventry Works Sports Association was formed.[104] This organisation was founded by twenty-five of the city's leading engineering firms and established viable leagues for thousands of workers in 30 football and swimming teams, 17 cricket teams and 9 snooker and billiards teams. There were also sections for Rugby Union and tennis. The Association was given the seal of civic approval with both the Mayor and the local MP invited to the first annual presentation awards.

By the 1930s, although new leisure facilities continued to be financed by firms, the social committee and financial maintenance of clubs passed into the hands of working men. For example, the AC Sphinx company, which relocated its firm in the Luton area from Birmingham, constructed a new social club, complete with entertainment hall, bar and canteen, declaring that the 'management of the canteen should rest with the work people themselves'. The club was left under the management of a workers' entertainments committee and, after a £50 donation from the firm, was entirely financially independent.[105] Clubs also had a key advantage over public houses as once a club was registered the police could not enter the premises without a search warrant, a loophole in the law which encouraged the frequent evasion of licensing laws. Furthermore, while public houses could only sell liquor within a fixed set of hours during the day, clubs were permitted to open their bars at anytime during the day as long so the total permitted opening time during the day was not exceeded. Llewellyn Smith noted that it was only natural for 'men leaving the public house at ten to go on to a neighbouring club for an additional hour's drinking … some clubs are said to select their hours so as to fill up the intervals between the permitted hours of the surrounding licensed premises, and in this way can get rid of the two hours' break in the afternoon'. Llewellyn Smith found that the total number of registered clubs in London rose rapidly after the War from 639 in 1918 to 1,181 in 1932. His report concluded that 'in view of these advantages it is no matter for surprise that the registered club should be generally a flourishing institution, and that much of its attractiveness should lie in its power to supply liquor to its members under easy conditions.'[106]

Conclusion

The leisure habits of working-class males in 1939 differed in a number of respects from those of their counterparts in 1860. The city centre, which traditionally had hosted the key working-class leisure activities, was no longer the unrivalled venue for entertainment for working men by 1939. The contestation over space with the Salvation Army or the civic authorities became less of an issue with the creation of self-sufficient working-class suburbs that had grown up to serve the large engineering firms in the Midlands and the Southeast. There can be little doubt also that men's leisure became more private and home centred, though still very separate from their wives' preferred recreational activities. However, historians who have argued that this somehow shaped a fundamental change in working-class attitudes to leisure push the point a little too far. The privatised, 'neurosis-ridden' and compliant worker stranded in suburbia is an image that is easily conjured up. Once we investigate male workers' activities outside of the home and within the wider context of the new suburbs, we can glimpse a similar autonomous and manipulative culture found in the Victorian period. The proliferation of the works' magazine and club during the interwar period, then, resembled the development of rational recreation during the nineteenth century. Many work-based magazines and clubs passed into the hands of employees, who set their own agendas and adopted their own leisure preferences. Moreover, in a challenge to the view that working-class males became more 'privatised' and passive workers, employees continued to manipulate the leisure opportunities available to them. Thus in his research on interwar 'factory leisure', Jones concluded that 'even if workers were without direct control, factory sports could have been appropriated by the working class for their own ends. Employees attended social functions on their own terms, even using them for drinking and other boisterous activities.'[107]

Notes

1 J. White, 'The summer riots of 1919', *New Society*, 13 August 1981, pp. 260–1; J. Jenkinson, 'The 1919 riots', in P. Panayi, *Racial Violence in Britain, 1840–1950* (Leicester, Leicester University Press, 1993).

2 *The Times*, 21 July 1919.

3 For the revival in civic ceremony during the early twentieth century, see P. J. Waller, *Town, City and Nation. England 1850–1914* (Oxford, Oxford University Press, 1983), p. 314.

4 N. G. Orr, 'Keep the home fires burning: Peace Day in Luton 1919', *Family and Community History*, 2 (1999), 28.

5 Orr, 'Keep the home fires burning: Peace Day in Luton 1919', 28.

6 *Luton News*, 24 July 1919.

7 *Luton News*, 24 July 1919.

8 J. Haydu, *Between Craft and Class. Skilled Workers and Factory Politics in the United States and Britain, 1890–1922* (California, University of California Press, 1988), p. 156.

9 *Aeroplane*, 5 December 1917.

10 *Midland Daily Telegraph*, 13 March 1919.

11 *Midland Daily Telegraph*, 19 April, 23 July, 1919.

12 *Midland Daily Telegraph*, 17, 18 March 1919.

13 B. Beaven, 'Shop floor culture in the Coventry motor industry, *c.* 1896–1920', in D. Thoms, L. Holden and T. Claydon (eds), *The Motor Car and Popular Culture in the 20th Century* (Aldershot, Ashgate, 1998), p. 198.

14 *Midland Daily Telegraph*, 18 July 1919.

15 Lady Godiva herself was portrayed by the daughter of one of the city's senior councillors; see *The Times*, 21 July 1919.

16 Coventry Local Studies (hereafter CLS), A. Heap, 'Newspaper cuttings', vol. 9, pp. 134, 138.

17 *Midland Daily Telegraph*, 22 July 1919.

18 *Midland Daily Telegraph*, 18 March 1919.

19 *Midland Daily Telegraph*, 25 March 1919.

20 *Midland Daily Telegraph*, 20 May 1919.

21 Public Records Office (hereafter PRO), MUN 5/55/300/47, 'The Labour Situation, week ending 16 July 1919'.

22 *Coventry Standard*, 5 September, 25 July, 1919.

23 *Coventry Graphic*, 25 July 1919.

24 Mansfield has recently argued that conservatism and local patriotism was easier to maintain in rural communities; see N. Mansfield, *English Farm Workers and Local Patriotism, 1900–1930* (Aldershot, Ashgate, 2001).

25 *The Times*, 3 October 1934.

26 *The Times*, 3 October 1934.

27 H. Llewellyn Smith (ed.), *The New Survey of London Life and Labour. Life and Leisure*, vol. 9 (London, P.S. King & Son, 1935), p. 42.

28 A. Olechnowicz, 'Civic leadership and education for democracy', *Contemporary British History*, 14 (2000), 16.

29 A. Olechnowicz, *Working-Class Housing in England between the Wars. The Becontree Estate* (Oxford, Clarendon Press, 1997), p. 153.

30 J.W.R. Whitehand and C.M.H Carr, 'England's interwar suburban landscapes: Myth and reality', *Journal of Historical Geography*, 25 (1999), 483.

31 P. Scannell and D. Cardiff, *A Social History of British Broadcasting*, vol. 1: *1922–1939. Serving the Nation* (Oxford, Blackwell, 1991), p. 365.

32 M. Clapson, 'Working-class women's experiences of moving to new housing estates in England since 1919', *Twentieth Century British History*, 10 (1999), 345.

33 S. Constantine, 'Amateur gardening and popular recreation in the 19th and 20th centuries', *Journal of Social History*, 14 (1981), 396.

34 R. McKibbin, *Classes and Cultures. England 1918–1951* (Oxford University Press, Oxford 1998), p. 188.

35 J. Stevenson, *British Society 1914–45* (London, Penguin, 1984), p. 222.

36 CLS, 'Newspaper cuttings 1916–23', vol. 2, p. 17.

37 CLS, *Coventry Corporation Boundary Commission Extension Act 1927. With Minutes of Evidence*, 1927, pp. 7, 10. For Coventry's rapid population rise, see also A. Shenfield and P.S. Florence, 'Labour and the war industries. The experience of Coventry, 1943–5', *Review of Economic Studies*, 12:1 (1944–5).

38 CLS, 'Newspaper cuttings 1916–23', vol. 2, p. 37.

39 CLS, 'Newspaper cuttings 1916–23', vol. 2, p. 2.

40 *Midland Daily Telegraph*, 17 June 1936.

41 *Midland Daily Telegraph*, 15 July 1936.

42 *The Times*, 24 December 1936.

43 *The Times*, 24 December 1936.

44 CLS, 'Newpaper cuttings, 1916–36', vol. 2, p. 1.

45 A.D.K. Owen 'The social consequences of industrial transference', *Sociological Review*, 29 (1937), 348.

46 *The Times*, 24 December 1936. For the general issue of the settlement of migrants in the Midlands and the Southeast, see P. Scott, 'The state, internal

migration, and the growth of the new industrial communities in interwar Britain', *English Historical Review*, 461 (2000).

47   For a 1945 perspective on urban planning and citizenship, see A. Homer, Planned communities: The social objectives of the British new towns, 1945–65', in L. Black et al., *Consensus Or Coercion. The State, The People and Social Cohesion in Post-War Britain* (Cheltenham, New Clarion Press, 2001).

48   W. Boyd (ed.), *The Challenge of Leisure* (London, New Education Fellowship, 1936), p. 206

49   W. Deedes, 'Social problems of the new housing estates', *Journal of State Medicine*, XLV:1 (1937), 19, 20.

50   E. Barker, 'Community centres and the uses of leisure', *Adult Education*, XI:1 (1938), 10.

51   *Cov Magazine*, 1:6 (August 1939).

52   *Cov Magazine*, 1:4 (June 1939).

53   *The Times*, 30 August 1935.

54   J. Benson, *The Working Class in Britain, 1850–1939* (London, Longman, 1989), p. 109.

55   McKibbin, *Classes and Cultures*, pp. 166, 197. For a more detailed investigation on the more central role that gardening played in male working-class leisure, see Constantine, 'Amateur gardening and popular recreation'.

56   Llewellyn Smith (ed.), *The New Survey of London Life and Labour*, p. 68.

57   For an analysis of the increase in working-class demand for allotments, see S. Badger, 'Household consumption, gender and the working class: The Black Country and Coventry, 1930–1970', unpublished paper, December 2000.

58   C. Cameron, A. Lush and G. Meara, *Disinherited Youth. A Report on the 18+ Age Group Enquiry Prepared for the Trustees of the Carnegie United Kingdom Trust* (Edinburgh, T & A. Constable, 1943), p. 109.

59   A. Hughes and K. Hunt, 'A culture transformed? Women's lives in Wythenshawe in the 1930s', in A. Davies and S. Fielding (eds), *Workers' Worlds. Cultures and Communities in Manchester and Salford, 1880–1939* (Manchester, Manchester University Press, 1992), p. 96.

60   L. Kuper (ed.), *Living in Towns. Selected Research Papers in Urban Sociology of the Faculty of Commerce and Social Science University of Birmingham* (London, Cresset Press, 1953), pp. 58–61.

61   Coventry Record Office (hereafter CRO), Acc 1647/1/8, Paul Thompson Oral History Archive.

62   *Coventry Herald*, 15 February 1935.

63   *Coventry Herald*, 8 March 1935.

64   *Coventry Herald*, 23 August 1935.

65   R. Sinclair, *Metropolitan Man. The Future of the English* (London, Allen & Unwin, 1937), pp. 96, 106.

66   F. Zweig, *The British Worker* (Harmondsworth, Penguin, 1952); J. H. Goldthorpe, D. Lockwood et al., *The Affluent Worker. Industrial Attitudes and Behaviour* (Cambridge, Cambridge University Press, 1968); subsequent historians who have

claimed that working men withdrew to some extent from traditional public leisure spheres have included McKibbin, *Classes and Cultures*, p. 198; Scannell and Cardiff, *A Social History of British Broadcasting*, p. 366.

67 McKibbin, *Classes and Cultures*, p. 198.

68 Scannell and Cardiff, *A Social History of British Broadcasting*, p. 366.

69 N. North 'Middle class suburban life styles and culture in England, 1919–1939' D.Phil. thesis, Oxford, 1989, p. i.

70 J. Hill, *Sport, Leisure and Culture in Twentieth Century Britain* (London, Palgrave, 2002), p. 133.

71 For examples of how industrialists during the interwar period shied away from civic involvement, see Kenneth Richardson Oral History Archive, University of Coventry; for more on the new industrialist, see J. Crump, 'Recreation in Coventry between the wars', in B. Lancaster and T. Mason (eds), *Life and Labour in a 20th Century City. The Experience of Coventry* (Coventry, Cryfield Press, 1986), p. 269.

72 S. G. Jones, *Sport, Politics and the Working Class. Organised Labour and Sport in Inter-War Britain* (Manchester, Manchester University Press, 1992), p. 62.

73 *Cov Magazine*, 1:1 (March 1939). For a full list of Coventry social clubs and associated magazines, see Crump, 'Recreation in Coventry between the wars', p. 284.

74 McKibbin, *Classes and Cultures*, pp. 142, 6; For Coventry car workers' recollection of the large number of work-based social clubs, see Coventry Record Office, Acc 1647/1/13 and 1647/1/27.

75 Crump, 'Recreation in Coventry between the wars', p. 268.

76 See prize-giving events in *Alfred Herbert News*, 1927–1940.

77 CRO, Acc 240/2/9, 'Coventry Sports and Social Association Records', 1943–53.

78 Tom Harrisson Mass-Observation Archive (hereafter THMO) 1625, 'Drunk' March 1942; for the marginalised public houses in new estates, see Crump, 'Recreation in Coventry between the wars', p. 263.

79 R.R. Hyde, *Boy in Industry and Leisure* (London, G. Bell & Sons, 1921), p. 196.

80 J. Hinton, *The First Shop Stewards' Movement* (London, George Allen & Unwin, 1973); J. Haydu, *Between Craft and Class*.

81 *The Limit*, 1 (July 1918).

82 *The Limit*, 4 (October 1918). For an analysis of the vast war profits made by White and Poppe, see B. Beaven, 'The Growth and Significance of the Coventry Car Component Industry, 1895–1939', Ph.D. thesis, De Montfort University, 1994, ch. 2.

83 Jones, *Sport, Politics and the Working Class*, p. 62.

84 C. Dellheim, 'Business in time: The historian and corporate culture', *Public Historian*, 8 (1986); J. Griffiths, '"Give my regards to uncle Billy": The rites and rituals of company life at Lever Brothers, c. 1900–1990', *Business History*, 37 (1995). However, Griffiths now prefers to see the magazines as less of an

influence on workers' culture than he had earlier estimated; see J. Griffiths, 'Exploring corporate culture: The potential of magazines for the business historian', *Business Archives*, 78 (1999).

85 CLS, A. Heap, 'Newspaper cuttings', vol. 7, p. 165.

86 CLS, A. Heap, 'Newspaper cuttings', vol. 7, p. 165.

87 *Siddeley Deasy. Employers Quarterly*, 1:4 (January 1918), 22.

88 *Siddeley Deasy. Employers Quarterly*, 1:1 (January 1918), 1.

89 *The Limit*, 19 (January 1920), 7.

90 *The Limit*, 13 (July 1919), 6.

91 *The Limit*, 14 (August 1919), 7.

92 For a fictional account of a works' day trip, see R. Tressell, *The Ragged Trousered Philanthropists* (1914; Flamingo, London, 1993), ch. 44, 'The Beano'.

93 *The Loudspeaker*, June 1925, p. 9.

94 CRO Acc 16471/1 Paul Thompson Oral History Archive.

95 *The Rudge Record*, vol. II, 1908–1919, July 1919, p. 7.

96 *The Loudspeaker*, March 1925, p. 7.

97 For examples of golf tournaments, see GEC's in-house magazine *The Loudspeaker*, 1935–39.

98 Crump, 'Recreation in Coventry between the wars', p. 273.

99 One moral reformer condemned the 'mania dancing' and blamed a compulsion for pleasure and excitement on the 'moral laxity caused by the Great War'; *The Times*, 16 February 1931; McKibbin, *Classes and Cultures*, p. 394.

100 Llewellyn Smith, *The New Survey of London Life and Labour*, p. 64.

101 Robert Roberts, *The Classic Slum. Salford Life in the First Quarter of the Century* (Harmondsworth, Pelican, 1971), p. 233.

102 *The Times*, 2 December 1933.

103 Llewellyn Smith, *The New Survey of London Life and Labour*, p. 130.

104 Crump, 'Recreation in Coventry between the wars', p. 276.

105 *Bedford and Hertfordshire Saturday Telegraph*, 12 January 1935.

106 Llewellyn Smith, *The New Survey of London Life and Labour*, p. 123.

107 Jones, *Sport, Politics and the Working Class*, p. 63.

5

Male youth, work and leisure, 1918–39: a continuity in lifestyle

The interwar period witnessed a shift in attitudes towards the long-standing 'problem' of male youth leisure. As with the Victorian period, working-class youths were regarded with suspicion by the authorities, who worried that the latest degenerate leisure craze could result in tomorrow's national failing. However, the difference from the Victorian era lay in the methodologies employed to investigate male youth behaviour. For the first time, thanks to new research emanating from the United States of America, male youths became the focus of a more systematic analysis by academics. The Chicago School's quasi-sociological research attempted to theorise male youth behaviour through the investigation of both family blood ties and contemporary leisure and work influences.[1] These ideas and research methodologies were taken up enthusiastically by academics such as Cyril Burt, who focused their attentions particularly on male delinquency.[2] Although contemporary academic interest in interwar youth began to flourish after the First World War, mainstream historiography has been dominated by the social unrest and unemployment problems that faced the government during the 1920s and 1930s. More recently, a number of historians have investigated youth life styles, particularly in relationship to working-class culture.[3] This chapter extends this analysis and engages with contemporary debates on the youth problem emanating from official and unofficial bodies. First, we shall investigate the research and provision of male youth leisure during a period in which unemployment had reached unprecedented levels and there was increasing domestic and international tensions. Second, the chapter will explore key traits in youth culture, challenging the premiss that new work and leisure patterns fostered a new youth lifestyle peculiar to the interwar period.

Research into the 'youth problem' and the provision of leisure

Between 1918 and 1939, a wide spectrum of official and unofficial bodies developed an interest in male youth culture. Research into nineteenth-century youth had largely been the domain of the concerned philanthropist conducting investigations into poverty and its impact on the urban boy.[4] The Chicago School's new approach to theorising youth behaviour gave British academics added impetus to their research, which ultimately sought to investigate how appropriate work and leisure patterns could help shape good citizenry. First, the British Government, anxious about rising youth unemployment and its implication for citizenship, established a number of official enquiries and youth schemes to help shape young male work and leisure patterns.

Alongside these official reports a second, unofficial genre of youth writing emerged from those who worked in government-sponsored youth schemes and later wrote of their experiences, offering advice on future social policies during the 1930s. For example, S. F. Hatton's *London's Bad Boys* (1931) and H. A. Secretan's *London Below Bridges* (1931) are both reminiscences of youth workers and their attempts to shape male youths into 'useful' citizens. The style of writing differed from the official government-sponsored surveys as they tended towards reportage, full of anecdotes, incidents and not a small amount of sympathy for their subjects. Another unofficial commentary on youth adopted an altogether more traditional and aggressive tone and stemmed from a fear that Britain's elite and civilised culture was under threat from new forms of American leisure and work patterns, something which British youths were condemned for embracing. It is the findings of this elitist group of researchers that we shall examine first.

The most dominant strand of thinking on youth during the interwar period remained with the traditionalists, who had found a voice in the 1930s through the Cambridge-based 'Scrutiny' group led by F. R. Leavis.[5] The target for the Scrutiny group and like-minded social observers was Americanisation and its degenerate influence on British identity and culture. For Leavis, youths were the most susceptible to the imported degenerate culture of America which threatened to undermine and replace the respectable and elevating values of British civilisation. America had corrupted popular leisure patterns with cinema-going, radio listening, cheap literature, advertising, standardisation and mass production. According to Leavis, 'it is a common place that we are being Americanised' and that British civilisation was 'levelling-down'.[6] Youths were at the centre of this Americanisation as not only were they subjected to imported leisure pursuits but also, in the realm of the workplace, they were integral to the standardisation and mass production methods of the 1930s. One social observer commented that 'an industrial economy based on master craftsmen, with their attendant labourers, is giving way before one based on the fool-proof automatic machine ... the economic results are calculable, the psychological results are as yet little understood'.[7] Viewed through the golden haze of a false nostalgia, this new and soul-destroying Americanised form of work was often compared unfavourably to the work practices of a previous generation which reputedly produced the respectable artisan worker. A. E. Morgan, a contemporary sociologist, claimed that in the engineering trades tens of thousands of juvenile workers, 'condemned to endless repetitive processes', were in the ascendent. Losing out were 'truer' skilled engineers, who were men of 'tradition and pride': 'He has not gained his skill without undergoing a strenuous period of work and study. The tragedy of engineering to-day is that so much of it is the easy knack which all but a half witted or deformed child can pick up in a trice.'[8] The youth moved, then, from a standardised and monotonous work culture to a standardised Americanised leisure culture, seeking excitement and adventure in the mass distribution of popular literature and films. This greater Americanisation and standardisation in the youth's work and leisure, so the argument went, brought a deterioration in their moral outlook. Roy and Theodora Calvert in *The Law Breaker* claimed that 'we are passing through a crisis in morals' since the traditional values that 'regulated and controlled men's actions for generations' were being smothered by imported American values.[9]

However, alongside this traditional strand of thinking, there emerged a more positive view of youth, drawn to understanding youth delinquency and harnessing the male youth's 'gregarious nature' for the good of the nation and Empire. This often forgotten, though nonetheless influential, counterbalance to the traditional view emerged from youth workers who were generally sympathetic to youth – even to the extent of sometimes romanticising youth delinquency. For example, far from seeing a rise in juvenile crime as the deterioration of traditional values, *The Times* in 1933 reported Baden-Powell's claim that 'it was rather a promising sign, because he saw in those banditry cases, robbery with violence, smash and grab, little "adventures". There was still some spirit of adventure among those juveniles and if that spirit of adventure could be seized and turned in the right direction they could make them useful men.'[10]

A similar theme was taken up by H.S. Bryan, the Derbyshire Medical Officer, who criticised a juvenile court for punishing young offenders for stealing, likening them to great figures of the British Empire such as Drake, Captain Cook and Clive. In this bizarre analogy, Bryan maintained that the very characteristics which made these men great – the spirit of adventure, courage, leadership and ingenuity – were all practised by the delinquent youth, albeit when stealing from local shops. Bryan argued that, instead of the youths being punished, these fine British traits should be nurtured, and even cited A.S. Neil's controversial Summerhill school as the most conducive environment to achieve this.[11] However, at the root of this new sympathy was a notion shared with the traditionalists that some form of intervention was required to strengthen both the physical and moral fibre of the nation's stock of youth, particularly in a period of international tension. Social observers sympathetic to the 'little adventures' of male youths were keen to secure these natural manly traits for the defence of the Empire, in the face of new leisure pursuits that could undermine the traditional 'street wise' youth. In a study entitled *London's Bad Boys*, S.F. Hatton believed that it was 'dangerous to be too severe' in repressing the boy's 'primitive instincts', pointing out that the 'Victorians failed miserably in that respect'. In addition he declared:

> I deplore all attempts to effeminize young manhood, and I am ashamed of some of the youths of today who are more given to the softer delights of the cinema and dance hall, than the more vigorous and manly sporting instincts of boxing, football, and such-like pastimes. There is a definite tendency for the young man of to-day to be soft.

To counter the 'soft' leisure attractions of the cinema, Hatton listed nine characteristics which he thought all teachers and youth workers should possess and bring to their work. Of these traits, which included confidence, courage and cheerfulness, Hatton singled out manliness as the most important characteristic to instil into the impressionable male youth. Importantly, a youth worker should be vigorous, healthy and athletic, as this would appeal 'to all that latent manhood struggling for expression in the boys themselves', something which Hatton clearly believed the cinema was incapable of stimulating.[12] Hatton echoed a fairly widespread call for greater intervention, particularly in the face of growing international tension during the 1930s, as he claimed that 'we take more care over the breeding of our horses and dogs, and relatively less of the breeding of our people, than any civilized nation under the sun.'[13] There were, then, some intellectual shifts in contemporary thinking on male youths' work and leisure activities. Although the traditional Victorian attitude to youth held some sway, more sympathetic youth workers argued that elements of the vibrant young male lifestyle could be harnessed for the good of the nation. The interwar period, as we shall see, also saw shifts in social policies towards male youths, with increased government intervention into the 'leisure problem'. The added interest in the role youth could play in developing good citizenry was given an added impetus by the international instability of the interwar period.

The First World War had seen the Government abandon its traditional laissez-faire stance and intervene in a range of socio-economic issues in British life. The perceived 'youth problem' proved no exception. The massive expansion of the munitions industries, particularly in the engineering industries in the Midlands and the Southeast, stimulated demand for semi-skilled labour. Munitions work was ideally suited to the youth labourer and was similar to the monotonous semi-skilled employment of the evolving consumer industries that youths had entered from the late nineteenth century.[14] However, there was considerable anxiety during the war that there would be 'serious demoralization' among the demobilised youth workforce after hostilities had ceased. For some youth workers, the war had twisted youths' moral and spiritual values, and consequently 'it may be easy to change from the khaki into civilian clothes at demobilization, but it is not so easy to change the mental garb'.[15] The Lewis Committee, established in 1917 to investigate the anticipated problem, predicted that the reduced labour required after re-conversion from munitions to peacetime consumer goods would result in a large number of unemployed juveniles 'hanging about the streets; and their numbers will be rapidly increased as new generations of children left school'.[16] The Committee's solution was the formation of Juvenile Unemployment Centres in 1918, in which unemployed youths between fifteen and eighteen were required to attend in order to claim state benefit. Between 1918 and 1919, seventy local educational authorities established 166 centres in Britain. Attendance at the centres fluctuated throughout the interwar period, with over 24,000 youths attending in any one week in 1919, waning to just over 10,500 in 1926. In 1931 the power to withhold unemployment benefit in the event of a refusal to attend was weakened with the changes to unemployment insurance regulations. The legislative changes made a proportion of young people ineligible to claim the dole, an alteration which seriously dented attendance during a period of increasing unemployment.[17]

Significantly, the centres were intended to be full-time providers of 'informal' education; other technical and formal forms of education were to be delivered at technical colleges. The limited form of education offered suggests that the Committee was more concerned with clearing the streets of youths and instilling discipline in their work and leisure time than with the provision of vocational skills. Furthermore, staff at the centres differed from college lecturers in that they were often former army instructors, who, working with a teacher, were expected to take classes with a student ratio of approximately 1:100.[18] Not surprisingly, the centres exhibited militaristic overtones, with one inspector in Luton reporting that the ex-military instructor was very good on physical training and discipline but 'rather weak' at teaching general subjects. Despite the overtly military connotations, attendance and discipline at the centres were notoriously poor. The problem institutions faced was that, for the most part, they were dealing with youths who had previously been employed in relatively well-paid munitions jobs and enjoyed the independence that this had brought. For example, one researcher interviewed a number of youths attending a London centre and found that they believed that they were the 'unlucky ones who are robbed of their liberty'.

> Their friends have the job which is the stamp of manhood and womenhood; they have their few shillings to spend on the pictures or going to a dance … but these unfortunates, bereft of all these desirable things, are kept in the old-time bondage of the school house with its association of subordination to other wills and set ways.[19]

This frustration often led to disorder in the centres; as one former teacher recalled, 'a great deal of material damage was done by rank hooliganism in these centres and the person in charge had very definitely to face many unpleasant situations.' His own unpleasant experience involved an attempt to maintain order in the centre when one particularly infamous group of lads, calling themselves the 'Juvenile Sabini Gang', attended en masse with the sole intention of disrupting the proceedings.[20] In addition to property damage and indiscipline, absenteeism was also a frequent occurrence with, for example, nearly half the boys in Salford attending their local centre for no more than two weeks. [21]

Although the centres staggered on into the 1930s, their perceived ineffectiveness in shaping unemployed boys into 'rational' forms of work and leisure aroused fears that the 'youth problem' was the underlying factor in a number of sporadic social disturbances in interwar Britain. Immediately after the First Word War the Peace Riots, according to Hatton, a London youth worker, prompted his local county council 'to examine the problem of the adolescent on the street'.[22] Hatton also cited disaffected youths as a major source of agitation in the General Strike of 1926, since

> the disturbances were not caused by the seasoned workman out on strike to prove his genuine sympathy with his unfortunate brothers in the coal fields – the Union men behaved splendidly and with great restraint often under considerable provocation – it was the gangs of youths who caused disorder and the damage, and it was they who stormed the buses and the lorries.[23]

In an attempt to quell the disorder, which was particularly intense in the King's Cross area, Hatton threw open the resources of his centre for members and non-members alike, organising football matches, cricket matches and boxing 'to keep them quiet rather than rioting'.[24] Significantly, the provision of leisure was seen as one solution to the 'youth problem', a problem that reached new heights in 1931, when over thirty towns experienced fierce clashes between the police and unemployed demonstrators.[25] Unemployment had, for many contemporaries, crystallised the 'leisure problem', since an unprecedented number of young males had excessive time on their hands. It was estimated that over 120,000 juveniles between fourteen and eighteen were unemployed, a statistic that provoked one group of researchers to declare that the youth's leisure activities were the most pressing social problem of the era.[26] By the 1930s, new 'Occupational Centres' and 'Community Service Clubs' were founded for both unemployed youths and adults to provide 'purposeful activities' for their 'excessive free time'. Centres were reliant on government grants from the National Council of Social Services, donations from local businesses and membership fees. The partial reliance on membership fees as a source of funding had important implications for the type of activities offered, since the centre had to attract rather than coerce youths and adults into joining. Indeed, one contemporary study tracked the change in emphasis from the strictly educational classes to 'Institutes of Leisure':

> The most common type of Evening Institutes with their schoolroom atmosphere and regulation classes and 'grouped courses' have not been successful. Most Educational Authorities are alive to these difficulties, and many are sympathetically modifying the somewhat drastic rules and regulations for evening classes for young people. Many are also recognising the need for a friendly and less formal atmosphere and in co-operation with voluntary bodies are sending tutors into the clubs. Some are considering the establishment of 'Club Institutes' or 'Institutes of Leisure', social and educational centres to which young people can be proud to belong.[27]

Unlike the Juvenile Unemployment Centres, attendance was not linked to benefits and the accent was on leisure rather than disciplined learning and physical educational drills. Moreover, in an attempt to create a more community centre feel to the organisation, youths and adults could continue with their membership even after they had found employment. For the organisers it was important not only to introduce youths to rational, useful and stimulating forms of leisure but also to facilitate these activities through into their adult life. This view was enshrined in government official policy through the National Council of Social Services, which, in its nineteenth annual report, declared 'that there is just as much need in the large cities as elsewhere for workers' clubs catering for the leisure needs of men and women whether they are unemployed or working, and depending for their success on a combination of social amenities and opportunities for creative activity in crafts, drama, music, gardening and the like'. Management of the centres varied, though most after a short time were adopted by local businesses, which donated considerable sums and which, in return, exercised close supervision over the management of the organisation. The fact that local businesses around the country were prepared to invest in unemployment centres during an era of economic depression demonstrates how seriously contemporaries viewed the 'youth leisure problem'. However, the rigid managerial structure of the centres did not prove attractive to working-class youths, a factor noted by a Liverpool youth worker, who wrote that club organisation was

> essentially undemocratic. It seems to have been based on the theory that unemployed men were unfitted to take any responsibility for their own Clubs and that Management Committees, by definition, knew what was good for

the men better than the men knew themselves. It meant, in practice, that there was usually a wide gulf between the desires of the members and the decisions reached by the management committees. Even the Wardens were unable to bridge this gulf effectively, because there was within the Centres themselves no body with effective powers of voicing and interpreting the wishes of the general body of members.[28]

Government's intervention, then, into the provision of leisure for unemployed and working youths was not an outstanding success. Established as a response to the sporadic social disorder after the First World War, the Juvenile Unemployment Centre and its successor the Occupational Centre failed to attract youths due to the often militaristic overtones in the early centres and the autocratic management that ran through most organisations.

The failure of Juvenile Centres and the tense international climate of the late 1930s did nothing to ease the Government's anxieties over the perceived 'youth problem'. The continued appetite for racial and eugenic ideas, fanned by the rise of Nazism, ensured that the moral and physical health of the nation's youth was intrinsically linked, in some peoples' minds, to the fortunes of the Empire. During one conference on the 'Challenge of Leisure', one speaker, though deploring Hitler's attempt to influence German youth, appeared to find the process a necessity given the political climate of the time:

> We have been forcibly reminded at this conference of the Challenge thrown down to us by the thorough way in which the European dictatorships have gripped the life of their youth. However gravely we may deplore much of what lies behind this, we cannot but note the significance of such things as the absorption of the 14–18 class of Germany into the Hitler Jugend for the employment of their leisure. Hitler knew the strategic importance of this for the building up of his Germany ... The time is long overdue when, as a nation, we must in our own British way face this problem.[29]

The fear that the nation's youth would not be mentally and physically fit for combat prompted the Government to introduce the Physical Training and Recreation Act of 1937 which permitted the allocation of public money to finance voluntary organisations in the provision of leisure facilities. Indeed, many of the swimming baths, playing fields, gymnasiums and lidos that mushroomed during the late 1930s were financed in this fashion. One motivation, then, was to prepare physically the nation's male youths for war, and a glance across to the continent suggested that Britain could not afford to lose any time.[30] *The Times* believed that the state's involvement in youths' leisure could improve the health and status of the nation and pointed to Germany's 'Strength through Joy' and Italy's 'After Work' programmes as examples of good practice. The continental lead in promoting physical fitness was enthusiastically taken on by *The Times* as it claimed that at last 'England has learned the value of physical culture. We have learned that a good deal of our expensive education is pure waste, because children have not the strength to benefit from it'.[31] In almost an echo of Masterman's plea to stop the human decay at the heart of the British Empire at the beginning of the twentieth century, the sociologist Morgan declared that 'human material' requires 'careful husbanding', as

> In the past there has been an abundance of men and women and they have been squandered. If this country is to continue as the heart of a great empire it cannot afford to allow its resources to run to waste. Apart from the suffering which appeals to the humanitarian sense, we are compelled on purely economic grounds to act swiftly, if we are to compensate for loss of quantity by improvement of quality.[32]

For Morgan, it was the purpose of the state and voluntary youth organisations to provide healthy activities for youths which would instil a sense of civic and national pride, masculinity and responsibilities at work. Thus, 'fitness must be physical, mental and moral. Fitness must be for citizenship, for manhood, for work.'[33] Certainly the Government, influenced by its continental counterparts and the domestic campaign that developed, took an active interest in leading a 'health crusade' to improve the 'national physique' by establishing the National Fitness Council in 1937.[34] Although the Council's brief was to ensure that local educational authorities and voluntary bodies worked together more efficiently, it was attacked by liberals as a harbinger of militarism and by those in sport for threatening the voluntary principle which had long been a feature in British recreation.[35] The much maligned National Fitness Council proved to be largely ineffective and was eventually superseded by a war-time body, the National Youth Committee.

The failure of the National Fitness Council to coordinate the myriad of voluntary groups and local municipal initiatives had highlighted the state's inability to deal with the 'youth problem', an issue which the onset of war had apparently magnified. It had been estimated that almost 1.75 million youths aged between fourteen and eighteen were without 'opportunities to use their leisure in a healthy and intelligent way'.[36] In a period of national crisis, it did not take long for the belief that millions of youths were indulging in inappropriate recreation to spark off moral panics. *The Times*, which was always a reliable mouthpiece for the anxious citizen, solemnly reported that the National Youth Committee was soon to circulate a memorandum to the local educational authorities,

> drawing their attention to the grave social symptoms which are appearing in some parts of the country, and recommending what action can be taken to deal with them. The juvenile gang is reappearing: juvenile courts in London have had busy sessions; restrictions on amusements have thrown thousands in the evenings on to the streets, which in their turn are blackened. It is something that the public should already be aware of the youth problem; it is even more that there now exists legislation to protect the child worker which was unknown in 1914.[37]

From the aftermath of the First World War into the 1940s, the Government, through a mixture of coercion and volition, had from time to time attempted to shape the work and leisure patterns of male juveniles. However, unlike its continental counterparts, the Government deemed its role minimal and that the vast majority of youth work should be delivered by the voluntary sector. The voluntary principle, which had its origins in the rational recreation movement of the nineteenth century, still held great sway and was jealously guarded by the proliferation of youth organisations, which were wary of Government interference. Pride was taken in the fact that planning was kept to a minimum; as one sociologist proudly proclaimed, 'it is not our English way to think far ahead, although we have an uncanny instinct for eventually finding the right direction by groping'.[38] We will now turn to the range of youth organisations on offer and their fortunes during the interwar period.

Viewed in context, youth antipathy towards government-inspired schemes was not surprising, as male teenagers were even less inclined to join youth organisations than they were prior to the First World War.[39] This was an unwelcome trend for many contemporary researchers, who often saw the voluntary run boys' club as the forum in which responsible leisure pursuits, leadership skills and good citizenship could be learnt. The club filled the increasing amount of leisure time enjoyed by both employed and unemployed youths and provided a distraction from commercialised entertainments and 'ready-made pleasures'.[40] Cameron's research group argued further that it was not enough simply to offer leisure facilities to the youth; clubs must 'integrate all activities and projects to serve the common end

– that of purposeful citizenship'. Likewise, one youth worker described the Boy Scouts as appealing 'to the natural instincts of a boy' while at the same time aiming 'at the production of what is called "citizenship"'.[41] In other words, leisure was perceived as *the* fundamental building block in the construction of good citizenship for the interwar youth.[42] This position was enthusiastically supported by *The Times*, which suggested that the club could teach working-class youths the virtues of good citizenship through emulating the public-school ethos:

> A vast number of boys in the formative years after leaving school are in desperate need of guidance and help if their characters are to be shaped right and they are to develop into good citizens … As Major Astor says, in a letter which appears this morning, boys clubs give working-lads "some thing of the same chance the more fortunate contemporaries get at their public schools … " They cultivate a club spirit (no bad substitute for the public school spirit) and comradeship and fair play.[43]

Despite the notion that pervaded the 1930s that the youth performed a pivotal role in the future citizenship and health of the nation, organised clubs, whose function was to shape young minds and bodies, faced an uphill battle to attract membership. Fowler has shown that the interwar years were difficult times for the numerous youth organisations that attempted to provide some 'rational recreation' as an antidote to the growing commercial leisure sector. Following the fortunes of four youth organisations in Manchester, he noted that all were hit by the emergence of the relatively affluent youth who could afford to attend the cinema at least twice a week, go to the seaside on holiday and ride his bicycle at weekends, significantly reducing his contact time with the club. Some clubs, such as the Oldham Lad's Club in Manchester, had by 1939 attempted to innovate and adapt by installing a film projector and permitting boys to smoke on the premises.[44] As Fowler suggests, it is questionable how far even successful boy's clubs were able to instil the particular values of the club, be it religious or patriotic. In a contemporary study of youth by Cameron, it was found that youths who had been members of organised groups 'spoke highly of them, but it appeared that their attachment to them was based more on some specific activity which they could participate than on the principles and ideals of the movement. A good football team might be the chief attraction of a Boy's Club.'[45] Other clubs, though, such as the Scouts and the Rovers, were not prepared to modify their activities and continued to place character-building and patriotism at the heart of their programme of leisure. Consequently, as Fowler notes, the movement failed to attract either investment or a mass following, which 'was undoubtedly the result of its overtly militaristic methods and ethos'. This formula, which had been tried, tested and failed in government-inspired Juvenile Centres, was clearly shunned by youths in favour of less oppressive and relaxed organisations.[46]

An insight into the type of club and leisure activities that youths preferred is provided by Cameron's *Disinherited Youth*. Although the study intended to focus on the unemployed youth, improved economic conditions meant that 'a number of the men were in fairly regular employment during the course of the Enquiry, so that their leisure-time activities were largely those of the normally employed young industrial worker'.[47] This more extensive analysis of the type of leisure found at the heart of youth culture ensured that the team of researchers inadvertently uncovered an underground network of clubs catering for youths and adults. In cities such as Cardiff, Liverpool and Glasgow, they found that alongside the 're-spectable' organisations there existed small clubs which, although generally licensed, were merely houses converted into bars. These types of clubs were situated in the poorer parts of cities and were housed in a variety of buildings including empty shops, cellars or basements and in wooden huts. The clubs were utilised by both employed and unemployed males, while a good proportion of membership was under twenty-five years of age, with Cameron estimating that at least 40 per cent of club members in Glasgow could be classified as youths. However, researchers discovered that the 'unofficial' clubs were regularly targeted by the police, who believed many of the clubs 'to be bogus, inasmuch as there is an air of irresponsibility about their management' as they were purely 'places where drinking facilities are available'.[48] Although most of these clubs benefited from the more relaxed club licensing laws, the major attraction for youths and adults was that they were all run by an elected committee of stewards and had an obligation to share any surplus profits among members. The regular sharing of profits removed the problem of large accumulated surpluses and maintained healthy membership levels as, on average, members could receive an annual profit share-out amounting to between ten shillings and one pound per member. Indeed, healthy membership subscriptions were vital as the only other revenues were gleaned from drink sales and sometimes billiard-table profits. These 'unofficial' clubs also encouraged saving among the very poor for specific events. Cameron found that in Glasgow, club members would pay sixpence each week for the 'Wembley' fund, which would facilitate the hire of a charabanc to see the England versus Scotland football match at Wembley and go sightseeing in London after the game. Nevertheless, leisure pursuits within the 'unofficial' clubs tended to revolve around drinking, billiards and gambling, activities which the club explicitly sanctioned. This relaxed environment was a far cry from the public-school ethos found at some 'official' organised youth movements that emphasised the virtues of patriotism, obedience and leadership. Indeed, unlike more organised youth groups, 'unofficial' club activities reflected male working-class leisure interests, as the facilitators were members from their own communities. Cameron noted that the unofficial clubs

> provide a special example of spontaneous growth in a section of the community which is not attracted to any of the longer established and better known institutions. Very few members of these clubs have any contact with other forms of social, political or religious organisation. They are not unsocial, but they view with suspicion any overtures which they think may lead to interference with their personal autonomy.[49]

Given the suspicion of organisations from outside their own communities, it is perhaps unsurprising that youth movements struggled to recruit when they were in competition with the 'unofficial' club that had grown spontaneously from working-class areas. The popularity of the unofficial or cellar club troubled more 'respectable' organisations, which were keen to expose their apparent degenerative influence, particularly on working-class youth. Indeed, there were calls from youth and men's organisations to establish an official register of clubs in the hope that the undesirable type might be eliminated. In the same hostile spirit, the Federation of Men's Clubs in Liverpool undertook an investigation into whether the 'cellar' clubs were suitable for affiliation. They concluded that fewer than 20 per cent were eligible for immediate affiliation, while over 50 per cent were 'purely betting clubs, or they sold intoxicants, or their premises and equipment were so poor as to make active collaboration with the Federation's activities quite impossible'. Significantly, few of the 20 per cent of cellar clubs deemed by the Federation as acceptable were willing to affiliate, being determined to retain their own autonomy over the management of the club. It is clear, then, that there was a reluctance among working-class youths to join 'respectable' organisations, when offered the choice between official and unofficial clubs.[50]

There was, then, a deep suspicion of official clubs among male youths during the interwar period. This mistrust was often exhibited through either boycotting youth movements in favour of informal clubs, or joining organisations for their sports and leisure facilities rather than the values espoused. The advantage of the unofficial club was that it had been established from within working-class communities and provided male youths with a foothold into adult male leisure activities found in the traditional working-men's clubs. Certainly, the unofficial clubs provided a recognisable frame of reference for youths since, unlike official youth movements, they did not attempt to transform their leisure pursuits into rational and citizenship-enhancing activities. Thus far, we have seen how youth culture was fairly impervious to both government and youth movements' attempts at shaping their leisure hours. The next section will examine further the nature of interwar youth culture and assess the impact that new leisure opportunities had upon male youth culture.

Britain's first teenagers?

In his innovative study of interwar youth, David Fowler has argued that changes in disposable income and leisure supply, along with the emergence of a youth consumer market, helped create Britain's first teenagers during the interwar period. The surprising level of disposable income, during a time of economic depression, was due to the high proportion of interwar youths initially opting for relatively highly paid 'blind alley' jobs prior to finding more long-term apprenticeship work. In a challenge to the received wisdom that the first teenage youth culture emerged hand in hand with the birth of 1950s' rock and roll, Fowler concludes that 'a distinctive teenage culture, based upon access to commercial leisure and on the conspicuous consumption of leisure products and services which were clearly aimed at the youth as much as at adults was clearly evident in Manchester and other cities as early as the 1920s and the 1930s.'[51] This is a welcome corrective to the existing historiography, which assumed youth culture was a product of 1950s Britain. In addition, Fowler argues that wage-earning youths possessed and exercised a new-found autonomy in their work and leisure time during the 1930s.[52] However, whether interwar youth culture was as distinctive and unique as Fowler has claimed is questionable. The remainder of this chapter will draw comparisons between the late-nineteenth-century youth culture outlined in Chapter 3 and the youth culture that emerged during the interwar period. Particular areas identified for comparison will be the type of work that young males were engaged in and how social commentators evaluated its impact on their organised and informal leisure activities.

As we have seen in Chapter 3, youth employment in 'blind alley jobs' was not a new development of the interwar period, but an essential component in the emergence of the new industries of the late nineteenth century. Indeed, Burgess has noted that the Victorian anxieties about the morally damaging effects of 'blind alley' jobs continued to consume policymakers and social observers alike. For one research group in the 1930s, the new industries, with their mechanisation and specialisation, had resulted in the 'simplification' of the work process where 'juveniles are able to quickly to master the routine jobs with little or no mental effort'.[53] It was estimated that a semi-skilled youth in a car factory could learn all aspects of the mechanised work routine in one and three-quarter hours. Youths in blind-alley jobs were 'trained' only in the 'process immediately in hand', scarring the young worker with a monotonous nature that he would import into his 'dull' leisure pursuits.[54] In effect, the debate on juvenile labour continued to be dominated by the wider concerns of monotonous work routines, poor leisure choices and its impact on citizenry. The First World War only served to heighten these fears since the labour shortages and the repetitive nature of munitions work accelerated the demand for juveniles and increased concerns over what would happen to youths in later life. Thus, disturbing parallels that had been drawn in the late nineteenth century between the wasted human capital and the degeneration of Britain's major cities continued to have a resonance during the interwar period.[55] By 1918, the new industries that had been established in the Midlands and the Southeast had become the largest employer in some of the towns. The rapid development of the bicycle, motor and electrical industries required a pool of predominantly young semi-skilled males, a demand which sometimes upset the sex balance of populations. For example, in Coventry it was estimated in 1914 that there were approximately 2,000 more males than females, an imbalance which was considered to be a direct consequence of the new industries. From a population of just over 100,000, almost 21,000 workers were engaged in the bicycle, motor and allied trades. Of these 21,000 workers, the vast majority were semi-skilled males, with fewer than 3,000 females recorded as working in the sector.[56] Indeed, by the late 1930s, only an average of 63 apprentices per year qualified in the Coventry motor industry and allied trades.[57] In addition, while the cost of housing rent was particularly high in these areas, male youths retained a considerable degree of financial independence if they remained at home with their parents and contributed to the family budget.[58] Thus the male youth employed in a 'blind alley' job and earning relatively good wages was not unique to the interwar period, but should be seen as a phenomenon that began in the late Victorian era. Indeed, there was a high degree of continuity in youth work patterns between 1870 and 1945, reflected in the enduring contemporary anxieties over the social consequences of the 'youth problem'.

If there are some clear continuities in work patterns between 1870 and 1945, then equally we can identify some significant strands of youth culture that survived and shaped young males' leisure during the interwar period. Much of male youth leisure activities continued to revolve around the street and park and also around places that they were not generally supposed to go. Furthermore, just as late-nineteenth-century youth conformed to a particular fashion style – bell-bottom trousers, large leather belt and 'floppy hair' style – the interwar youth continued to don specific clothes for the 'monkey parade'. Butterworth noted that young men would spend a considerable amount of time in preparing their clothing before stepping out on their 'nightly parade'. The suit, which was almost always a 'pay as you wear' purchase, was carefully preserved since 'the crease is a fine art, the trousers have been well pressed under the mattress by night and scrupulously folded in brown paper by day'.[59] Although Fowler has suggested that parades were on the decline, few contemporary observations or sociological surveys conducted in the 1930s appear to accord with this view.[60] An academic study on male youths' work and leisure patterns noted that approximately 20 per cent of the lads surveyed said that most of their free time was spent walking about the streets. The majority of those interviewed, however, spent at least part of their leisure time on the streets, with Sunday identified as the most popular day for this activity. The report's authors noted that 'certain clearly defined streets were selected for the parade' as, apart from the dance hall, they provided the best way of meeting girls. 'Usually both lads and girls went about in twos and threes; some colour was added to the evening by their casual encounters.' Significantly, the report remarked that 'in certain cases the streets were more attractive than the homes the lads had left'.[61] A. E. Morgan's report for King George's Jubilee Trust Fund, entitled *The Needs of Youth*, unusually devoted a whole section to 'loafing' and the monkey parade. Despairing of their irrational use of leisure, Morgan, unlike his nineteenth-century counterparts, played down the 'dangerously uncivilised' character of loafing and concluded 'positively it may be harmless; negatively it is tragic. It is tragic because it is a measure of the waste of human worth which we permit'.[62] Left to their own devices, male youths would waste their time loafing on street corners engaged in frivolous talk. James Butterworth, a youth-club owner in London, astutely noted the conversations of youth gangs that were hanging around shop doorways in the early 1930s:

> Each will relate how, with advantage, they told the manager off at work – what he said and what everybody said, all of which is probably untrue or greatly garbled. Smutty jokes, retailed with repetition of limited language, will be followed by the fiercest of arguments about favourite films, stars, cup chances, league places, goal scorers, racing tips and betting news.[63]

The centrality of the street to male youth culture can be explained, to some extent, by the continuation of the environmental conditions that helped shape male youth gang culture in the first place. Although some working-class districts had been established on the outskirts of cities, most working people lived in or around the city centre in tightly packed terraced housing from the late nineteenth century to the end of the Second World War.[64] The living conditions of the poorer working-class families were not vastly different to those of the late nineteenth century, with overcrowding being one of the most compelling reasons why the street remained so attractive.[65] Male youth's attraction to the street gang did, of course, wane, with the onset of adulthood. By their late teens and early twenties, Butterworth noted that interest in girls divided the groups as gang members begged their peer group 'temporarily to be excluded' for they had 'gone birding'.[66] It would not be long before the gang lost its purpose and was replaced by a younger generation of teenage youths. The novel *Love on the Dole* captures this turning point particularly well when the teenager Harry Hardcastle leaves his gang and begins to 'court' Helen Hawkins, a young factory hand:

> He was growing older perceptibly; no longer did he seem to hanker for the company of the other boys. Indeed, there was a change in the demeanours of them all; they all were more or less subdued. Its cause was not far to seek. Of a Saturday evening nowadays only a ghost of their erstwhile boisterousness remained; no more did they fling money about carelessly. A new generation had taken their places by Hulkington's the grocer's shop; the same

in the Saturday picture theatre queues. The younger boys evinced the same habits, the same prodigality; different boys, that was all.[67]

While the street gang continued to be a forum in which male youths could assert their masculinity, the interwar period did usher in the dance hall, a new form of leisure which swept the country. The 'dance craze' took off when dance halls began opening in working-class districts of major cities during the 1920s. Unlike in the prewar era, dancing became a more casual activity, often taking place in informal venues, two factors which made the 'dance craze' extremely attractive to working-class youths. One report on interwar leisure noted:

> The dance halls are within the range of nearly everybody's purse, and typists, shop assistants and factory girls rub shoulders with them. Girls wear smart dance frocks in the latest fashion, while the men usually wear lounge suits. Dancing is informal, and without the elaborate preparations customary before the war. People drop into a palais after the day's work or on Saturday evenings as casually as they go to the cinema. Dances held at swimming baths, municipal halls and at various club-rooms, are usually sure of a good attendance. The price of a ticket is seldom over 2s.[68]

The dance hall craze soon began to be perceived as part of the youth problem, particularly as youths came under rather more scrutiny there than when they were on street corners. One moral reformer condemned the 'mania dancing' and blamed the compulsion for pleasure and excitement on the 'moral laxity caused by the Great War'.[69] Robert Roberts offered an insight into the 'mania' when he remembered that 'in the explosive dancing boom after the war, the young from sixteen to twenty five flocked into the dance halls by the hundred thousand: some went "jigging" as often as six times a week.'[70] This has led some historians to pronounce that this new commercial form of leisure helped shape interwar youth into the 'first teenagers' since no other generation of male youths experienced the postwar dance craze. Certainly many of the commercial dance halls relentlessly promoted their venture, offering novelty items and special demonstrations by professional dancers, while youths were encouraged to 'follow' popular bands.[71]

However, despite these overtures the teenage males and females who flocked to the halls do not appear to have changed their behaviour to suit the new commercialised venues. The street corner 'gang' mentality persisted and sometimes spilled over into fights. One youth worker at a dance hall remembered that on one particular evening two gangs, who had kept their distance all night, suddenly broke into a fight over a local girl. 'Chairs were raised and thrown, and a few moments of pandemonium raged.' He then, 'after a deal of argument and not a little adroitly applied physical force, separated the gangs and got them fighting into the street'.[72] However, although fighting was an occasional feature of dance hall entertainment, the overriding incentive to attend was to meet the opposite sex. Once again, however, the courting rituals of the street gang were replicated in the dance hall with groups of lads and girls adhering to a strict self-imposed sex demarcation that would last almost to the end of the evening. Hatton recalled that prior to the evening a gang of lads would eagerly talk about the forthcoming dance and which girls would be attending. This bravado, however, crumbled at the start of the evening of the dance:

> Watch them at the dance itself, all the girls one side of the room, waiting and anxious to dance, all of the lads huddled together in groups in the corners, looking sheepish and awkward as can be, much too shy to make a move; absolutely longing to mingle with the lasses but as bashful and blushing as a Dickens heroine. It is a most difficult thing to get the lads and lasses to intermingle freely, and is usually about three dances from the end of the evening before one can get them all together and happy.[73]

The street and the dance hall provided very public arenas where young men could display and assert their masculinity. Other new forms of leisure such as the cinema and radio also became integral to male youth culture between the wars. However, as we shall see in Chapter 6, these new forms of mass communication and entertainment did not necessarily transform youth culture, but instead accentuated existing traits.

The interwar period also saw a repeat of concerns that youths were abusing new and emerging technologies. Just as Victorian youths were castigated for subverting the protocols of bicycle riding, a small but significant minority of their 1930s' counterparts began 'joy riding' motor cars. Joyriding, where a group of youths used a car for temporary use without the consent of the car owner, became a serious problem in the 1930s. O'Connell has argued that 'while the middle class professional could signify his masculinity through the ownership of the latest attractive motor car, joyriding offered his young working-class counterpart an opportunity to express, albeit fleetingly, his own manliness'.[74] Just as the bicycle in the late nineteenth century had provoked a moral panic about its misuse by youths, social observers began to comment on the menace of the motor car. Roy and Theodora Calvert, who produced a study on crime and punishment in the early 1930s, commented that the motor car had been an 'active help' to the young lawbreaker. In what was almost an echo from the bicycle moral panics from the late nineteenth century, they suggested that the car allowed 'hundreds of thousands of people who formerly lived in crowded areas which were easily protected to move to more scattered houses in the suburbs which are much more difficult to police'. The fear that undesirable youths from the slums were spreading into the suburbs was brought into sharp focus by the increase in joyriding during the 1930s. The Calverts noted that in the suburbs 'people make a practice of leaving in the streets expensive motor-cars, into which anyone can step, put his foot on a pedal, and drive away'.[75] The temptation for some youths was too great, particularly as until the early 1930s the public was forbidden by the police to lock their cars as they were required to be made available in the event of an emergency.[76] Evidence suggests that youths who 'borrowed' cars did so to impress friends or women, and did not systematically damage cars, drive dangerously or at excessive speed. Indeed, the newly 'acquired' car was often a modern addition to the monkey parade, where young people would parade in their best clothes in the hope of pairing off with a member of the opposite sex. Contemporary reports criticised these 'car ghouls' who drove 'about the thoroughfares ogling and smiling at young girls parading the pavements'.[77] Cases of joyriding emerged in most of the major cities throughout 1930s' Britain. In 1931, 5,086 cars were stolen in London and 4,869 recovered, suggesting that the vast majority of these cars had been taken for a relatively short period of time. In Birmingham, the local paper blamed the rise of joyriding cases on 'irresponsible youths', while the increase in the problem in Glasgow prompted the police to create a special detachment of officers to deal with the offence.[78]

Conclusion

It is tempting to mark out the 1930s as the decade which saw the first teenagers emerge. Academics and youth workers began writing about the 'new' type of adolescent that had appeared on the streets and in the clubs, who seemed to have adopted different a lifestyle to his forebears. However, these pronouncements perhaps tell us more about the shift in thinking by academics, theorising youth behaviour that once would have been dismissed as unworthy of serious attention. For the first time researchers came to recognise that, like it or not, perhaps youths did possess an identifiable culture. Male youths had, of course, since the late nineteenth century possessed a distinct youth culture which had reflected modern changes in work and leisure patterns. As Chapter 3 has demonstrated, male youths at the end of the nineteenth century had considerable financial independence, gaining employment in 'blind alley' jobs similar to those the future generation of male youths would recognise in the interwar period.[79] Cultural continuities in work and leisure appear as the most dominant feature of interwar youth culture. Substitute the cinema for the music hall, and in the late nineteenth century you have a broadly similar male youth leisure profile, which included street 'loafing', a commercial market for youth literature, and the existence of a proliferation of organised clubs and societies. The predilection of youths to manipulate their environment to their own advantage should also be seen in a wider context since this reflects an important trait found in adult working-class culture. However, in one key respect the interwar period did witness an important break from the Victorian period. It became the era of mass communication, the subject of the next chapter.

Notes

1 J. Hill, *Sport, Leisure and Culture in Twentieth Century Britain* (London, Palgrave, 2002), p. 115.

2 C. Burt, *The Young Delinquent* (London, University of London Press, 1925).

3 Historians who have focused particularly on the interwar period include A. Davies, *Leisure, Gender and Poverty. Working-Class Culture in Salford and Manchester, 1900–1939* (Milton Keynes, Open University Press, 1992); D. Fowler, 'Teenage consumers? Young wage earners and leisure in Manchester, 1919–1939', in A. Davies and S. Fielding (eds), *Workers' Worlds. Cultures and Communities in Manchester and Salford, 1880–1939* (Manchester, Manchester University Press, 1992), p. 148; D. Fowler, *The First Teenagers. The Lifestyle of Young Wage Earners in Interwar Britain* (London, Woburn Press, 1995); K. Burgess, 'Youth employment policy during the 1930s', *Twentieth Century British History*, 6 (1995).

4 H. Llewllyn Smith, *The New Survey of London Life and Labour. Life and Leisure*, vol. 9 (London, P.S. King & Son, 1935), p. 140.

5 G. Pearson, *Hooligan. A History of Respectable Fears* (London, Macmillan, 1983), p. 27.

6 F.R. Leavis, *Mass Civilisation and Minority Culture* (Cambridge, Minority Press, 1930), pp. 7–8.

7 H.A. Secretan, *London Below Bridges. Its Boys and its Future* (London, Geoffrey Bles, 1931), pp. 58–9.

8 A. E. Morgan, *The Needs of Youth. A Report to King George's Jubilee Trust Fund* (Oxford, Oxford University Press, 1939), p. 59.

9 E. R. and T. Calvert, *The Lawbreaker. A Critical Study of the Modern Treatment of Crime* (London, Routledge, 1933), p. 60; Pearson, *Hooligan. A History of Respectable Fears*, p. 28.

10 Quoted in Pearson, *Hooligan*, p. 34.

11 H. S. Bryan, *The Troublesome Boy* (London, A. C. Pearson, 1936), pp. 31–2.

12 H. S. Hatton, *London's Bad Boys* (London, Chapman & Hall, 1931), pp. 48, 132.

13 Hatton, *London's Bad Boys*, p. 78.

14 See Chapter 3.

15 J. Butterworth, *Clubland* (1932; London, Epworth Press, 1933), p. 21.

16 R. Pope, 'Adjustment to peace: Educational provision for unemployed juveniles in Britain, 1918–19', *British Journal of Educational Studies*, 27 (1979), 70–3.

17 Morgan, *The Needs of Youth*, pp. 94–5.

18 Pope, 'Adjustment to peace: Educational provision for unemployed juveniles in Britain, 1918–19', 70.

19 Morgan, *The Needs of Youth*, p. 97.

20 Hatton, *London's Bad Boys*, p. 74

21 Pope, 'Adjustment to peace: Educational provision for unemployed juveniles in Britain, 1918–19', 70–3.

22 Hatton, *London's Bad Boys*, p. 95

23 Hatton, *London's Bad Boys*, p. 75.

24 Hatton, *London's Bad Boys*, pp. 75–6.

25 Pearson, *Hooligan*, p. 38

26 E. B. Castle, A. K. C. Ottaway and W. T. R. Rawson, *The Coming of Leisure. The Problem in England* (London, New Education Fellowship, 1935), p. 14.

27 Castle et al., *The Coming of Leisure*, p. 18.

28 C. Cameron, A. Lush and G. Meara, *Disinherited Youth* (Edinburgh, T. & A. Constable, 1943), p. 112.

29 S. Nairne, 'The leisure of the adolescent', in W. Boyd (ed.), *The Challenge of Leisure* (London, New Education Fellowship, 1936), p. 167.

30 Hill, *Sport, Leisure and Culture in Twentieth Century Britain*, pp. 151–3.

31 *The Times*, 13 February 1937.

32 Morgan, *The Needs of Youth*, p. 2.

33 Morgan, *The Needs of Youth*, p. 283.

34 *The Times*, 8 February 1939.

35 Hill, *Sport, Leisure and Culture*, p. 152.

36 *The Times*, 6 October 1939.

37 *The Times*, 6 November 1939.

38 Morgan, *The Needs of Youth*, p. 368.

39 Fowler, *The First Teenagers*, p. 138.

40 Castle et al., *The Coming of Leisure*, p. 35.

41 Nairne, 'The leisure of the adolescent', p. 169.

42 Cameron et al., *Disinherited Youth*, p. 123.

43 *The Times*, 19 September 1933.

44 Fowler, *The First Teenagers*, pp. 138–40.

45 Cameron et al., *Disinherited Youth*, p. 118.

46 Fowler, *The First Teenagers*, p. 159.

47 Cameron et al., *Disinherited Youth*, p. 100.

48 Cameron et al., *Disinherited Youth*, p. 114.

49 Cameron et al., *Disinherited Youth*, p. 115.

50 Cameron et al., *Disinherited Youth*, p. 115.

51 Fowler, 'Teenage consumers?', p. 148; Fowler, *The First Teenagers*, p. 1.

52 Fowler, *The First Teenagers*, p. 170.

53 Castle et al., *The Coming of Leisure*, p. 16.

54 Morgan, *The Needs of Youth*, p. 41.

55 Burgess, 'Youth employment policy during the 1930s', 25.

56 *Coventry Herald*, 6 February 1914.

57 Morgan, *The Needs of Youth*, p. 61.

58 *Coventry Herald*, 22 August 1913.

59 Butterworth, *Clubland*, p. 40.

60 Fowler, *The First Teenagers*, p. 107. Fowler draws evidence from Rowntree's findings from York. This account tends to exaggerate the contrasts with the late nineteenth century and contradicts more persuasive evidence offered by youth workers and academic research surveys.

61 Cameron et al., *Disinherited Youth*, p. 108.

62 Morgan, *The Needs of Youth*, p. 276.

63 J. Butterworth, *Clubland* (London, Epworth Press, 1932), p. 41. For a similar account of a street gang, see Hatton, *London's Bad Boys*, p. 38.

64 See Chapter 4.

65 H. A. Secretan, *London Below Bridges. Its Boys and its Future* (London, Geoffrey Bles, 1931), p. 75.

66 Butterwoth, *Clubland*, p. 43.

67 W. Greenwood, *Love on the Dole* (1933; Harmondsworth, Penguin, 1981), pp. 79–80.

68 H. Llewellyn Smith, *The New Survey of London Life and Labour. Life and Leisure*, vol. 9 (London, P.S. King & Son, 1935), pp. 64–5

69 *The Times*, 16 February 1931.

70 R. Roberts, *The Classic Slum. Salford Life in the First Quarter of the Century* (Manchester, Manchester University Press, 1971), p. 232.

71 Cameron et al., *Disinherited Youth*, p. 105.

72 Hatton, *London's Bad Boys*, p. 27.

73 Hatton, *London's Bad Boys*, p. 47. For a similar account, see Roberts, *The Classic Slum*, p. 233.

74 S. O'Connell, *The Car in British Society. Class, Gender and Motoring 1896–1939* (Manchester, Manchester University Press, 1998), p. 103.

75 Calvert, *The Lawbreaker*, pp. 59–69.

76 Calvert, *The Lawbreaker*, pp. 59–60.
77 O'Connell, *The Car in British Society*, p. 105.
78 O'Connell, *The Car in British Society*, p. 104.
79 See also Davies, *Leisure, Gender and Poverty*, p. 82.

6

The era of mass communication: working-class male leisure and 'good' citizenship between the wars

Mass commercial leisure came of age between the wars. A visit to at least one mass commercial leisure venue, be it a football match, music hall or cinema, had by 1939 become an important weekend ritual for many working men.[1] Since professional sport and the music hall had their foundations in Victorian society, contemporary observers tended to divert their critical gaze towards the new technological developments that could dispense 'popular' leisure to an unprecedented number of people. The explosion of commercial literature, the cinema, and the inception of public broadcasting were all significant new cultural developments that permeated the daily lives of working-class people. Technical innovation, and with it the growth of more sophisticated propaganda techniques, marked the interwar period as the era of mass communication. For the British establishment, this brought unprecedented access to working-people through print, film and wireless. On the other hand, it was thought that this new technology also had the potential for weakening the ties between the state and the individual. Once again, at the centre of this debate was the role that appropriate leisure habits could have on stimulating good citizenship, a matter of heightened importance during the socio-economic and political turmoil of the 1930s. The success or otherwise of the establishment in projecting propagandist entertainment advocating social cohesion in print, film or wireless programmes has also been the subject of significant histori-cal controversy. This chapter will investigate the expansion of commercial literature, cinema-going and finally radio broadcasting in order to establish whether working-class males really did embrace a more 'homogeneous', less class-specific culture, as some historians have argued.[2]

The impact of reading on leisure patterns between the wars has often been overlooked by historians, as it was essentially a home-based activity. Although it had always featured in some part of working-class leisure patterns, after 1914 a rapid increase in the number of books published and a significant growth in libraries suggest that reading played a greater role in working people's lives.[3] Contemporary surveys suggested that working-class families would spend between 1 and 2 shillings a week on reading matter, a fair proportion of their income, considering books could be loaned for a few pence.[4] The number of books published increased from 8,666 in 1914 to 14,904 in1939, while the number of book sales rose from 7.2 million in 1928 to 26.8 million in 1939.[5] It was during this period that the publishing industry transformed its practices, introducing aggressive marketing techniques and new styles of production. The novel became a 'commodity' carefully packaged and reduced in size with a view to creating a successful series. Books were effectively marketed like any other consumer product, with colourful and dramatic covers and illustrations. Novels would also be heavily advertised in newspapers and be the subject of poster campaigns.[6] The increase in demand for books can also be identified in the library figures for the period. Although the free library movement had begun in the mid-nineteenth century, the establishment of free lending libraries by civic authorities was haphazard. It was only during the interwar period that the vast majority of working people acquired access to a local, well-stocked and free library. This is borne out in the British figures for books issued in public libraries, which increased from 54.3 million in 1911 to 247.3 million by 1939.[7] These figures, however, hide a number of different traits in reading habits, which were determined particularly by social class and gender. The following section will explore these differences in an attempt to identify and explain the most popular genres among working-class males and their motivation for reading during this period.

There can be little doubt that the publishing boom extended reading as a regular habit to all levels of society. However, the belief that an enlarged reading public somehow blurred social tastes or distinctions in 1930s' Britain is somewhat misleading, particularly since publishers attempted to shape the presentation and content of their books to attract specific social groups. For example, Penguin Books, perhaps the most famous publisher of this era, were keen to cultivate a strong middle-class readership. Conscious of the new mass production era it was working in, Penguin made a direct effort to link its new publications with cultural improvement. Through its publication of middlebrow novels and the contemporary social commentary found in the Penguin Specials, Penguin steered away from sensationalist and 'vulgar' novels, and therefore the popular mass markets. Thus although Richard Hoggart had, after the Second World War, declared that Penguin had its roots among the common man, he had earlier admitted that their books were principally read by 'sixth formers, young clerks, teachers, undergraduates, adult students, trade unionists and solitary serious readers'.[8] The 1930s also saw the establishment of the Left Book Club, another publishing organisation which was proclaimed by some to have received enthusiastic support from the working class. Victor Gollancz, the publisher, claimed that 'in one place thirty unemployed are contributing a penny a month so that, jointly and through one of them, they may become a member'.[9] In reality the subscribers to the Left Book Club came from the same social background as the readership of Penguin described by Hoggart. Indeed, the first four books chosen – Thorez's *People's Front in France*, Palme Dutt's *World Politics, 1918–1936*, Strachey's *The Theory and Practice of Socialism* and *Spain in Revolt* – were, according to Symons, merely products of Communist propaganda and unlikely to appeal to a mass working-class reading public.[10] George Orwell's novel *Coming Up for Air*, first published in 1939, satirises the Left Book Club and perhaps captures the spirit of some of their meetings. In one meeting the audience at the lecture was essentially composed of liberal middle-class women intent on improving their minds, a wide-eyed school teacher who was 'drinking it all in', and a range of political activists from the left. The local Labour Party activists who had for years been campaigning on local issues could not 'make head nor tail' of the international crisis that had swamped the political scene in the 1930s, while the more interested younger Communists were itching to interject with ideological queries and comments when question-time started. The ordinary working-class man and woman were noticeable by their absence. Such was the readership of the Left Book Club.[11]

If publishers such as Penguin or Victor Gollancz were perceived to be fulfilling a culturally educative role, how was popular literature received? Like most mass commercial leisure ventures, there was an initial outcry regarding the impact that new mass-produced cheap literature would have on its readership and British culture as a whole. As reading was not a new leisure medium, the moral panics were less pronounced than for

innovatory media, though, as we shall see, it did generate the same underlying anxieties. The most vocal critique of mass reading habits was that
of F. R. Leavis, an academic who feared that the standardisation and mass
production of the novel would inevitably be accompanied by a 'process
of levelling-down'.[12] Taking up this theme, one report, which concerned
itself with the 'problem' of leisure in England, worried that in the era of
mass-produced literature,

> the untrained adult is at the mercy of the cheap libraries and the publishers
> of widely advertised best-sellers. In order to make a personal selection from
> the enormous number of books available to-day, even the best-educated man
> must have acquired a critical taste and a considerable amount of what the
> Americans call 'sales resistance'. If he does not select, the selection will be
> done for him by book societies, reviewers, and advertisers.[13]

The report's belief that uneducated working-class readers could be manipulated by a cynical publishing industry reveals an underlying assumption
that working people were not making conscious choices over the type of
literature they preferred. However, as we shall see, working-class males and
females had distinct tastes in literature that reflected more general traits
in working-class culture.

Perhaps the best insight into working-class reading patterns can be
found in the Mass-Observation (M-O) research which investigated the
reading habits of working people between 1937 and 1945. M-O's interest
in popular literature stemmed from an anxiety that the democratic system
was breaking down and that there was a fundamental dislocation between
the people and parliament. M-O researchers were confident that surveys
on popular reading habits would be at least one measure of how working
people engaged with the wider world.[14] M-O's early research into popular
reading habits uncovered a whole subculture of literary outlets that were a
far cry from the standard bookshop. For example, one respondent informed
a researcher that 'much more can be found about what people like reading
from public libraries, two penny libraries and grubby little sweet shops
than Charing Cross Road'.[15] The pay-as-you-read twopenny libraries were
run, on the whole, by newsagents, tobacconists or department stores as a
sideline to attract the new reading public into their shops. These types of
library were extremely popular and better stocked with light fiction than
their public-library counterparts, a situation which led some cultural elites
to compare cheap commercial libraries with 'their worn greasy novels' to
'tuppenny dram shops'.[16] This was a view perhaps shared by Orwell, who

described a twopenny library in his novel *Keep the Aspidistra Flying*. The library had been established by a bookseller a little way from his main premises where quality books were sold, as the twopenny library 'would frighten away the book-lovers who came to the shop in search of "rare" books'. Although Gordon Comstock, the book's main character, deplored this spread of 'low-brow' literature, a dip in his career had driven him to work in

> one of those cheap and evil little libraries ('mushroom libraries', they were called) which are spreading up all over London and are deliberately aimed at the uneducated. In libraries like these there is not a single book that is ever mentioned in the reviews or that any civilised person has ever heard of. The books are published by special low-class firms and turned out by wretched hacks at the rate of four a year, as mechanically as sausages and with much less skill ... the shelves were already marked off into sections – 'Sex', 'Crime', 'Wild West', and so forth.[17]

The growth of the twopenny libraries was significant as, due to their commercial instincts, these types of library were less anxious about the wider 'cultural implications' of catering for working-class tastes. This contrasted with the civic public libraries, which were closely watched by town councillors and still carried over elements of a nineteenth-century rational recreation ethos when considering the purchase of new books. Such was the growth of the twopenny library between the wars that Berwick Sayers, President of the Library Association, observed that 'we have almost the spontaneous appearance in thousands of shops of departments for lending light literature; so much so that it would seem the lending of reading matter is becoming an auxiliary of every business'.[18]

Not surprisingly, most working people tended to borrow, from a variety of outlets, rather than purchase books. However, even with the relatively simple process of borrowing books, librarians observed that working people conducted themselves in the library in a distinctive manner and followed similar methods of selecting books. It is worth citing one M-O researcher's evidence at length, as it sheds some light on working people's relationship with libraries and reading:

> There is little experimenting, little adventure among unfamiliar types of literature. It seems almost that there is a state of rut. Moreover people tend to follow the taste of the majority, at public libraries often picking books from those which have just been returned by other borrowers. Thus the same books are constantly kept in circulation, whilst others especially the classics

remain on the shelf. People stick to their own type, and have prejudices in some cases against other types. If you give people short stories, said one librarian – 'they look at you as though you had given them margarine instead of butter'. People take on an average less than a quarter of an hour to choose books ... Many books are taken from the shelves in the process of choosing, and returned hastily after an average of about 13 seconds.[19]

These observations about working people's use of the library cut across gender lines, though men particularly exhibited greater discomfort in the public library environment. The rapid selection of books which had recently been loaned points to a fear of ridicule by either their contemporaries or library staff if an unusual book was taken out. However, unease was particularly acute in civic public libraries, whose formalised protocol contrasted with the twopenny libraries, which were more relaxed and seemed to have tolerated groups of lenders 'chatting' in the aisles.[20] One report on young men's leisure noted that '2d. or "step in libraries"' were much more frequented than the public library as there were less complications in joining. The report discovered that many of the men 'were aware of the existence of the public libraries but were unaware of how to become members'. Indeed, it is significant that many of the working-class men who visited the library did not use its primary function of loaning books. The report observed that most working men 'did not get beyond the reading room, where they scanned the newspapers for 'situations vacant' and for Sports and Betting News'. For lending, however, men preferred twopenny libraries which were 'more numerous and convenient'.[21] Once the books were in their possession, working-class readers tended to treat literature differently from their middle-class counterparts, who often felt pleasure in possessing books. There was a reluctance to buy anything but cheap literature and, probably due to cost and the ethos of twopenny libraries, usually a failure to distinguish between magazines and books. Significantly, working people would treat books like magazines, sharing them among both neighbours and work colleagues and not expecting their return.

There was also commonality between the working-class male and female reading public in the types of books selected to buy or loan. Although 'relaxation' was cited across the social classes as the prime reason for reading, it appears that when the choice of reading is also considered, the vast majority of male and female working-class readers were also motivated to read for 'escapist' purposes. Drink had always been traditionally cited as achieving the 'quickest way' out of city life, but in this era of mass publishing the novel proved a popular method of escape, with the added bonus that it could be consumed without the morning-after feeling.[22] In an interview with an M-O researcher in London, one librarian noted that 'the vast majority of readers prefer fiction to non-fiction. At Fulham public libraries the fiction issues form an average 71% of the total.' The Second World War also galvanised demand for escapist fiction, a trend noted by one bookseller who reported that 'war has greatly stimulated reading', which was 'partly due to the black-out'. He also explained that there was little demand for books about politics or war.[23] Although the working-class appetite for fiction was accentuated by two wars and the explosion in the publishing industry after 1914, there had long been a tradition of their preference for 'sensational' fiction.[24] Where M-O researchers found a divergency in working-class reading habits was in the type of escapist fiction that appealed to males and females. One researcher reported that

> crime books, mysteries or 'thrillers' are more important than any one type, and relatively more popular among men than women. Adventure and cowboy stories are also more read by men. Women prefer romance and the more sentimental type of novel … classics are read by few, and the more serious modern authors are read comparatively little.[25]

In addition, as we have seen, working-class males' choice of literature was, on the whole, made outside the confines of the public library and instead in the twopenny libraries. It is here, according to one report, that the vast majority of working men bought a plentiful supply of crime and horror, which could be obtained in almost all twopenny libraries in the poorer areas.[26]

Social class, then, helped shape preferences, not only in the choice of literature but also the institutions used to loan or purchase the material. Moreover, working-class men were less inclined to use the public library, which tended to overload the reader with rules and protocol. Instead, the reading room, often much to the complaint of library staff, was the base where information on sport and betting tips could be gleaned. Apart from the newspapers, working men favoured the 'crime', 'thriller' and 'sensational' fiction end of the market. The working-class fascination with escapist melodrama stretched back to the nineteenth century and was to continue into the twentieth through the publishing boom between the wars and, importantly, through the medium of film. It is to this relatively new form of leisure pursuit that we will now turn.

The most significant mass commercial institution during the interwar period was undoubtedly the cinema. Although film had its origins in the pre-First World War era, Philip Corrigan has described 1914 as 'the moment of cinema'. The number of cinemas had grown rapidly in all of the major cities in Britain and at that point overall audience figures were estimated to be some 350 million a year in a population of 40 million. In 1917, an independent inquiry undertaken by the National Council of Public Morals (NCPM) attempted to take stock of the rapid acceleration of the industry. It concluded that cinema-going had become, for many working people, a popular and dearly held leisure routine, and estimated that approximately 100,000 people were employed in the trade.[27] At first glance, the rise from 4,000 cinemas in 1921 to about 4,300 in 1934 does not seem to match the phenomenal increases of earlier years. However, these figures hide a significant transformation, as by the 1930s the small open hall cinemas had generally been phased out to be replaced by the large and ostentatious 'picture palaces' owned by 'the big three': the Odeon, Gaumont–British and Associated British Cinemas. Unlike earlier forms of cinema, the 'picture palace' was a truly mass form of entertainment: not only were the interiors of cinemas considerably enlarged, in some cases to seat over 4,000 people, but the domineering influence of 'the big three' also ensured that audiences were watching the same films with the same stars up and down the country.[28] By the mid-1930s, then, 'the pictures' was the most popular form of leisure activity, with annual admissions to the cinema totalling 963 million and box office receipts of approximately £41 million.[29]

As the most popular leisure activity, cinema-going unsurprisingly became the centre of a number of moral panics linked to its supposed negative impact on citizenship and morality in the British working class. These anxieties were embodied in a group calling themselves the Birmingham Cinema Enquiry, who established the organisation after a conference in Birmingham in 1930. The group, which became known as the National Cinema Enquiry, was led by the Vice-Chancellor of Birmingham University and comprised magistrates, doctors, teachers and clergymen, most of whom tended to hold a rather hostile position towards the cinema even before investigations had begun. It was clear from the start that the group perceived a perilous tension between the cinema and the future of British citizenship. Grant Robertson, the Enquiry's leader, outlined their underlying concerns: 'The basis of our British civilization, and I do not put it too strongly, is built upon some very fundamental ideas, and certain fundamental standards, and standards upon which we have built at any rate our British life. If these go, what remains?'[30] Although the Enquiry campaigned for tighter censorship, the Government was reluctant to become involved, declaring that the current arrangements with the British Board of Film Censors were working well. After their repeated failure to provoke Government intervention, the influence of the National Cinema Enquiry petered out after 1935.[31]

While the National Cinema Enquiry's research was established with the sole purpose of investigating the cinema, film-going invariably became a significant issue in more general contemporary surveys of working-class leisure patterns. For some contemporary researchers the glamorous film and the luxurious conditions of the new picture palaces engendered an apathy within the working class and a dislocation from their immediate socio-economic environment. In one report, *The Coming of Leisure* published in 1936, it was noted that

> standards of value and emotional reactions of large numbers of people are being moulded unconsciously by the standards implicitly embodied in the fictitious characters for whom the emotional sympathies of the audience are won, while their critical faculties are dulled by the glamour and the general conditions in which films are shown.[32]

In the same year another survey, entitled *The Challenge of Leisure*, reported that

> it is obvious that most films present common problems in a peculiar and non typical form and solve them, too often, in an arbitrary and illogical manner, with the result that many millions of cinema-goers may easily be educated to accept submissively the vicarious satisfaction of instincts and desires which could and should be actually satisfied. The unreal world presented for our entertainment in the great majority of films may make us less capable of living a satisfying and useful life in the real world which awaits us outside.[33]

Finally, the perceived passivity of the cinema-audience was the main criticism of film-going in Rowntree's report on life and leisure in 1930s' York:

> Undoubtedly the cinema shares with other forms of entertainment the danger that it may become to some merely a way of escape from monotony rather than a means of recreation. True recreation is constructive, and wholesome recreation implies *re-creating* physical, intellectual, or moral vitality. As one among several ways of spending leisure, visits to the cinema may be

re-creative. But some cinema 'fans' rely on the cinema too exclusively as a way of passing their leisure hours. It becomes for them a means of *escapism* rather than of *re-creation*, and this arrests their development.[34]

The implications were clear: during the frenzied domestic political turmoil of the 1930s, a considerable number of working-class males were lulled into apathy, too consumed with the world of film fantasy to embrace their democratic duties as British citizens. Film was perceived as a new and potent influence on working people, which, according to Leavis, could damagingly encroach upon higher and more civilised cultural planes. Thus cinema-going entailed the audience surrendering 'under conditions of hypnotic receptivity, to the cheapest emotional appeals, appeals the more insidious because they are associated with a compellingly vivid illusion of actual life'. Leavis went on to say that mass film-going was helping to shape a standardised popular leisure which could eventually infect and jeopardise elite civilisation.[35] A solution to this problem, in some quarters, was for more active state intervention to ensure that good citizenship and the film industry worked in harmony. Writing immediately after the Second World War and in the shadow of the 1930s, the sociologist J. P. Mayer made a plea for the state to formulate a cultural policy, asserting that it was 'possible to make the film medium into an active and dynamic instrument of an all-round citizenship'. Although he rejected the elitist cultural positions adopted by writers such as F. R. Leavis, Mayer did advocate active state intervention to realise an improved mass culture that was both uplifting and civically aware.[36]

However, the role and duties of the British citizen were further confused by the impact and popularity of Hollywood films, which were considered to be importing an alien American culture to British shores. *The Times*, never one to underestimate a moral decline, reported in 1932 that 'the United States' film industry has done more to Americanize the world than ever Julius Caesar and his legions to Romanize it'.[37] For some contemporaries the new American 'talkies' were not only corrupting English speech but also introduced hot-headedness and sensationalism, which were, according to one youth worker in the 1930s, 'foreign to our national temperament'.[38] Indeed, it was young male youths who were considered the most at risk since it was thought that a significant minority were replicating American habits and, at worst, gangster behaviour on British streets. One newspaper commentator articulated the received wisdom of the early 1930s when he declared that 'it is impossible to deny the enormous and pernicious effect that the innumerable crook films from Hollywood have had on the adolescent with lawless tendencies.' He concluded that the imported American films were increasingly perverting young male minds with 'the muck which exalts lawlessness into a virtue and the murderer and racketeer into heroes'.[39] Mayer believed that his research had uncovered not only discernable differences in film tastes according to gender and class, but also the fact that the adolescent working-class boy was more likely to absorb uncivilising traits associated with lowbrow pictures. Certainly boys favoured the action films. One thirteen-year-old boy wrote that 'the picture I like best is the *Eve of St. Mark*. Why I like it is because it has fighting in it. I like fighting pictures. The picture I dislike is *Rose-Mary*. I dislike it because it is so much singing and Romance.' This and other responses from boys in his study provoked Mayer to pose the question, 'how can their minds resist the emotional temptations that films offer? How can they become appreciative of life, its obligations, its beauties, its disappointments? They are "movie-made", even before they begin to live.'[40]

However, despite these fairly widespread anxieties, researchers consistently failed to find links between juvenile crime and the cinema. Cyril Burt, perhaps not the most liberal researcher of his era, found that the imitation of gangster films by adolescent males was 'exceptional and rare' and concluded that in general 'the picture house provides an alternative, not a provocative, to mischievous amusement'.[41] In this view he was supported by a number of police authorities who during the 1920s and 1930s dismissed the gangster film's perceived link with crime, pointing to the reduced intemperance in British cities during this period.[42]

With its great numerical impact, it is tempting to suggest that the act of cinema-going and the influence of the films themselves fundamentally reshaped working-class leisure patterns. For some historians, the cinema was another agency spawned in the late nineteenth and early twentieth centuries that further fragmented working-class culture along the fault lines of geographical region, generation and gender. Davies has argued that access to commercial leisure was 'structured by class, income, gender and age', which could dictate whether men or women were able to participate in these new forms of mass leisure.[43] The cinema's influence on working-class culture has been taken a stage further by a number of leading historians who have argued that popular British films intentionally and successfully promoted social consensus. Richards and Aldgate have shown that 'stars' such as Gracie Fields and George Formby became national symbols who advocated support for existing institutions, rather than working-class heroes who might have exposed the social tensions of the 1930s. Furthermore, Richards has concluded that 'the public seem on the whole to have been happy with the films they were given during the 1930s, and those films for the most part played their role in maintaining consensus and the *status quo*.'[44] For Stevenson and Cook the cinema helped forge a 'British culture' with which differing social classes could identify and thus serve to prevent the social tensions and revolutionary fervour of continental Europe during the interwar period.[45] This theme has been taken up more recently by Sedgwick, who has argued that, combined with a passive working-class culture, the cinema helped forge social stability during the 1930s:

> A reading of the provincial daily newspapers of the period, with their combination of national, international and local news and local advertisements, leaves little doubt that at a local level Britain was a socially and politically cohesive and coherent nation. Even in the face of mass unemployment and poverty, local institutions such as the town council, the courts and police acted with legitimate authority and maintained order. It is quite clear that a complaisant working-class culture pervaded in Britain ... Within this environment, cinema performed the important role of diffusing widely an aesthetic experience which served the dual function of increasing the general level of well-being while reinforcing the status quo.[46]

Given the central role of cinema in the development of working-class culture and leisure, we shall first explore the view that attendance was structured by disposable income, generation and gender considerations.

Fortunately for the historian, the anxiety that the cinema provoked among social commentators generated a number of surveys across the country on the impact of film-going on the British public. The Carnegie Trust's study of young unemployed in Glasgow, Liverpool and Cardiff, Rowntree's investigation in York and the *New Survey of London Life and Labour* all singled out cinema as an important influence and attempted to categorise patterns of attendance. The evidence gleaned from contemporary surveys on popular cinema-going habits illustrates that attendance patterns were not overly shaped by issues of poverty. A lack of income, though cited by historians as a barrier to cinema attendance, does not appear to be an overriding factor. The cinema was extremely cheap: half of the seats during the 1930s cost less than 6d, a price which even gave access to social groups historically unable to access commercial entertainment on a regular basis.[47] Such was the importance of cinema to working people that even those who occasionally lacked sufficient funds to visit the cinema were supported by their peer group. H. A. Secretan, a youth worker in London, reported that teenage male youths would perceive a visit to the cinema as an important group activity that was worthy enough to subsidise among themselves. He observed that sometimes one youth would find, due to unemployment or bad luck, that he would be out of coppers:

> probably he will feign a headache and say he means to sit at home. No word will be said but when they get to the booking office, one will slip in front and buy two tickets, with the casual 'I've got yours, chum.' The others will pay up their proportion of the cost later for the gang shares and shares alike. Such is true comradeship below the bridges.[48]

The Carnegie Trust's research into the unemployed confirmed these observations when it discovered that about 80 per cent of the unemployed men attended the cinema at least once a week and 25 per cent of these attended more often. Respondents to the survey regarded films as important topics of discussion within their peer group. Indeed, the report observed that 'it appears just as necessary for many of these young people to be able to discuss the latest film as it is for other people to be able to talk about the best seller in literature'.[49] Thus, such was the cultural significance of the cinema, those on low incomes made every effort to attend at least once a week.

Where perhaps differences between those on low incomes and the so-called affluent workers did lie were in the type and location of the cinemas visited. The survey reported that the more affluent workers attended the cinema during the evening at the more lavish venues in the heart of the city, while the unemployed cut their cloth accordingly and visited the suburban cinemas for the cheaper matinée showing.[50] Even working-class communities in regions which had suffered from the worst consequences of the 1930s' depression continued to patronise the cinema. For example, William Woodruff, recalling his financially austere childhood in Blackburn, remembered that he was able to gain admittance to the local cinema 'by handing over two empty, clean, two-pound jam jars' to the cashier.[51] Indeed, for children especially, jam jars appear to have been an accepted currency for cinemas across many parts of the country.[52] One historian of South Wales has noted that even in the poverty-stricken mining towns the cinema was 'cheap and accessible' and 'was generally within reach of the poorest sections of the community'.[53] Moreover, there is not a clear correlation between worker affluence and increased cinema-going since those in the North of England were twice as likely to visit the cinema as those in the South. These striking regional variations continued into the postwar era; in 1950–51 it was estimated that the average person in Preston went to the cinema 53 times a year compared with the 27 visits of the residents in the comparatively prosperous Coventry.[54]

There is evidence, however, that generation and gender did structure cinema-going. Although younger males and females were fairly entrenched in the cinema-going habit, older married women were more likely to attend than their husbands. A survey in 1946 reported that 68 per cent of sixteen to nineteen-year-olds, compared with only 11 per cent of those over sixty, went to the cinema at least once a week.[55] Older married women appear to have adopted the cinema as a break from the daily chores of housework and shopping, visiting the matinée showing before the children came home from school. *The New Survey of London* reported that about 70 per cent of the weekly cinema audience consisted of women and girls, and that it was 'not an uncommon sight to see women slipping into the cinema for an hour, after they have finished their shopping'.[56] In addition, women and girls were also more likely than men to attend the cinema by themselves. Older males, on the other hand, 'tend to go only when they have nothing better to do, or when they have a girl friend to take out'. Indeed, Richards concluded that a large proportion of the population that attended the cinema were the young urban working class, who were more likely to be women than men.[57] It is clear, then, that the explosion of the cinema on to the mass commercial leisure scene had a greater impact on youth and older women than on adult males. The cheap prices and the flexibility of the matinée showings allowed women to adopt the cinema at the early stage of its development and ensure that it was one of the few 'respectable' leisure institutions available to them. For adult males, on the other hand, the cinema was one of many commercial institutions competing for their custom. The gendering of the cinema experience should not, however, be overestimated. Robert Roberts remembered that it was one of the first leisure institutions in which men and women would attend together. 'Many women who had lived a kind of purdah since marriage (few respectable wives visited public houses) were to be noted now, escorted by their husbands to the "pictures", a strange sight indeed and one that led to much comment at the shop.'[58] Moreover, for unattached young men and women, it was the ideal place to meet members of the opposite sex.

Although we can identify agencies such as region, generation and gender which helped shape audience patterns, the experience of cinema-going was not shorn of class distinctive traits. While the cinema attracted all classes, as Richards has pointed out, cinema-going was not a classless form of leisure. In cinemas where there was a socially mixed audience, differing admission prices would ensure that social distinction was often preserved within the auditorium. The stratified seating arrangements in the cinema ensured that seats in one auditorium could cost from as little as 3d to as much as 2s 6d.[59] Indeed, some middle-class patrons urged cinemas to extend the social ordering of film-goers to the streets outside, requesting the formation of orderly and separate queues according to seat prices.[60] The increasing numbers of middle-class film-goers patronised the more purpose-built venues in the suburbs with their elegant decor and tea rooms, a far cry from the traditional 'flea-pit' institutions found in working-class neighbourhoods. Cinemas, then, were often class-specific institutions with working-class audiences exhibiting rather different behavioural traits to their middle-class counterparts. Whereas middle-class patrons would 'make the cinema a genteel recreation and choose their films with care, boycotting anything with a dubious title', working-class audiences were altogether more gregarious and less discerning.[61] In addition, traditional concerns within working-class culture, such as respectability, did, however, come to the surface, as W. E. Bakke and Robert Roberts recalled. Bakke noted that 'one interesting feature of the cinema audience is its sense of class distinction. Two theatres in Greenwich were spoken of by skilled workers as "Not attended by a very good class of people".'[62] Similarly, Roberts reported that during the early years of the cinema,

> would-be patrons of two-penny seats literally fought each night for entrance and tales of crushed ribs and at least two broken limbs shocked the neighbourhood. In the beginning cinema managers, following the social custom of the theatre, made the error of grading seats, with the cheapest at the back of the house. For a short time the rabble lolled in comfort along the rear rows while their betters, paying three times as much, suffered cricked necks and eye strain at the front. Caste and culture forbade mixing. A sudden change-over one evening, without warning, at all the local cinemas caused much bitterness and class recrimination.[63]

Despite the differing cinema-going habits that were determined by age and gender, the cinema was more than simply a house to view pictures and had become an important cultural institution within the working-class neighbourhood. Indeed, the cinema, rather like its predecessor the music hall, was a crucible in which certain traditional working-class behavioural traits were allowed to flourish. We must now examine these in detail, since they directly engage with claims that the cinema's influence helped engender a passivity and acceptance of social structures among the working class.

As we have seen, there is an important strand of historiographical opinion which perceives that the cinema was a significant agency in shaping working-class values and assumptions. Historians who adopt this perspective see popular British films as performing a pivotal role in transferring the underlying message of social cohesion to the masses. Aldgate's work on the propaganda potential of 1930s' films such as *Sing As We Go*, where Gracie Fields triumphantly leads a cheerful and very compliant unemployed workforce back to a reopened mill, demonstrates that film makers were consciously attempting to engender an acceptance of existing institutions in a society which was far from stable.[64] This important reading of films by historians should not, however, cloud important issues such as the motivation for film-going and audience behaviour while in the cinema. Kuhn has recently argued that because film studies have privileged the film text, 'not only the reception of films by the social audiences but also the social-historical milieux and industrial and institutional settings in which films are consumed' have been downplayed.[65] There is a great leap from identifying a film's underlying socially inclusive message to asserting that cinema helped nurture a socially cohesive culture during the 1930s. For this to occur we must accept that the audience's role was largely a passive one in which the film's underlying message seeped into the targeted group's consciousness. Harper's research on audiences' responses to 'lowbrow' films in the 1930s suggests that audiences were far from passive consumers of leisure, with working-class men in particular keen to express their film tastes to contemporary researchers.[66]

Male audience members were just as keen to express their views about films in the confines of the cinema auditorium and this casts doubt on the assumption that cinema-going was a straightforward process where 'people in their billions went to the cinema primarily to watch films, normally under conditions of quiet and comfort'.[67] Contemporary cinema managers, however, would not perhaps have recognised this rather cosy image of the cinema of the 1920s and 1930s. Audience participation, often of a rowdy kind, such as catcalls, wolf whistles and guffaws, was commonplace and demonstrated the less than passive mood of the viewers. William

Woodruff remembered that cinema-going in the interwar period was 'a wild affair where a man kept order with a long bamboo pole. If we were caught blowing rice or rock-hard peas at the pianist, or spitting orange pips from the balcony, or whistling too long at the kissing scenes, we ran the risk of getting whacked over the head – a real hard whack.'[68] Indeed, Mayall has shown in his work on Birmingham that cinema management was not for the faint-hearted, as there was often a struggle to maintain order and discipline among the audience.[69] In addition, it is clear that for working-class people a trip to the cinema was not motivated solely by the desire to see a picture, a situation which cuts across generation and gender boundaries. For working-class male adolescents it was the camaraderie of the group and the gregarious behaviour that went on inside the picture house that was for many the cinema's chief attraction. A disgruntled adult cinema-goer in Birmingham sheds light on young male activity in the cinema when he complains about the 'gangs of young "roughs" whose sole entertainment appears to be to see who can make the "cleverest" remarks and shout them out during a programme ... Fortunately, these disturbances are rarely met in better cinemas, but they are a continued source of annoyance in cheaper houses.'[70]

Likewise, one early police report on the activities of a cinema in London noted that the young men and women gathered in the cinema's coffee shop with no intention of watching a film: 'Many young girls and youths between the age of 16 and 18 have assembled there indulging in horseplay causing annoyance to pedestrians and nine males have been charged with insulting behaviour.'[71] A further report confirmed that the cinema coffee shop 'appears to be a place of meeting for young courting couples, many of whom partake of refreshments and leave without visiting the pictures'.[72] Clearly, for these youths film-watching was not the chief motivation for attending the cinema complex. However, it is an undercover policeman's report on the behaviour of a cinema audience which raises doubts over whether the underlying messages of films were successfully transmitted to a receptive audience:

> In the ground floor there were seats filled with couples of opposite sexes, all closely embraced and not in the slightest way interested in the pictures which were being shown on the screen. Many of the couples lay in a reclining position in lounge seats which occupied one corner of the building ... I frequently saw the manager walking about various parts of the house and apparently taking no action whatever regarding the conduct of couples lying

in indecent attitudes. The film which was being shown on the screen at the time I was in the 'cinema' was very interesting but many couples were taking no interest whatever in the picture, but were embraced in each other's arms apparently oblivious to what was appearing on the screen.[73]

Despite the policeman's insistence that the film was a very interesting one, the couples in this cinema seemed to have had more pressing matters on their minds.[74] What, in fact, working-class youths were doing was transferring the audience participation of the music hall and the horseplay of the street into the arena of the cinema. The film, in this context, was of secondary importance. Likewise, when a teenage girl in one contemporary social survey could not recall the plot of a film she had seen twice, the researcher suspected that the respondent visited the local cinema with the prime intention of meeting local boys. The regular habit of cinema-going ensured that films did not have a lasting impact on their audience, a situation confirmed by Kuhn, who in a recent study has argued that 'for the typical young cinema-goer of the thirties … going to the pictures was a part of everyday life: easy sociable, pleasurable – and still fondly remembered.'[75] Indeed Fowler discovered that 'cinemas were by no means simply institutions where a passive working-class audience would sit in silence and receive unquestioningly all the images and messages peddled in the films.'[76]

If film propaganda had difficulty distracting impressionable youths from their more preferable activities, how did older working-class people react? Surviving evidence gleaned from the few studies of cinema audiences suggests that working-class youths and adults shared similar behavioural traits in the auditorium that distinguished them quite markedly from their middle-class counterparts. During one week in 1934, a reporter for *Film Weekly* observed three very different cinemas audiences in London. He noted that in the large West End cinema the audience was 'a lively, good-humoured and intelligent house' in which couples took more interest in the film than in themselves and that 'audible comment on the film was conspicuous by its absence'. Moving on to a cinema located in a middle-class suburb, the reporter observed that the afternoon matinée had attracted a small, largely female audience who disturbed his concentration of the film with 'the clatter of jugs and requests for more milk and fresh buns from the harassed attendant'. Finally, he moved on to a 'different class of cinema in a less prosperous district'. He reported:

I encountered a packed house and a perfect roar of sound. Every single person present constituted him or herself a loudly vocal critic of the fare provided. I have never heard so loud a noise accompanied by such violent behaviour. Yet an attendant explained to me that this was a comparatively quiet night. Only the fact I had seen the film before (about a year ago) made me aware that it was indeed a talkie and not the revival of some old silent film. Had I gone in to see the film and not the audience, I should undoubtedly have walked straight out again, for it was a very bad one – and not for a moment did sickly tolerance cloud the audience's recognition of its badness. No lapse was allowed to pass unnoticed. Yet despite their unusual method of showing it, they were utterly absorbed in the film. They missed nothing – their appreciation was all-embracing. It was an object lesson to other more expensive audiences. When I had entered the spirit of the thing I began to enjoy myself thoroughly – a perfect example of the effect of an audience on the appreciation of a film.

The audience behaviour reminded the reporter of 'the early years of film-going'; however, he added 'naturally, I do not commend this example of audience behaviour for wider circulation'.[77] Clearly, this form of cinema-going was a new and compelling experience for our intrepid reporter, who after initial doubts thoroughly enjoyed the occasion. Indeed, working-class cinema-going consisted of more than just simply watching the picture: it was 'a night out'. The film was important, though watching a 'bad' film in a vocal and energised atmosphere was, it seems, as entertaining as watching a critically acclaimed picture.

For working-class adults, a visit to the pictures could mean that the film was one of a number of entertainments on offer. The newer purpose-built picture palaces employed page boys, usherettes, doormen and chocolate girls and offered a luxurious environment, some cinemas containing cafés, restaurants and bars.[78] As we have seen, the new cinema complexes proved more of an attraction to older working-class women than to their male counterparts, who still preferred traditional masculine pursuits. However, evidence suggests that the groups of females who visited the cinema perceived film-watching as one of a number of activities associated with the cinema. Once again, the cinema coffee shop was the focal point of the afternoon, with many women preferring this leisure activity to the film itself.[79] Likewise, older men would often attend the cinema as it was part of a weekly routine. One survey noted that 'it was perhaps inevitable, but none the less unfortunate, that many [men] acquired a habit of attending the cinemas regardless of the standard of films.[80] This particularly in-

furiated film aficionados, who complained that people would '"pop in" at
any old time without regard to what films are showing' and on leaving the
auditorium were often unable to recall the film title, plot or any actors in
the picture.[81] In addition, as Orwell observed, cinemas, particularly in areas
hit by the 1930s' depression, were densely populated by unemployed men
whose first concern was to find a warm and dry place away from inclem-
ent weather. He reported: 'In Wigan a favourite refuge was the pictures,
which are fantastically cheap there. You can always get a seat for fourpence,
and at the matinée at some houses you can even get a seat for twopence.
Even people on the verge of starvation will readily pay twopence to get
out of the ghastly cold of a winter afternoon.'[82] These sentiments were
shared by a correspondent to *Film Weekly* who commented that dole and
cinema queues were both growing rapidly in 1934.

> The reason is simple. The cinema is an entertainment which is within reach
> of all. Even the man with only a few coppers in his pocket can have two
> or more hours enjoyment and forget his worries for a time. It is impossible
> to get the same value for money elsewhere. In my opinion it is wrong of
> people to condemn the out of work man for spending time and money at
> cinemas. The entertainment is a tonic.[83]

The working class's use of the cinema, then, was perhaps more complex
than some historians have described, a situation that confirms William
Farr's observations of cinema audiences during the 1930s. In 1936 Farr
was a member of the British Film Institute when he wrote, 'the millions
of people who visit cinema each week – and very many go more than
once a week – go to be entertained. With some the motive may not even
be as explicit as that; they go to the cinema as a way of spending the
evening.'[84]

It has been argued here that film choice and the influence of propaganda
on working-class audiences ought not be overstated. Audience behaviour
and motives for cinema-going suggest a far from passive response from
working people regardless of gender and generational divides. Furthermore,
the theory that cinema helped engender a social cohesion in British society
through the messages embedded in popular films tends to underestimate
the audience's power of choice. Cinemas and film makers were, after all,
commercial institutions that relied on popular support. Social surveys noted
that working-class audiences were drawn towards certain genres of film that
were essentially escapist in narrative. In terms of the most popular films,

one cinema manager declared that crime and adventure were the biggest
successes, followed by comedy and Westerns. He complained that

> the crowd you get here doesn't like anything that makes it think ... prefers
> mostly blood and thunder and sophisticated comedy. Spencer Tracy and Gable
> get over well. The Marx Brothers fell flat; they just don't see the point. What
> I think is the best policy is just to get people into a seat and simply pour
> entertainment into them.[85]

When asked by social surveys why they preferred certain types of
film, 'escapism' was the most featured response by working-class audiences, irrespective of age or gender..[86] In another survey, unemployed
men explained that the 'pictures help you live in another world for a
little while'.[87] Even in South Wales, workers' film groups struggled to
find much support for showing didactic left-wing films, even when they
targeted older and committed trade unionists. It soon became apparent
that the hardened politicised trade unionist much preferred Hollywood
films since, as one historian has noted, 'the typical working-class cinema-
goer in the depressed south Wales valleys of the 1930s was already fully
cognisant with the lives and struggles of the workers without having to
see them drearily restaged on the screen'.[88] Indeed, a rare insight into male
working-class film tastes is provided by a group of unemployed miners
in Blaenavon who filmed, acted in and produced their own silent film in
1928. The film included a 'highway robbery, high upon the windswept
moors of Blaenavon, a duel in a garden, a dramatic escape of a lovely
heroine from a picturesque Welsh castle, set amid the romantic mountains
of Gwent; a family feud, a wicked Major and a highwayman.'[89] Clearly,
this melodrama and escapist action were far removed from the day-to-day
realities of Welsh coalmining.

The cinema, then, was the most important commercial entertainment
in working-class communities, integrating effortlessly into working people's
leisure habits, surpassing the popularity of the music hall and becoming
a key cultural institution. Although older males were less enthused than
their younger counterparts and female devotees, there can be no doubt that
the popularity of the cinema cut across gender and generation and was
infused with working-class traits. Audience behaviour, at times, resembled
the horseplay of the working-class neighbourhoods, while – like the music
hall – the cinema became a meeting place for men and women alike. The
preference in films also shows a continuity in working-class entertainment

tastes, with the escapist and often crude comic plots of popular films representing a smooth transition from the similar music hall genre. The escapist
nature of the cinema also ensured that the film makers' messages of social
cohesion were left behind in the cinema auditorium. Contemporaries and
subsequent historians have underestimated the ability of working people
to consume mass commercial leisure on their own terms and within their
own forged environments. The cinema, then, must be seen in a broader
cultural context, which, like its predecessors such as rational recreation and
music hall, evolved from attempting to shape working-class leisure patterns
to becoming more responsive to the demands of popular culture.

The final form of mass communication that this chapter will investigate,
one linked to the commercial leisure boom in entertainment, is the radio.
Like reading and cinema-going, national broadcasts during the 1930s have
been cited as helping to preserve a social cohesion that protected Britain
from the social unrest manifest on the continent. Although radio sets were
available from the 1920s, widespread working-class radio ownership only
really took off during the late 1930s. Three million households possessed
a radio in 1930, a figure which had tripled by 1939 and accounted for
approximately three-quarters of the households in Britain.[90] Even families
in the poorest areas, it seems, were able to afford the battery-powered
'entry' model of radio set, which would cost, by the early 1930s, a couple
of pounds or 1 or 2 shillings per week on hire purchase.[91] Orwell noted
on his travels to Wigan Pier that 'twenty million people are underfed but
literally everyone in England has access to a radio'.[92] From radio's very
inception the establishment realised that such a popular form of home
entertainment was also a powerful form of communication. Indeed, the
radio could potentially rectify the perceived damaging effect that new commercial forms of leisure such as the cinema had on active citizenship in
Britain. The British Broadcasting Corporation, which in 1926 became the
first major public corporation of the twentieth century, was charged with
this responsibility. Although independent from government, the BBC was
responsible to a government minister, the Paymaster General. John Reith,
the first Director-General of the BBC, was an enthusiastic proponent of
the BBC's role of educator in civic values. Dismissing the suggestion that
radio was essentially a form of entertainment and maintaining that it was an
important role in cultural education, Reith remarked that 'few people know
what they want and very few what they need'.[93] The intention to cleanse
aspects of popular culture by carefully marshalling its output was echoed by

another BBC employee, Roger Wilson. In the mid-1930s, Wilson outlined the BBC's policy relating to light entertainment, and explained that

> listeners were provided a standard of taste in amusement. They may or may not like it, but at least it is a standard by the side of which they can set their non-broadcast entertainment and reach a critical decision. If listeners come to the conclusion that they can be entertained without vulgarity, taste in humour may change.[94]

In many respects, Reith and his fellow policymakers advocated the position that the state should act as guardian of the nation's culture, an assumption which was first put forward by Matthew Arnold in the nineteenth century and had permeated twentieth-century thinking through the work of Leavis.[95] For all three strands of thinking, the preservation of high culture was imperative as it was linked with good citizenship and the incorporation of the working class into the social, economic and political institutions of British society. The social tensions that provoked Arnold's discourse in the nineteenth century were as tangible to Leavis and Reith in the socially divided 1930s. However, the radio heralded a solution to the perceived cultural degeneration, a solution which, for some progressives, could foster good citizenship and democracy. John Grierson, a progressive 1930s' documentary film maker, noted that the twentieth century had brought a certain pessimism, since

> because the citizen under modern conditions could not know everything about everything all the time, democratic citizenship was therefore impossible. We set to thinking how a dramatic apprehension of the modern scene might solve the problem, and we turned to the new wide-reaching instruments of radio and cinema as necessary instruments both in the practice of government and the enjoyment of citizenship.[96]

This solution lay in what was termed the science of the 'neotechnic age', and was enthusiastically taken up by Reith's BBC, which asserted the right to broadcast a range of political, religious, monarchical and ceremonial events drawing working-class people into a realm that hitherto had been exclusively for the privileged. In the most thoroughgoing analysis of the BBC, Scannell and Cardiff have noted that 'particular publics were replaced by the *general* public constituted in and by the general nature of the mixed programme service and its general, unrestricted availability'.[97]

Such was the pervasiveness of the radio, its ability to speak directly to working-class families in their homes, that historians have credited sound broadcasting as a stabilising influence on the nation. In a famous comment on the lack of revolutionary fervour in 1930s Britain, Orwell placed the radio alongside other small luxuries enjoyed by the working class which dampened dissent:

> Of course the post-war development of cheap luxuries has been a very fortunate thing for our rulers. It is quite likely that fish-and-chips, art-silk stockings, tinned salmon, cut-price chocolate (five two-ounce bars for sixpence), the movies, the radio, strong tea, and the football pools have between them averted revolution.[98]

More recently, Stevenson has contended that 'in many ways radio merely made more effective the national cohesion already established by the press, the railways and mass education before 1914 ... in 1926 it had provided one of the crucial mediums of government control.'[99] The private nature of radio listening, of course, creates problems for the historian attempting to assess its impact upon working-class families and their relationship with citizenry and democracy. However, a sense of its impact can be registered by examining *how* and *why* people listened to the radio, and by considering its function within the working-class family.

From the inception of radio during the 1920s, its purchase and operation of the radio had largely been the preserve of males in both middle-class and working-class households. For women, particularly when in the 1930s radio sets became more sophisticated and reception improved, the radio was a welcome distraction while performing domestic duties. For men it was a new toy. One social commentator during the 1920s commented that 'it seems to women that the last thing men want to do with their wireless set is to listen in. They want to play with it, fiddle with it incessantly, just as they do with their cars.'[100] It is also clear that the BBC's attempt at culturally educating the masses with 'highbrow' discussion programmes and classical concerts required an attentive audience sitting quietly around the radio. Although this image is often invoked, supported by contemporary photographs of families gathered around the radio for announcements of national importance, the reality of the matter was that for working-class families the radio was often background entertainment. Unlike in middle-class families, which were more discriminating in their radio listening, in working-class households, for the most part, the radio was switched on for most of the day to provide some distraction from the daily chores.[101] This, of course, could be particularly annoying for anyone in the household who actually wanted to listen to something attentively, as one late 1930s' survey on listening habits in South Wales discovered:

> Seven Toscanini concerts will during the month of May be thankfully received by many homes in this area. There will be homes where he will be treated respectfully by people of a minority which is growing. But in most of our homes he will have to 'rough it' and take his chance in the hurly-burly with Music Halls, Sing-Songs, Serials – and all the fun o' the fair. As he conducts women will knit and sew whilst waiting patiently for something they would much prefer, but can't get because the most musically minded son of the house insists on having what his father says is 'nothing more than a row'. The concert is interrupted by the coming and going in the room of other members of the family, each of whom asks: 'what's the row now?' Father growls 'ask me another' and the solitary listener groans inwardly. Neighbours call, enter the room and, not knowing Toscanini, state and discuss their business without lowering their voices.[102]

Thus, whereas the middle-class listener would be tuned in for specific programmes and turn off the radio when they ended, in the working-class household, one report despaired, 'little or no discrimination was shown in the choice of items. Very often the set was turned on in the early morning and left running for the greater part of the day.' The report did note that male listening habits were fairly pronounced, in that 'serious' programmes were not among their listening preferences:

> Plays and talks were for the most part rejected or, if some interest was evinced, it was usually stifled by complaints from other members of the family. Anything more serious than Saturday Night 'Music Hall' was dismissed as 'Highbrow' … Most men could recite with little difficulty the names of the various dance bands and their leaders. They could state the exact times when these were to be heard. They did not confine themselves to the home stations, but travelled far and wide to satisfy their thirst for 'swing' and 'rhythm'.

For the young, radio listening was not simply a home-based activity, as public houses capitalised on the interwar dance craze and invited customers to listen to radio broadcasts on their premises. For example, one northern public house during the 1920s asked patrons to 'come and spend an evening with us and listen to the World's greatest concert Artistes. All the latest news and the finest concerts given every evening.'[103] This was a far cry from the BBC's model family listening in silence to culturally fulfilling programmes. In addition, Reith's high ideals of high cultural enlightenment fell flat since, for working-class families, the radio was an additional household appliance which could aid their existing recreational interests rather than replace them. Furthermore, Reith had not bargained for listeners tuning in to the continental stations that had adopted 'American' type broadcasting techniques. This less formalised broadcasting, offered by stations such as Radio Normandie (established in 1931) and Radio Luxembourg (established in 1933), scheduled shorter programmes, which played popular music, hit parades and British and American comedy without the grand culturally elevating medicine prescribed by the BBC. These independent stations relied on advertising for funds and were conscious of the need to tap into popular tastes, a situation which saw a significant number of working-class listeners switch from the BBC, particularly during their dry Sunday programming schedules.[104] Indeed, in 1938 the most comprehensive survey of listening habits, conducted by two of the leading advertising societies, estimated that on Sundays Radio Luxembourg and Radio Normandie attracted audiences of about 4 million and 2.5 million respectively. The BBC's reduced output on Sundays (broadcasting began at 10.30 a.m.) and its sombre musical content ensured that in every contemporary listening survey commissioned before the Second World War the commercial radio stations generally recorded higher listening figures than the BBC.[105]

According to Nott, by the mid-1930s commercial radio provided a 'complete and national service which offered a viable alternative to the BBC'.[106] Moreover, the corporation faced criticism from the press for its oppressive image and 'general condemnation' from working-class listeners for its Sunday programming. It was within this context that in 1936 Reith reluctantly commissioned a listener survey into the habits and tastes of the radio audience. The survey's results, though unsurprising, confirmed that social class rather than gender structured the listening habits of the nation. With few regional differences, the researchers discovered that a higher proportion of the middle class than the working class liked listening to Shakespeare, while more working-class listeners wanted more variety programmes. Social class also appeared to be the determining factor on whether a listener switched over to the commercial stations on a Sunday, since 47 per cent of the working-class and 28 per cent of the middle-class audience tuned into either Radio Luxembourg or Radio Normandie on a Sunday. Although similar surveys on commercial radio listeners did find significant regional variations in audience size (possibly due to reception problems), they concurred with the BBC's research, which indicated that the listener's social class often informed his or her radio choices. Indeed, evidence suggests that the commercial stations targeted the working- and lower-middle-class audience, broadcasting popular programmes at strategic times of the day to capture these groups' work routines.[107]

Conclusion

The nineteenth-century term 'pleasure seekers' was never more apt than as a description of working-class mass leisure habits between the wars. Contemporary anxieties of degeneracy in a higher culture and citizenry pervaded the two decades, while more recent historians have claimed that the new forms of mass communication, literature, cinema and radio were powerful forces of social cohesion. This chapter has argued that there can be little doubt that a significant section of the entertainment in print, film or on the airwaves was, consciously or not, actively supportive of the status quo and social stability. However, the assumption that this propaganda was successfully transmitted to a wide-eyed public is problematic. Working-class men during this period were manipulating their environment for their own ends and finding a commercial sector willing to respond. Be it in literature, cinema or radio, working-class males imposed their own layer of meaning and enjoyment, a trait in their culture which stretched back into the nineteenth century.

Notes

1   S. G. Jones, *Workers at Play. A Social and Economic History of Leisure 1918–1939* (London, Routledge & Kegan Paul, 1986), p. 38.

2   J. Stevenson and C. Cook, *Britain in the Depression. Society and Politics 1929–39* (London, Longman, 1994), ch. 14. For a more detailed critique of this revisionist position, see the section below on the impact of cinema.

3   D. Vincent, 'Reading in the Working-Class Home', in J. K. Walton and J. Walvin (eds), *Leisure in Britain, 1780–1939* (Manchester, Manchester University Press, 1983).

4   *Cov Magazine*, 1:2 (April 1939), 1:4 (June 1939).

5   J. Stevenson, *British Society 1914–45* (Harmondsworth, Penguin, 1984), p. 398.

6   J. McAleer, *Popular Reading and Publishing in Britain 1914–1950* (Oxford, Clarendon Press, 1992), p. 54.

7   Stevenson, *British Society 1914–45*, p. 398.

8 N. Joicey, 'A Paperback Guide to Progress: Penguin Books 1935–1951', *Twentieth Century British History*, 4 (1993), 41, 56.

9 J. Symons, *The Thirties. A Dream Revolved* (London, Faber & Faber, 1960), p. 94.

10 Symons, *The Thirties. A Dream Revolved*, p. 94.

11 G. Orwell, 'Coming Up for Air', in *The Complete Novels* (1939; Harmondsworth, Penguin, 1983), p. 519.

12 F. R. Leavis, *Mass Civilisation and Minority Culture* (Cambridge, Minority Press, 1930), p. 8.

13 E. B Castle et al., *The Coming of Leisure. The Problem in England* (London, New Education Fellowship, 1935), p. 52.

14 C. Madge and T. Harrisson, *Britain* (Harmondsworth, Penguin, 1939), p. 9.

15 Tom Harrisson Mass-Observation Archive (THMOA), microfiche 41A–46, File Report 1937–49 'Book Reading in Wartime. Report on material obtained from publishers, book clubs, libraries and book sellers'.

16 McAleer, *Popular Reading and Publishing in Britain*, pp. 47, 79.

17 G. Orwell, *Keep the Aspidistra Flying* (London, Secker & Warburg, 1936), pp. 246–7.

18 Quoted in McAleer, *Popular Reading and Publishing in Britain*, p. 58.

19 THMOA, microfiche 41A–46, 'Book Reading'.

20 McAleer, *Popular Reading and Publishing in Britain*, p. 82.

21 C. Cameron et al., *Disinherited Youth. A Report on the 18+ Age Group Enquiry Prepared for the Trustees of the Carnegie United Kingdom Trust* (Edinburgh, T. & A. Constable, 1943), p. 101.

22 University of Sussex, Mass-Observation Archive, *Report on Books and the Public. A Study of Buying, Borrowing, Keeping, Selecting, Remembering, Giving and Reading Books* (File Report 1332), July 1942.

23 THMOA, microfiche 41A–46, 'Book Reading'.

24 Vincent, 'Reading in the working-class home'.

25 THMOA, microfiche 41A–46, 'Book Reading'.

26 Cameron et al., *Disinherited Youth*, p. 101.

27 Public Record Office (hereafter PRO), HO 45/10811/312397/1 'Cinema Commission Inquiry', 1917.

28 P. Corrigan, 'Film entertainment as ideology and pleasure: A preliminary approach to a history of audiences', in J. Curran and V. Porter (eds), *British Cinema History* (London, Weidenfeld & Nicolson, 1983), pp. 27–8.

29 Jones, *Workers at Play*, p. 37.

30 J. Richards, *The Age of the Dream Palace. Cinema and Society in Britain 1930–1939* (London, Routledge, 1984), pp. 58–60.

31 Richards, *The Age of the Dream Palace*, pp. 58–60.

32 Castle et al., *The Coming of Leisure*, p. 68.

33 W. Boyd (ed.), *The Challenge of Leisure* (London, New Education Fellowship, 1936), p. 132.

34 B. S. Rowntree, *Poverty and Progress. A Second Social Survey of York* (London, Longman, 1941), pp. 46–7.

35 Leavis, *Mass Civilisation and Minority Culture*, pp. 10, 30.

36 J. P. Mayer, *British Cinemas and their Audiences* (London, Dennis Dobson, 1948), p. 249.

37 *The Times*, 5 March 1932.

38 H. A. Secretan, *London Below Bridges. Its Boys and its Future* (London, Geoffrey Bles, 1931), p. 86.

39 *Truth*, 6 September 1933.

40 Mayer, *British Cinemas and their Audiences*, pp. 130–1.

41 C. Burt, *The Young Delinquent* (London, University of London Press, 1925), pp. 147–50.

42 Richards, *The Age of the Dream Palace*, p. 62.

43 A Davies, 'Cinema and broadcasting', in P. Johnson (ed.), *Twentieth Century Britain* (London, Longman, 1994), pp. 265, 270; A. Davies, *Leisure, Gender and Poverty. Working-Class Culture in Salford and Manchester: 1900–1939* (Milton Keynes, Open University Press, 1992), p. ix.

44 T. Aldgate, 'Comedy, class and containment: The British domestic cinema of the 1930s', in Curran and Porter (eds), *British Cinema History*, p. 270; Richards, *The Age of the Dream Palace*, p. 324.

45 Stevenson and Cook, *Britain in the Depression*, ch. 14.

46 J. Sedgwick, *Popular Filmgoing in 1930s Britain. A Choice of Pleasures* (Exeter, University of Exeter, 2000), p. 47.

47 P. Miles and M. Smith, *Cinema, Literature and Society* (London, Croom Helm, 1987), p. 164.

48 Secretan, *London Below Bridges*, p. 84.

49 Cameron et al., *Disinherited Youth*, p. 104.

50 Cameron et al., *Disinherited Youth*, p. 104.

51 W. Woodruff, *The Road to Nab End. An Extraordinary Northern Childhood* (London, Abacus, 2002), p. 176.

52 A. Kuhn, *An Everyday Magic. Cinema and Cultural Memory* (London, I. B. Tauris, 2002), p. 48.

53 S. Ridgwell, 'Pictures and proletarians: South Wales miners' cinemas in the 1930s', *Llafur*, 7:1 (1996), 70.

54 R. McKibbin, *Classes and Cultures. England 1918–1951* (Oxford, Oxford University Press, 1998), p. 422.

55 McKibbin, *Classes and Cultures*, p. 420; see also M. Chamberlain, *Growing up in Lambeth* (London, Virago, 1989), p. 26.

56 H. L. Llewellyn Smith, *The New Survey of London Life and Labour. Life and Leisure*, vol. IX (London, P. S. King & Son, 1935), p. 46; Jones, *Workers at Play*, p. 60.

57 Richards, *Age of the Dream Palace*, p. 15.

58 R. Roberts, *The Classic Slum. Salford Life in the First Quarter of the Century* (Manchester, Manchester University Press, 1971), p. 175.

59 Kuhn, *An Everyday Magic*, p. 2.

60 *Film Weekly*, 14 September 1934.

61 Richards, *Age of the Dream Palace*, p. 17; S. Harper, 'A middle-class taste community in the 1930s: The case of the Regent Cinema, Portsmouth', *Historical Journal of Film, Radio and Television* (forthcoming).

62 Richards, *Age of the Dream Palace*, p. 16.

63 Roberts, *The Classic Slum*, p. 176.

64 Aldgate, 'Comedy, class and containment: The British domestic cinema of the 1930s', pp. 268–70.

65 Kuhn, *An Everyday Magic*, p. 4.

66 S. Harper, *Picturing the Past. The Rise and Fall of the British Costume Film* (London, British Film Institute, 1994), p. 61.

67 Sedgwick, *Popular Filmgoing in 1930s Britain*, p. 6.

68 Woodruff, *The Road to Nab End*, p. 176.

69 D. Mayall, 'Palaces for entertainment and instruction: A study of early cinema in Birmingham, 1908–18', *Midland History*, 2 (1985), 98.

70 *Film Weekly*, 16 February 1934.

71 PRO, MEPO 2/7497/8, 'Report on the Rank Picture Show', 1916.

72 PRO, MEPO 2/7497/7, 'Report on Rank Cinema', 1916.

73 PRO, MEPO 2/7497/13, 'Report on Rank Cinema', 1916.

74 For more examples of this type of behaviour, see N. Hiley, '"Let's go to the pictures": The British cinema audience in the 1920s and 1930s', *Journal of Popular British Cinema*, 2 (1999); J. Hill, *Sport, Leisure and Culture in Twentieth Century Britain* (London, Palgrave, 2002), pp. 59–63.

75 A. Kuhn, 'Cinema-going in Britain in the 1930s: Report of a questionnaire survey', *Historical Journal of Film, Radio and Television*, 19 (1999), 540.

76 For contemporary survey on teenage leisure and Fowler's conclusions on the impact of cinema, see D. Fowler, *The First Teenagers. The Lifestyle of Young Wage-Earners in Interwar Britain* (London, Woburn Press, 1995), p. 132.

77 *Film Weekly*, 9 November 1934.

78 McKibbin, *Classes and Cultures*, p. 423.

79 M. Abendstern, 'Expression and control: A study of working-class leisure and gender 1918–39. A case study of Rochdale using oral history methods', Ph.D. thesis, University of Essex, 1986, p. 109.

80 C. Cameron, *Disinherited Youth*, p. 104.

81 *Film Weekly*, 4 January 1935.

82 G. Orwell, *The Road to Wigan Pier* (1937; Harmondsworth, Penguin, 1974), p. 72.

83 *Film Weekly*, 6 March 1934.

84 W. Boyd et al., *The Challenge of Leisure*, p. 131.

85 G. Cross (ed.), *Worktowners at Blackpool. Mass-Observation and Popular Leisure in the 1930s* (London, Routledge, 1990), p. 135.

86 C. Cameron, *Disinherited Youth*, p. 104.

87 E.W. Bakke, *Unemployed Man. A Social Study* (London, Nesbit, 1933), p. 182.

88 Ridgwell, 'Pictures and proletarians: South Wales miners' cinemas in the 1930s', p. 78.

89 *Film Weekly*, 7 November 1928.

90 P. Scannell and D. Cardiff, *A Social History of British Broadcasting. Volume One 1922–1939. Serving the Nation* (Oxford, Blackwell, 1991), pp. 260–2.

91 Stevenson, *British Society 1914–45*, p. 408.

92 Orwell, *The Road to Wigan Pier*, p. 80.

93 Stevenson, *British Society 1914–45*, p. 410.

94 Boyd, *The Challenge of Leisure*, p. 139.

95 M. Arnold, *Culture and Anarchy* (Cambridge, Cambridge University Press, 1932).

96 Quoted in Scannell and Cardiff, *A Social History of British Broadcasting*, p. 13.

97 Scannell and Cardiff, *A Social History of British Broadcasting*, p. 14.

98 Orwell, *The Road to Wigan Pier*, p. 80.

99 Stevenson, *British Society 1914–45*, p. 410.

100 Scannell and Cardiff, *A Social History of British Broadcasting*, p. 358.

101 McKibbin, *Classes and Cultures*, p. 458.

102 Quoted in Scannell and Cardiff, *A Social History of British Broadcasting*, p. 373.

103 Abendstern, 'Expression and Control', p. 111

104 Cameron et al., *Disinherited Youth*, p. 102; Morgan, *The Needs of Youth*, p. 245.

105 The leading advertising societies were the Institute of Incorporated Practitioners in Advertising (IIPA) and the Incorporated Society of British Advertisers (ISBA), which jointly produced the *Survey of Listening to Sponsored Radio Programmes* in 1938; J. J. Nott, *Music for the People. Popular Music and Dance in Interwar Britain* (Oxford, Oxford University Press, 2002), p. 72.

106 Nott, *Music for the People*, p. 67.

107 Nott, *Music for the People*, p. 73.

7

Male leisure and citizenship in the Second World War

It is perhaps fitting that in a book which considers male leisure and notions of citizenship, the final chapter should investigate the impact of the Second World War on working communities. Never before had the leisure of the working class been so systematically scrutinised by the state through a network of intelligence officers and researchers. The era of total war had propelled the civilian to centre stage and the British Government watched nervously to see how he or she would respond to enemy bombardment. As we have seen, male leisure patterns were of concern to the establishment and were closely bound to narratives of social citizenship throughout the period under study. The Second World War saw this process intensified. Good citizenship would not only maintain morale levels but also prepare the nation for the new and very different society following post-war reconstruction. The war also brought about a greater awareness of female citizenship, which was often framed in a very different fashion to the qualities associated with the 'good' male citizen. This chapter begins with a discussion of how historians have traditionally interpreted the war as a force for change in social relations and cultural values. The study will then explore how the government established a network of intelligence officers and researchers to investigate working-class leisure activities in a bid to define 'good' citizenship and morale. The final question addressed is whether total war and the ensuing national crisis created the conditions in which working people were more willing to conform to government-defined 'acceptable' modes of citizenry and leisure.

Orthodox accounts of the home front during the Second World War have stressed the new sense of social unity that a common enemy brought. It is argued that the social conflict of the prewar period was eclipsed by a greater understanding between the classes, a situation engendered, in no small way, by the working class's central role in war production. The origins of this interpretation can be traced back to Richard Titmuss's postwar study, which claimed that the military debacle at Dunkirk, the Blitz and the real threat of invasion that followed fostered a sense of shared danger which was transmogrified into a sense of 'doing one's bit' for the nation and of 'pulling together'. Writing almost immediately after the euphoria of victory, Titmuss declared that the 'mood of the people changed and, in sympathetic response, values changed as well'.[1] The premiss that total war brought an unprecedented understanding between the social classes and a more enlightened social policy formed the central plank of Marwick's four-tier model of the impact of war. Citing contemporary newspaper reports which regularly reminded their readers that a new era of social cooperation had emerged due to wartime conditions, Marwick maintained that a period of social levelling occurred between 1939 and 1945. 'Over a brief period of time substantial sections of British society were thrown into a gigantic cocktail shaker, even if shortly the snooty vermouth might insist on separating off from the humble gin.'[2] More recently, Ziegler, writing about wartime social relations in the capital, claimed that 'nothing could destroy overnight a system that had grown up over centuries, but London was more nearly classless at this period than ever before or since.'[3]

Angus Calder was the first historian to express doubts about the social-cohesiveness model of the Second World War in his book *The Myth of the Blitz*. This seminal study demonstrated how the key propaganda institutions created a powerful myth of the social unity of the British during wartime. While Calder confined his research to the organs of propaganda, historians such as Summerfield began to question whether war did in fact bridge the gaping socio-economic divide between the working and middle classes and create a greater understanding between social groups. Through a detailed analysis of wages, savings and spending patterns, Summerfield argued that the true beneficiaries of the war were generally middle class. Wealthy investors who had the means to channel their savings into lucrative long-term financial portfolios made for a stark contrast with the working class, who, due to spiralling prices, saved little and lived on a subsistence basis.[4]

Recently, however, there have been attempts to resurrect more traditional interpretations of the nation's wartime spirit. For example, Mackay has argued that '"the negative" features emphasized by revisionist historians, although indisputably present, were not on such a scale as to invalidate the orthodox picture of a people who became actively committed to the project their leaders put before them.' He concludes that both the people and the authorities operated 'within a mental framework of common identity and shared destiny – "the invisible chain" – that determined civilian morale'.[5] Clearly at the heart of this debate is our understanding of *how* morale was generated in working communities.[6] One possible way forward would be to combine an analysis of official communiqués to the public offering advice on 'good' citizenship with an investigation of the impact of that advice on working-class morale and leisure patterns.[7] Government advice was closely tied in with wartime propaganda designed to uplift public morale, particularly during the dark days of the Blitz. Moreover, as we have seen, a large part of becoming a 'good' citizen was the adoption of 'appropriate' leisure activities, and in this respect narratives of citizenship did not differ from peacetime. However, during the period 1850–1939 notions of 'good' citizenship offered from above were largely rejected or sidestepped by working men preferring a more immediate frame of reference located within their own culture. Clearly, then, tracking the impact that war had upon male leisure and notions of citizenship will shed light on the extent to which working people embraced a shared social unity.

Government Intelligence: citizenry, morale and the Mass-Observers

Total war brought to the forefront questions about community identity and national solidarity, since diversity and division within a nation during times of crisis were seen as problematic. The focus on what it was to be a 'good' citizen became even more intense during this period as social citizenship was the concept which linked individuals to the state or nation. As with earlier notions of social citizenship, social cohesion was the chief objective, a goal which became even more imperative during a period of national crisis. The Federation of British Industries, for example, pronounced that the Blitz had 'already linked London's east and west in a new sense of civic unity and responsibility', while in December 1940 Seebohm Rowntree declared that there was a 'growing spirit of friendliness

between class and class'.[8] Social citizenship, as we have seen in the previous chapters, had overriding moral characteristics that emphasised the
obligations of the individual. Although these moral characteristics altered
over time, the purpose of social citizenship was to determine a person's
behaviour as a member of the nation. One difference that war brought,
however, was that the scope of citizenship was widened further after
1939. Between 1850 and 1939 notions of citizenship expressed by social
commentators, youth workers and government officials were generally
framed for the male worker due to their perceived increasing public role
in British society during this period. However, the more prominent role
of women in the war brought their behaviour, particularly in their leisure
time, under closer scrutiny.

Although there had been isolated outbreaks of moral panic over the
sexual morality of women during the Great War, the Second World War
witnessed a more concerted attempt to define the private sphere of women.[9]
While narratives of social citizenship had attempted to encourage male virtue
in public life, a strand of citizenship during the Second World War was
directed towards improving women's maternal duties and sexual activities.
In particular the 'slum' mother was targeted, as according to the Ministry
of Health they were 'idle, verminous, extravagant, ungrateful, prone to
heavy drinking, unable to sew and mend, ignorant of basic nutrition and
reliant upon the can-opener and prepared foods'.[10] In a similar vein, *The
Times* noted that the evacuation of working-class mothers and children
into middle-class suburbs and rural retreats had uncovered an underbelly
of degeneration in the great urban cities. A leading article in *The Times*
contended that some working-class mothers knew little of the 'rudiments
of cooking and housecraft' and subsequently raised animalistic children
who were frequently 'destructive and defiant, foulmouthed, liars and pilfer-
ers'.[11] Moreover, not only was the nation's health at risk; government was
also concerned that its attempt to create a unified community that put
national interests first was being undermined by fun-loving and sexually
expressive women. Indeed, it was no coincidence that womens' pub-going
activities were the subject of at least two lengthy reports carried out by
the Mass-Observation unit (M-O) in 1943. In the first report, the observer
noted that 'flirtation and public accosting by girls clearly not in the class
of professional prostitutes has become a fairly frequent occurrence ...
girls of the artisan and working class [of] respectable appearance can be
seen in central London with allied soldiers.'[12] This moral panic over the

perceived sexual laxity of women has led Rose to assume that this purely moral rhetoric could take on gendered inflections, and that consequently 'class was less important than virtuous behaviour in defining the members of the national community'.[13] However, if we step back from the contemporary discussion on female 'pleasure seekers', it is clear that all other areas of working-class life, such as the family, work and male leisure, were subject to the same intense scrutiny from government officials and social observers. It is apparent that although social citizenship during the Second World War developed gendered strands, they were constructed to encounter 'problems' only associated with the working class.[14] It was working-class men and women who were most public in their leisure activities, be it the cinema, dance hall, public house or the street. The public sphere, clearly important before the war, took on a new significance since it was one of the few ways in which the authorities could measure civilian morale during the conflict.

Although discourse on the state of civilian morale features in both contemporary and academic accounts of the Second World War, both perspectives have had to grapple with the difficult problem of how to define and research the popular mood of the nation. As a result, although civilian morale is often referred to, its source and function are rarely analysed. Evidence gathered by the Government and M-O, which undertook extensive research into civilian morale during the blitz, provides the historian with an opportunity to assess how the Government framed notions of citizenship to encourage 'good' morale and reflect upon how the 'people' responded. However, historians have viewed this evidence with some scepticism, since the Government and the M-O movement were unclear what morale actually was and how it should be defined.[15] Criticised at the time as the work of an uninformed 'intelligentsia',[16] M-O focused upon people's attitudes and behaviour in the aftermath of the raids and was concerned with immediate and specific considerations. Except at the most peripheral level, it did not concern itself with more sophisticated methodologies centring upon longitudinal or comparative studies.[17] This was perhaps not surprising since it was not until 1943 that the Home Office itself came to recognise that the factors affecting post-raid morale must necessarily be located within a broad conceptual framework.[18] Government officials also found it difficult to define the precise nature, and therefore variations in the level, of public morale. As Addison notes, 'morale was the woolliest and most muddled concept of the war'.[19] The Mass-Observers relied upon a range of quasi-psychological and more general assessments of the public mood. Sometimes these were of a highly scientific nature relating to individuals, while other assessments sought to summarise group attitudes and behaviour. Even with the benefit of hindsight, official histories of the Second World War acknowledged that morale 'cannot be easily classified, let alone measured, especially by those who lack the perspective that only time can give'.[20]

Since the government officials and M-O researchers who prepared intelligence documents for the British Cabinet largely comprised a small social and intellectual elite, the final reports tended to fall back on a preoccupation with regional stereotypes, disregarding other possible facets of working-class life. However, many of the preliminary findings that provided useful insights into working-class morale during the blitz were overlooked in the final reports due to preconceived notions of the working-class character. Despite their methodological limitations, the M-O reports do provide a useful basis upon which to analyse the public mood following periods of heavy air bombardment, particularly when placed within a comparative framework.[21] Moreover, although definitions are unclear, M-O appeared to define 'good' morale as a feeling of confidence and optimism within a community or social grouping.

The organisation's network of local voluntary workers and small core of full-time trained personnel accumulated a formidable body of information. One of the great strengths of M-O was its independence for as Harrisson noted, 'units of trained investigators were sent anonymously to blitz-towns to make overall reports, prepared regardless of any official accounts, departmental feelings or published glosses'.[22] As with any research, the M-O's trained observers were not free from the problems of subjectivity, despite Harrisson's pronouncements to the contrary. The M-O investigators' preconceived stereotype of regional working-class culture was influential in shaping their preferred public responses to a blitz attack and was fed back into model citizen behaviour espoused by the Government. To understand this process it is necessary to investigate the assumptions that underpinned the M-O organisation.

The Mass-Observation movement was founded by Tom Harrisson, Humphrey Jennings and Charles Madge, three left-wing intellectuals from middle-class backgrounds who established the organisation with the desire to develop a 'science of ourselves'. The main focus of the research was the British working class, as Harrisson, like many of his middle-class contemporaries, felt he knew more about the 'savages' of Borneo than the 'savages' of northern England. Whilst earlier social inquiries by researchers, such as Booth, Rowntree and Pember-Reeves, had been stimulated by concerns over working-class poverty, the M-O organisation emerged from the fear that there was an increasing dislocation between the people and parliament. As a result, in one of their first publications, Harrisson and Madge stated that

> It is the function of the 615 members of our democratic parliament to voice the wishes, feelings, wants, needs, hopes, opinions, grouses, aspirations and criticisms of 45,000,000 people. But this democratic system has broken down in other countries, and may break down in our own, because the 45,000,000 do not feel sufficiently strongly that they are able to speak through parliament. So they give it up as a bad job and resign themselves to being voiceless or get annoyed with the whole system.[23]

Madge and Harrisson's investigation of working-class attitudes was motivated by the belief that their efforts would help to preserve democracy and ward off the growing threat of fascism. The assumption that official reports from the media and the establishment on the state of the nation were at odds with what people actually thought helped shape the research methodologies that M-O adopted throughout its existence. This mistrust of officialdom ensured that M-O employed largely two main research methods designed to tap into an undercurrent of the public's thoughts and activities, which lay beneath the establishment's propaganda. The first technique comprised volunteers secretly noting down what they saw and heard, while the second relied on volunteers who were prepared to keep in-depth diaries of their activities and thoughts.[24]

Although during the Second World War M-O continued to critique Britain's political leadership for its remoteness, the organisation turned its attention towards producing maximum efficiency in government and industry. M-O defined 'efficiency' as gaining the maximum war effort from the population, an ambition which meant that M-O's original objectives – the desire to examine exactly what the British people were doing and thinking – became of paramount importance. This did not go unrecognised by the 'Home Intelligence' section of the Ministry of Information, which in 1940 commissioned M-O to survey the development and variations in morale.[25] The Government's interest in civilian morale stemmed from the belief that intense German bombing would initiate a large exodus from London and the provinces and that widespread panic would ensue. The civilian was compared unfavourably to the soldier, who was thought to be disciplined and trained in stress management. In contrast, the civilian was perceived as 'isolated, unattached and unorganised', being concerned more with self-preservation than with the national war effort.[26] The belief that mass panic and chaos would ensue immediately after the first air raids was, in fact, a widely held view during the interwar period, and was portrayed vividly in H. G. Wells's 1935 film *Things to Come*. This film was surprisingly re-released in 1940 as a second feature and served as a powerful reminder to the authorities that the public mood would require monitoring.[27] Early intelligence reports prior to any bombing in Britain appeared to support the Government's worst fears, as officers noted that few people followed official advice and instead 'did what they pleased'. In Bristol during one air-raid warning, it was noted that:

> wardens were walking about blowing whistles, but no one seemed to pay attention to them whatever. Many similar reports of public indifference to wardens' recommendations have been received. The incident is interesting as offering a possible indication of a crowd's action in circumstances of attack, i.e. they would herd straight into any obvious hollow regardless of its suitability for shelter or official recommendations to disperse.[28]

The Government's resolve to prepare for episodes of mass panic encouraged the search for intelligence from non-official channels, which in turn made them more sympathetic to the new research techniques that M-O could offer.

One of the major problems that M-O faced when assessing their morale report findings was to explain why there were variations in civilian morale. Since the researchers comprised largely middle-class volunteers, they had little understanding of the internal dynamics of working-class communities. In many respects, the M-O researchers simply reflected contemporary assumptions on the nature of working-class life.[29] Thus, in the 1930s after his social inquiry into the lives of working people in Britain, George Orwell concluded that 'the Northerner has "grit", he is grim, "dour", plucky, warm hearted and democratic; the Southerner is snobbish, effeminate and lazy'.[30] The postwar sociologist Ferdinand Zweig echoed Orwell's sentiments when researching the British worker in concluding that 'the worker in the North is like a hardy plant born against the background of a hard industrial struggle ... what is called the "industrial proletariat" *par excellence* is known in the North, but there is little of it in the South.'[31] Writing in a similar vein after the war, Titmuss implied that a certain northern endurance and hardiness may have explained the apparent good morale in Bootle during the Blitz:

> Many of these people had never known standards of home life, of space, quietness and stability, which other people accepted as a matter of course. They looked out on a world of disorder and instability with different eyes, for had they not grown up with hardship by their side during the years of unemployment? To them, leaking roofs, broken windows, no schools and a nightly trek to the open fields in spring-time meant less than the loss of a job.[32]

It is perhaps of little surprise, then, that when pressed to explain variations in civilian morale during the Blitz, M-O tended to resort to a-priori regional stereotypes and peculiar traits that the respective communities were reported to have possessed. For example, researchers recorded a high level of morale in Liverpool which was explained by the unique 'hardy' character of the city's population:

> Perhaps as important as the above conditioning, is Liverpool's previous peacetime conditioning of toughness and hardness. For many years there has been economic depression on Merseyside. There is some of the worst poverty and chronic unemployment in the country. The tradition of the sea is another toughening character of Liverpool ... apart from the general toughness associated with sea faring, there is a bi-product of some importance. Sailor's wives are used to living alone, without their husbands, for long periods. This stands them in good stead as compared with the wives of Coventry munition workers or Cockney bus conductors.[33]

Tom Harrisson later wrote that in Liverpool morale was preserved through 'a hardy northern tradition of endurance, which had come to climax within most memories with mass unemployment in 1931'.[34] Likewise, in assessing the initial response to the blitz in Southampton, a Mass-Observer concluded that 'the population of Southampton is to a high extent genuinely resident and locally interested. Southampton has deeper social roots than Coventry or Stepney. There is a certain tradition of local toughness, partly associated with the docks and the sea.'[35]

Another important factor which, according to M-O researchers, boosted civilian morale was the presence of the military. The 'cheerful effect' sailors and soldiers had on Liverpool were cited as possible influences on morale. It was found that the people of Liverpool welcomed the stationing of soldiers and sailors in the city, as they 'brought an atmosphere of revelry and holiday which they continued throughout air-raid warnings'.[36]

Plymouth was also highlighted as enjoying high morale due to the impact the navy had upon the town. One researcher noted a 'real cheerfulness everywhere' in Plymouth and observed that 'Plymouth nightlife [can] best be described as "terrific" mainly due to the navy. Pubs were open and crowded in the last hour. There was a great deal of singing, "Bless'em all" being the dominant song as in Liverpool.'[37]

By contrast, civilians who were deemed not to possess a 'hardy' character or who had not experienced a military presence within a city were, according to M-O researchers, susceptible to long periods of low morale. Thus Coventry, which had undergone a period of prosperity during the 1930s, was considered to lack a tradition of endurance, while Manchester was deemed to possess a 'background of softness' combined with a 'noticeable strain of selfishness and strict utilitarianism'.[38] These explanations for regional differences in civilian morale do not stand up to closer inspection once evidence from other areas is examined. For example, M-O had some difficulty in maintaining their thesis that regional characteristics and a military presence aided civilian morale when Southampton dipped to low levels of morale two weeks after the initial attack in November 1940.[39] Moreover, the M-O team were hard pressed to explain why Portsmouth, a city with a strong naval tradition deeply embedded in civilian life,[40] appeared to suffer from low levels of morale throughout the blitz. Six to nine days after the first blitz in 1941, it was reported that morale was 'not good': 'Portsmouth morale is the more striking in a town with a tough sea tradition. There are too many indicators pointing in the same direction to leave any doubt that there has been a serious emotional and confidence disturbance here.'[41]

Clearly, contemporary analysis and interpretation of blitzed cities by M-O researchers has its limitations. Despite these setbacks in determining an overarching hypothesis explaining variations in civilian morale, the M-O drew upon perceived working-class regional attributes when defining the characteristics of the 'good citizen'. Thus, in contrast with earlier notions of citizenship, the 'peoples' war' had encouraged public officials to celebrate perceived aspects of working-class culture in an effort to shape and maintain civilian morale. The moral codes framed in this very public sphere of citizenship were certainly masculine in nature and drew inspiration from the hardy male northerner stereotype propagated by the M-O researchers. While, as we have seen, women's ideal behaviour during the war was defined in the private sphere, be it their family responsibilities or sexual conduct, working-class male behaviour was framed in the public and highlighted the 'plucky, brave, heroic, self sacrificing' and, above all, 'cheerful' qualities of their culture. Although this was a war that involved all classes, it was the constant emphasis by social commentators from Priestley to Orwell that Britain was a unified land of 'ordinary people' which was perhaps most striking. Priestley maintained that the Blitz had produced a new and improved Londoner who had cast aside the social divisions of the interwar period when he wrote, 'in 1940–1, for once [we] felt free, companionable, even – except while waiting for the explosions – light hearted. It took bombs to deliver us.'[42]

Male leisure and civilian morale

In Britain generally, the importance of recreational institutions was belatedly recognised by the authorities. In the anticipation of a massive aerial attack, many public places in Britain were closed down on the outbreak of war.[43] There was also a moral dimension since some commentators argued that it was inappropriate that mass entertainment be provided when others were laying down their lives for their country. Such providers of entertainment could have stood accused of peddling frivolous distractions from a national crisis or even of lacking sufficient patriotism.[44] However, within a fortnight after the initial closure, cinemas reopened and in the following weeks theatres cautiously and sporadically opened their doors to the public once again.[45] In an about-turn, there was a sudden realisation that since the conflict had become labelled a 'people's war', aspects of popular culture could be actively celebrated to maintain morale. For example, a sanitised version of Victorian popular culture was portrayed in a number of films during and after the war, including *Variety Jubilee* (1943), *Champagne Charlie* (1944), *I'll be Your Sweetheart* (1945) and *Trottie True* (1949).[46] For example, the film *Champagne Charlie* depicts two rival nineteenth-century entertainers who join forces to defeat killjoys in the establishment who are intent on closing down music halls on decency grounds. Tommy Trinder, who plays George Leybourne the original Champagne Charlie, laments that 'they're trying to stop ordinary people having fun', a contemporary reference perhaps also to the draconian shut-down of music halls at the outbreak of war.[47] The importance of working-class leisure institutions was, however, recognised by intelligence officers who toured post-blitzed cities. A Home Office report on propaganda noted that 'in post blitz situations the function of entertainment in keeping up morale has sometimes been vigorously ignored'.[48] Indeed, after the Coventry blitz in 1941, the reconstruction and preservation of key popular leisure institutions was one of four recommendations designed to improve civilian morale after heavy bombardment.[49] By 1941, then, the Government had recognised that recreational institutions were an important form of escapism from the harsh realities of war and were fundamentally linked to variations in civilian morale. As we have seen in previous chapters, at the heart of working-class leisure patterns were the music hall, public house, club and the street, all important forums that were usually situated in working-class neighbourhoods towards the centre of the city. Even in cities such as Coventry where extensive suburbanisation had taken place, a large proportion of working-class people lived within close proximity to the city centre. As a consequence, such important leisure institutions were vulnerable to attack and dislocation.

Clearly, the topography of a city centre and the position of working-class leisure institutions within it would have a bearing on the impact that enemy bombardment would have on morale levels. For example, although Manchester received only three blitz-scale attacks, they were concentrated in the heart of the city, seriously affecting key institutions such as public houses, cinemas and public utilities, along with transport infrastructures which linked Manchester's centre with its suburban areas. An M-O report found that the local services, leisure institutions and transport were seriously affected and that the importance of these utilities in keeping up morale 'cannot be over-emphasised'.[50] The 'unco-ordinated' and 'overlapping' design of Manchester's city centre also ensured that just two severe bomb raids caused maximum devastation to the city's infrastructure and familiar landmarks. The morale-weakening effects that the destruction of Manchester's city centre had upon the population was described by an M-O volunteer: 'The concentration of damage, including town centre, is suggested as an important factor in reducing morale in Manchester, the damage has been less concentrated in Liverpool.'[51] Also the raids occurred on the Sunday and Monday before Christmas which, according to observers 'gave a tragic bitterness to the whole affair'.[52] Coventry's topographical features also ensured that the city's essential amenities were badly damaged. Commenting on the differences in topography between Coventry and London, one observer noted that in Coventry,

> the compression of damage in the city centre struck many as especially impressive. Here and there where social nuclei like the Cathedral and shopping

centre were destroyed, there was a powerful dual impact: a first sense of tragic loss, closely followed by a quite passionate interest, growing readily to pride. Again, London's size and scatter masked the effect: while many of London's oldest focal buildings never were destroyed ... in a place like Coventry the lot could go in one night. This struck at the heart of the community.[53]

In September 1940, a report on Coventry's city centre found an 'air of vitality and affluence', with 'smart clothes in the streets, prosperous looking homes, busy public houses, crowded shops, long queues outside the cinemas'.[54] A very different picture emerged in November after the first German bombardment. Approximately 100 acres of the city centre lay in ruins, with familiar landmarks such as the Cathedral, Empire Theatre and municipal swimming baths suddenly removed from public view.[55] Government officials on the scene were quick to identify the relationship between morale and leisure, as one civil servant noted that post-blitzed Coventry had few organised entertainments. Cinemas were open but with restricted hours, many public houses had been destroyed and, to cap it all, the city was suffering from a beer shortage.[56]

In contrast to Manchester and Coventry, less densely concentrated cities suffered less destruction of important working-class amenities. For example, one observer found that Liverpool's town centre had not been 'completely shattered or very seriously scarred', although 'in terms of morale the effect is undoubtedly great'. An M-O report remarked that in other towns the dislocation of utilities was 'found to have a major effect in lowering morale'. In Liverpool these consequences were limited to a few areas and a few days. Significantly, the report noted that Liverpool's city centre landmarks were not destroyed during the blitz:

> There is a subtle psychological tie-up between the citizens, however apathetic, and the *centre*, the heart of their city. Quite an important factor in Liverpool is the comparatively good layout of parts of the town, and the exceptional wide streets in many areas. This greatly reduced the dislocation of transport, which is a very important factor in keeping up the morale of big towns, especially among shoppers and industrial workers.[57]

Thus the preservation of the public utilities in Liverpool eliminated the practical problems that were evident in Manchester and Coventry, while the undamaged city centre landmarks provided a physical manifestation of continuity.

In order to make sense of the often contradictory M-O reports and pseudo-scientific interpretations of variations in regional civilian morale, it has been argued that analysis should be directed to the impact the raids had upon the functioning of a working community. Clearly, air attacks on city centres which provided essential amenities to close-by working-class communities severely damaged civilian morale in these areas. The acknowledgement that the destruction of key urban recreational institutions could lead to dangerous dips in civilian morale encouraged a more interventionalist approach by Government: they not only offered advice on appropriate leisure pursuits but also attempted to introduce working-people to a 'higher' more civilising culture. It is to this culture and the response of working men that we shall now turn.

Social observers' enduring interest in popular leisure perhaps reached a zenith during the war period. Not only was the nation in an immediate crisis with the fear that civilian morale could collapse at any moment, but it was also a period in which opinion-formers began to think about the cultural possibilities in postwar social reconstruction. These twin themes informed the thinking of writers such as Priestley, who argued that popular leisure patterns should contain creative and intelligent influences which would provide satisfaction and stability in the immediate crisis and beyond in the brave postwar world. In emphasising the creative over the 'passive' and 'numbing' forms of leisure, Preistley drew from traditions that had been deeply held in the labour movement since the Victorian era.[58] However, while socialist ideals during the Victorian period had largely been substitionalist, whereby the socialist culture could one day replace the corrupt and stupefying capitalist one, discourse on leisure during the 1930s and 1940s looked towards the state for leadership in recreational matters. Like Priestley, J. M. Keynes believed that popular knowledge and participation in the arts would foster good citizens by 'refining their sensibilities' and lead to an appreciation of the value in their cultural roots.[59] The state's intervention in almost all areas of life during the war gave added impetus to the 'statist' approach to tackling morale and the postwar development of leisure, and may explain why, in 1939, the Council for the Encouragement of Music and the Arts (CEMA) was founded.

CEMA was established by Earl De La Warr, President of the Board of Education, and was launched to promote the popular appreciation of 'higher' and civilised forms of recreation. Supported initially by a £25,000 grant from the Pilgrim Trust, the organisation gained official support in April 1940 when CEMA received a £50,000 subsidy from the Government.[60] Under the slogan 'The Best for the Most', CEMA's aim was to bring the arts to the working-class provinces at subsidised prices. Its activities included classical concerts performed in factory canteens and popular venues, and the creation of Art for the People Exhibitions which took famous British paintings to provincial towns. CEMA also sponsored acting companies, such as the Old Vic, to tour traditional working-class districts in Britain.[61] The duel aim of promoting 'civilised' values within a context of bolstering morale and preparing for reconstruction were clearly apparent in the Board of Education's request to the Treasury for the funding of CEMA:

> We are engaged in a war to defend civilisation. Such a policy can only have meaning if the people behind it believe intensely in the value and reality of their own cultural roots. It might be possible to make the country aware that its traditions are indeed bound up with conceptions of democracy, tolerance and kindliness. These things have little meaning in the abstract but are actual and concrete when expressed through national literature, music and painting; and such a consciousness might become the spearhead of national effort, both as a weapon of war and as a means of implementing a constructive peace.[62]

The CEMA-sponsored events which perhaps best encapsulated the organisation's ideals were 'Dame Myra Hess' Mid-day Concerts', held at the National Gallery, where 'ordinary' people were invited along for the price of only a shilling. After surveying the audience, the *Picture Post* enthusiastically celebrated the concerts as an example of how the civilised arts had produced a new understanding between the social classes, commenting that 'strange things happen in wartime'.[63] Indeed, Humphrey Jennings used the Myra Hess concerts as a pivotal sequence in his film *Listen to Britain* (1942), which carried the same message of social harmony through an all-round appreciation of high culture. These contemporary images of CEMA's activities have led some historians to assume that this state-funded leisure programme did successfully introduce the arts to an enthusiastic working class. Angus Calder has argued that 'certainly, classical music found a new audience ... people found it harder to use what spare time they had, and were willing to venture their new earnings on culture, to give it a try.'[64] More recently, Addison and Leventhal have claimed that CEMA was an unrivalled success, exceeding expectations and breaking down the financial and social barriers between the working class and the 'high arts'.[65] However, the great popularity of the Hess concerts masked the continuing social divisions that hampered CEMA's idealistic vision of successfully transmitting an 'elevating' culture. One social observer noted that most people in the Gallery were from a social background accustomed to classical music, while the touring orchestras were often met with indifference in the factory canteens. One band member noted:

> Everyone was eating and clinking cups of tea and getting up to fetch more during the concert ... [w]e stood unnoticed in the corner, wondering how to begin and feeling a little unwanted, but suddenly someone started clapping and it spread rapidly through the room to the accompaniment of cries of 'come on, get started' and so forth. After that all went well. We decided to stick to things that were simple and well-known.

This incident was far from untypical and also reflected a trend of bands resorting to more 'popular' and well known material in order to gain a response from the audience. However, this approach was met with some resistence from CEMA purists, who sniffily derided this new direction as 'altogether odious' and, if it continued, could see no point in differentiating between CEMA and the more popular (and therefore culturally inferior) Entertainments National Service Association (ENSA).[66] This evidence has rightly led Nick Hayes to argue that there was little transference of high culture across existing social barriers and that working people yearned for the familiar, 'with no great demand for radical change'.[67] Indeed, it is argued here that the 'familiar' or the continuation of pre-wartime conditions was a key factor in generating and maintaining morale. Thus the state's sponsorship of leisure schemes to promote good morale and citizenship was largely ineffectual given the working class's strong commitment to their own forms of entertainment.

Beneath the veneer of the propaganda that proclaimed that the war had brought a new popular appreciation of high culture, the prewar institutions within the working-class community remained significant frames of reference for many working men. Indeed, the failure of CEMA to impart high culture to the masses reflected a wider failure of government to penetrate and alter working-class leisure patterns even during national crises. The local official be it a local councillor, health worker or air-raid warden was looked upon with suspicion. Richard Hoggart's vivid account of interwar working-class culture described a world divided into 'Them and Us'. '"Them" includes the policemen and those civil servants or local authority employees whom the working-classes meet – teachers and the school attendance man, "the corporation", the local bench.'[68] The fear that mass panic would follow heavy civilian bombing placed the working class under greater scrutiny from officialdom, provoking further hostility or suspicion in working-class districts. According to one chief constable in the South of England, people in working-class districts were wantonly disregarding official advice during aid-raid warnings:

> The conduct of the public is becoming more callous and in spite of all possible action by both police and wardens, including the use of the loud-speaker on the police car, we cannot get the public to take cover. They will stand about in doorways and gossip at corners … [and] lounge about in a sort of absurd bravado.[69]

Other reports complained that after initial concerns when the sirens were first heard, many people 'stayed in bed through the sounding of the sirens and would not get up and seek shelter until they heard firing/bombs. Many slept on and weren't woken by the "all clear".'[70] If there was a general unwillingness to follow government advice, it was even more marked in leisure activities. With the initial closure of cinemas, music halls and thea-tres at the outbreak of war, the official government advice was to pursue more solitary pastimes. For example, Ministry of Information public leaflets extolled the merits of reading and warned civilians that music was only to be played at a 'reasonable time' and 'not without asking the warden's permission'.[71] The encouragement of solitary pursuits was taken up by the press, with *The Times* even reminding its readers of the 'pleasures of progressively filling up each blank square' of a crossword since it 'helped one to regain a sense of competence and efficiency, blurred by the day's experiences'.[72] The initial draconian ban on mass entertainment provoked fears that the mass entertainment industries would collapse. Indeed the head of the one of the largest dance-hall circuits and band agencies duly pronounced that 'he was finished'. However, despite government dictates, working-class people in particular preferred their 'mass' entertainment, a demand that enterprising dance-hall managers eagerly met. For example, one manager recalled how he covertly sidestepped the order that large public recreational venues cease to offer entertainment at the outbreak of war:

> We closed on September 3rd. In the morning we listened to the broadcast, and I called in what members of the staff there were to hear it. After the speech we realised we couldn't keep on. I told them [the staff] the situation and we all went into the ballroom and started taking the glass tops off the tables and clearing the room, making it ready as an air-raid shelter. Then the first warning went. All the people scampered down from the street. We gave a concert that afternoon and another at 7 in the morning, when that

warning went. We had a full night staff we were doing 24 hours on and 24 hours off. We gave a concert. I called for a pianist and for volunteers to do turns. I indulged in singing myself – a thing I never do. We had a knobbly knees contest, one old chap got up and sang 'Soldiers of the Queen', and we had kids dancing on the stage.[73]

Although the Government soon relaxed the ban on staging mass public entertainment events, working people were still reluctant to break from their regular leisure patterns, particularly during the early stages of the war. In Clitheroe, the Chief Constable informed the Home Office that 'enquiries show that during the evenings when the cinemas are giving shows and the receipt of the "ACTION WARNING" has been announced from the stage, practically no one has left, everybody being content to remain to see the show through.'[74] Likewise, in one report a Midlands chief constable noted that at a Coventry City football match an air-raid warning sounded during the game. 'There being 3,000 people present. The referee stopped the match and few persons left but others pressed for the game to go on which it did.' Although such loyal support was highly commendable, it served to remind the authorities that their advice and instructions often fell on deaf ears. The sheer numbers involved in all forms of mass entertainment rendered crowd management a very difficult task.[75] In general, then, CEMA and other government-inspired events and advice had a minimal influence on civilian morale and popular leisure patterns. This was particularly the case when contrasted with the traditional working-class institutions, such as the club, public house, music hall, dance hall and neighbourhood, which became vital in maintaining a collective purpose under wartime conditions. These institutions were especially poignant for working-class males, whose leisure tended to be located away from the home and in the public sphere.

The working-class male's reliance on traditional institutions contrasted with his middle-class counterpart, who tended to withdraw from public activities and gravitate towards the private sphere. In their report on wartime Oxford, M-O noted that working-class clubs such as the Cowley Workers Social Club experienced 'greater demands than ever', while the middle-class Conservative Club suffered a marked decline in use.[76] These observations reflected a general tendency for working-class males to increase their dependence on leisure activities during a time of crisis. A good example of this was the British Legion, which, M-O noted, had 'no difficulty in welcoming members from other branches. Here no doubt the club habit was already well developed, a ready-made link existed in all being members of one legion.'[77] The public house, however, remained the most popular leisure institution for men during the war. It has been estimated that at least three-quarters of the British men and half of its women visited the public house on a regular basis. This was despite the shortage of supply and increase in prices, indicating that the public house performed an important social function. The war had also altered drinking habits since the shortage of liquor had encouraged customers to start their drinking earlier in the evening to avoid missing out. Moreover, landlords began to dispense with the bar and saloon divide which had traditionally separated men and women drinkers.[78] The often smaller public bar began to fall into disuse since fuel shortages and an increase in women drinkers meant that the larger saloon bar became the nucleus of pub life.[79] Contemporary researchers were quick to identify the public house as a major influence on improving morale. As one M-O investigator in Oxford noted, the public houses were 'fairly popular', with pub-goers 'spending money freely and joining in the singing with gusto'. It was reported that drink had a considerable effect on morale. In a survey of a Plymouth pub the talk of raids decreased from 80 per cent to 40 per cent as more alcohol was consumed.[80] In a Home Intelligence report of October 1940, M-O noted that in Fulham pub-going had decreased up until the end of August 1940. However, once the Blitz started in September it noted that the habit 'had revived … pub going has in Fulham at least reasserted itself'.[81] Where public houses were shut the effect was generally negative on working-class morale. For example, after the severe raids on Plymouth in March 1941, it was reported that the absence of night life had cast 'an expectant gloom over the whole city'. This was also the case in Portsmouth, where the post-blitz reaction was to keep public houses shut. By contrast, in Southampton it was noted that the public houses in the working-class districts were doing very good business both at night and at midday.

Another important recreational institution was the music hall, which provided the opportunity for familiar entertainers from prewar Britain to raise morale significantly. One observer noted that, 'unlike the cinema, the music hall has been affected little if at all, by the war. Indeed at the moment the industry is experiencing a minor boom.'[82] However, investigators repeatedly noticed that there was a greater preponderance of men in the audience than before the war. It is difficult to account for these observations, but the increased attraction of the public house for women and the continued prioritisation of monies for male over female leisure in working-class households may provide some answers. The popularity of the music hall and its impact on civilian life did not go unnoticed by the establishment. For example, the Ministry of Information regularly connsidered the role of performers in increasing morale, thus:

> There are a considerable number of first rank stars who do recitation and orations of a semi-comic nature which generally contain a great deal of topical material and undoubtedly have a considerable impact. Perhaps most effective among these are the Western Brothers, Nosmo King, Ernie Lotinga, Jack Warner, Bill Bennett.[83]

The available evidence suggests, however, that where performers tried overtly patriotic material there was little laughter in response, suggesting the audience wanted an escape, not a reminder of the war. A wartime survey on popular entertainment in music halls concluded that sketches that included 'sexual references' and 'lavatory humour' were the most popular, whilst jokes with references to Germany and the war, on the other hand, 'were not on the whole successful'.[84] Good civilian morale, then, depended upon entertainment that provided a form of escapism from war and, in a more general sense, upon the community continuing to live and function as close to prewar times as possible.

Conclusion

At the outbreak of war the Home Morale Emergency Committee predicted that 'class feeling' was one of the most dangerous impediments to the maintenance of a favourable level of civilian morale.[85] Given that leisure was inexorably tied to citizenship and morale, official advice on people's wartime recreation consistently sought to engender class harmony. Under the stresses of war it was important that the population was consistently reminded that it was a 'people's war' in which, for the first time, culturally elevating leisure activities could be shared by everyone. The failure of CEMA and the general reluctance of working people to comply with initially draconian dictates regarding their personal leisure hours illustrates that perhaps the Home Morale Emergency Committee caught the mood of the nation from the outset. Official advice on civilian behaviour had little impact on the public at large since morale was essentially generated and maintained in working-class communities. Working-class leisure institutions played an important role in this, particularly for males since their leisure patterns had traditionally been situated in the public arena. Working-class morale visibly dipped when key utilities and leisure institutions such as the public house suffered extensive damage during air raids, a point that was consistently made by post-blitz investigators. Despite extensive government intervention in the provision of leisure, overall one is struck by the continuities of male leisure patterns rather than by the deep-rooted cultural changes that some historians have discerned.

Notes

1　R. Titmuss, *Problems of Social Policy* (London, HMSO, 1950), p. 508; see also J. Harris, 'War and social history: Britain and the home front during the Second World War', *Contemporary European History*, 1 (1992), 18.

2　A. Marwick, *Britain in the Century of Total War. War, Peace and Social Change, 1900–1967* (Harmondsworth, Penguin, 1968), p. 298.

3　P. Ziegler, *London at War 1939–1945* (London, Sinclair-Stevenson, 1995), p. 166.

4　P. Summerfield, 'The "levelling of class"', in H. L. Smith (ed.), *War and Social Change. British Society in the Second World War* (Manchester, Manchester University Press, 1986).

5　R. Mackay, *Half the Battle. Civilian Morale in Britain during the Second World War* (Manchester, Manchester University Press, 2002), pp. 248, 263.

6　Harris, 'War and social history', 28.

7　S. O. Rose, 'Sex, citizenship, and the nation in World War II Britain', *American Historical Review*, October 1998; G. Field, 'Perspectives on the working-class family in wartime Britain, 1939–1945', *International Labor and Working-Class History*, 38 (1990).

8　Cited in Marwick, *Britain in the Century of Total War*, p. 298.

9　This is a reference to the so-called 'khaki fever' during the First World War, where young women broke moral convention by openly pursuing young soldiers in their barracks. See A. Woollacott, '"Khaki-fever" and its control: Gender, class, age and sexual morality on the British homefront in the First World War', *Journal of Contemporary History*, 29 (1994).

10　Quoted in Field, 'Perspectives on the working-class family', 9.

11　*The Times*, 29 March 1943.

12　University of Sussex, Tom Harrisson Mass-Observation Archive (hereafter THM-O) 1835, 'Behaviour of women in public houses', June 1942.

13　Rose, 'Sex, citizenship, and the nation in World War II Britain', pp. 1166–8.

14　Field, 'Perspectives on the working-class family', 4.

15　M-O did explain in their report on Glasgow that 'by morale we mean primarily not only determination to carry on, but also determination to carry on with the utmost energy, a determination based on a realisation of the facts and with a readiness for many minor and some major sacrifice including life itself. Good morale means hard and persistent work, means optimism, maximum unity, reasonable awareness of the true situation and absence of complacency and confidences which are not based on fact and which are therefore likely to be terribly let down as time passes.' THM-O, File 600, 'Morale in Glasgow'.

16 Public Records Office (hereafter PRO), HO/199/442, 'Letter to H. Morrison from First Lord of the Admiralty A. V. Alexander MP'.

17 For a general analysis of the Mass-Observation's Organisation, see A. Calder, 'Mass-Observation 1937–1949', in *Essays on the History of British Sociological Research*, ed. M. Bulmer (Cambridge, Cambridge University Press, 1984).

18 PRO, Home Office 199/442, 'A note on the meaning and measurement of the morale in relation to air raids', 2 February 1943.

19 P. Addison, *The Road to 1945* (London, Pimlico, 1994), p. 121.

20 Titmuss, *Problems of Social Policy*, p. 337.

21 B. Beaven and D. Thoms, 'The Blitz and civilian morale in three northern cities, 1940–42', *Northern History*, 32 (1996).

22 T. Harrisson, *Living through the Blitz* (London, Collins, 1976), p. 13.

23 T. Harrisson and C. Madge, *Britain* (Harmondsworth, Penguin, 1939), p. 9.

24 Calder, 'Mass-Observation 1937–49', pp. 121–4.

25 P. Summerfield, 'Mass-Observation: Social research or mass movement?', *Journal of Contemporary History*, 20 (1985), 446.

26 Titmuss, *Problems of Social Policy*, p. 338.

27 Field, 'Perspectives on the working-class family', 7. For the response to *Things to Come* after it was re-released in 1940, see THMO, March 1940, 'Film Report', file 57. Also C. Frayling, *Things to Come* (London, British Film Institute, 1995), p. 77.

28 PRO, HO 199/276, 'Visit to Bristol and Cardiff', 2–6 August 1940.

29 The origins of regional stereotyping can be traced back to the Victorian era; see C. Dellheim, 'Imagining England: Victorian views of the north', *Northern History*, 22 (1986), 216–30.

30 G. Orwell, *The Road to Wigan Pier* (Harmondsworth, Penguin, 1974), p. 98.

31 F. Zweig, *The British Worker* (Harmondsworth, Pelican, 1952), p. 47.

32 Titmuss, *Problems of Social Policy*, p. 313.

33 PRO, HO 199/442, 'Report on Selected Blitz Towns M-O Reports Dec 1941–Jan 1942'.

34 Harrisson, *Living Through the Blitz*, p. 237.

35 THM-O, File Report 516, 'Report on Southampton 4 Dec 1940'.

36 PRO, HO 199/442, 'Report on selected Blitz towns M-O reports Dec 1941–Jan 1942', p. 6.

37 THM-O, File Report 559, 'Report on Portsmouth and Plymouth 29 Jan 1941'.

38 PRO, 'Report on selected Blitz towns M-O Reports Dec–Jan 1942', p. 10.

39 THM-O, File Report 529, 'Report on aftermath of town Blitzes Bristol, Southampton and Cheltenham'.

40 K. Lunn and R.Thomas, 'Naval imperialism in Portsmouth 1905–14', *Southern History*, 10 (1988).

41 THM-O, File Report 559, 'Report on Portsmouth and Plymouth 29 Jan 1941'.

42 Ziegler, *London at War*, p. 165.

43 A. Aldgate and J. Richards, *Britain Can Take It. British Cinema during the Second World War* (Edinburgh, Edinburgh University Press, 1994), p. 1.

44 M. Taylor, 'Leisure and entertainment', in J. Bourne, P. Liddle and I. White-head (eds), *The Great World War, 1914–45. Who Won? Who Lost?* vol. 2: *The Peoples' Experience* (London, HarperCollins, 2000), p. 378.

45 Marwick, *Britain in the Century of Total War*, p. 260.

46 S. Harper, *Picturing the Past. The Rise and Fall of the British Costume Film* (London, British Film Institute, 1994), pp. 110–11.

47 *Champagne Charlie*, film, directed by Albert Cavalcanti, UK, 1944.

48 THM-O, *Home Propaganda. A Report prepared by M-O* (n.d.), p. 47.

49 PRO, HO 207/1069, 'The Psychology of Coventry', November 1941.

50 THM-O, File Report 538, 'Report on Manchester and Liverpool 6 Jan 1941'.

51 THM-O, File Report 538, 'Report on Manchester and Liverpool 6 Jan 1941'.

52 Harrisson, *Living through the Blitz*, p. 244.

53 Harrisson, *Living through the Blitz*, p. 138. For first-hand accounts of the Coventry blitz, see G. Hodgkinson, *Sent to Coventry* (Bletchley, Maxwell, 1970); P. Donnelly (ed.), *Mrs Milburn's Diaries. An Englishwomen's Day-to-Day Reflections 1939–45* (Glasgow, Collins, 1981).

54 *The Times*, 9 September 1940.

55 D. Thoms, *War Industry and Society. The Midlands 1939–45* (London, Routledge, 1989), p. 128.

56 Thoms, *War Industry and Society*, p. 139.

57 PRO, HO 199/326, 'Report on the effects of heavy air raids on Hull June 1941'.

58 J. Hill, 'When work is over: Labour, leisure and culture in wartime Britain', in N. Haynes and J. Hill, *'Millions Like Us'? British Culture in the Second World War* (Liverpool, Liverpool University Press, 1999), p. 237.

59 R. Weight, 'State intelligentsia and the promotion of national culture in Britain, 1939–45', *Historical Research*, 68 (1996), 98.

60 Marwick, *Britain in the Century of Total War*, p. 299.

61 A. Calder, *The People's War. Britain 1939–1945* (1969; London, Pimlico, 1997), p. 372.

62 Quoted in Weight, 'State intelligentsia and the promotion of national culture in Britain', p. 85.

63 N. Haynes, 'More than "music-while-you-eat"? Factory and hostel concerts, "good culture" and the workers', in Haynes and Hill, *'Millions Like Us'?*, p. 211.

64 Calder, *The People's War*, pp. 372–3.

65 F. M. Leventhal, 'The best for the most: CEMA and state sponsorship of the arts in war-time', *Twentieth Century British History*, 1 (1990), 316; P. Addison, *Now the War is Over* (London, Pimlico, 1995), pp. 135–6.

66 Haynes, '"More than music-while-you-eat"?', p. 231.

67 Haynes, '"More than music-while-you-eat"?', p. 223.

68 R. Hoggart, *The Uses of Literacy* (Harmondsworth, Penguin, 1957), p. 72.

69 PRO, HO 199/316, 'Copy extract from fortnightly appreciation report of the Chief Constable of the Isle of Wight', 14 September 1940.

70 HO 199/276, 'Visit to Bristol and Cardiff', 2–6 August 1940.

71 PRO, INF 1/252, 'Propaganda department, Leaflets and Advice'.

72 *The Times*, 16 July 1940.

73 THM-O, 11A 'Jazz and Dancing', November 1939.

74 PRO, HO 199/316, 'Copy extract from fortnightly appreciation report of the Chief Constable of Clitheroe', 14 September 1940.

75 PRO, HO 199/316, 'Copy extract from fortnightly appreciation report of the Chief Constable of Coventry', 14 September 1940.

76 See A. Whiting, *The View from Cowley. The Impact of Industrialisation upon Oxford, 1918–39* (Oxford, Clarendon Press, 1983).

77 THM-O, File Report 761, 'Report on Oxford Clubs and Evacuee Participation 27 June 1941'.

78 A. Davies, *Leisure, Gender and Poverty. Working-Class Culture in Salford and Manchester* (Manchester, Manchester University Press, 1992), p. 61.

79 Calder, *The People's War*, p. 366.

80 THM-O, File Report 626, 'Second Report on Plymouth 1 April 1941'.

81 THM-O File Report 469 'Pubs in Fulham October 1940'.

82 THM-O, Live Entertainment and the War Box 3 File C, 'Music Hall and the War'.

83 THM-O, File Report 197, 'Report on Music Halls, 13 June 1941'.

84 THM-O, File Report 33 1937–49, 'Music Hall 1940'.

85 I. McLaine, *The Ministry of Morale* (London, Allen & Unwin, 1979), p. 93.

Conclusion

Contemporary discussion on the future of citizenship and male leisure between 1850 and 1945 was a fluid discourse, filtered through wider anxieties that gripped society at the time. While popular leisure patterns were often seen as an obstacle to 'good' citizenship, appropriate 'rational' leisure was perceived as the antidote to urban degeneracy. The book's focus on the Midlands has revealed that the citizenry were perceived as much as a problem in 'boom towns' as in poverty-stricken areas that have traditionally been associated with schemes of cultural regeneration. Indeed, towns that had become dominated by the 'new' industries were often at the heart of contemporary debates pertaining to the nature of leisure, work and citizenship. For the late Victorian urban elite, new industries had brought significant cultural and physical changes to the city, which bred anxieties over the future of civilisation in a mass society. Although less apocalyptic, their counterparts in the interwar period feared that increased suburbanisation would physically and culturally cut working people adrift from the town council and the civic responsibilities that flowed from it. Thus, although we see regional variations in working-class poverty and relative affluence, for contemporaries the 'problem' of leisure and citizenship remained constantly on the agenda and was distinctly expressive of class and gender relations.

While the book has sought to map the contemporary discourse on leisure, it has also undertaken to identify the significant characteristics of male working-class leisure and the key agencies that helped fashion it. Certainly, the fundamentals of class, gender and generation all had significant roles in shaping working people's experience of life, labour and leisure. When we compare the free time of women and men, there can be little doubt that working-class men were the chief beneficiaries of the increased leisure opportunities and surplus incomes in working-class families of the late nineteenth century. The era of mass commercial leisure compounded gender inequalities and set the tone for the twentieth century. Until the Second World War, working-class womens' experience of mass leisure was severely limited after marriage. Married women became attached to a localised neighbourhood existence which merged leisure time with household duties and 'neighbourhood gossip'.[1] Traditional gender inequalities at home legitimised male spending on leisure at the expense of the household, creating conditions in which gender tensions were often in the ascendant. However, outside the domestic sphere class identities assumed a more important role, particularly when external agencies attempted to advise, cajole and regulate popular entertainment.

Although the contexts changed, working-class male leisure was deemed a problem throughout the period. This study has outlined contemporary debates on citizenship and evaluated its impact on male leisure patterns. Although patterns of leisure undoubtedly changed with the demise of rational recreation and the subsequent rise of commercialised leisure, one is struck by the considerable degree of continuity in the years 1850–1945. There is a distinct trend of working males creating a culture, within leisure institutions such as the public house, football match and club, which was both class and gender exclusive. Within these leisure institutions there was also a strong emphasis on collective participation. This tradition, evident in the interaction between audience and performers in early Penny Gaffs, survived into the twentieth century in the form of crowd behaviour in the football ground. Significantly, it was the collective ethos that enabled working men to maintain some autonomy over their leisure experience and that was an important factor in negotiating an often alien cultural environment. Thus rational recreation failed to create the desired 'model citizen', while music hall and football both maintained the spectators' involvement even in the more regularised and commercial world of the early twentieth century. Indeed, the popular leisure habits enjoyed by male youths throughout the period demonstrate how commercial leisure neatly dovetailed into traditional informal street activities. In addition to their traditional informal 'loafing' around street corners, male youths regularly visited the football match, the music hall and, later, the cinema. However, contemporary fears that popular leisure would provoke public disorder on the streets had largely dissipated by the interwar period. A curtailment of civic street celebrations, the city's more fragmented suburban structure and redesigned leisure venues all helped curb the contestation over urban space that had surfaced during the nineteenth century. There can be little doubt also that men's leisure became more home-centred and private, though still very separated from their wives' preferred recreational activities. However, historians who have argued that this somehow produced a privatised and compliant worker stranded in suburbia have pushed the point too far.

Although the interwar period saw new ideas of what constituted acceptable behaviour, these did not remain unchallenged or exist within a political vacuum. The social citizenship schemes of the nineteenth and twentieth centuries consistently failed to enthuse a sceptical working class, who regarded their leisure time as beyond the bounds of legitimate interference. By the early twentieth century popular civic pride did exist but, crucially, it was generated from below. The popular civic pride fostered by successful Edwardian football teams saw a host of local dignitaries dispense with their own schemes of citizenship and make a headlong dash to endorse the 'peoples' game'. By the interwar period, citizenship schemes talked less about civilising the degenerate and more about the civic and ballot-box responsibilities of the working man during a period of increasing political tension. In addition, although mass commercial leisure remained the target for many schemes of social citizenship, critiques of institutions such as the cinema shifted from its considerations of degenerate influence to assessing its pacifying and apathetic effects.

Given these trends, subsequent historiography has tended to present leisure as playing an important role in either class subordination or resistance: two static opposing camps of analysis.[2] It has been maintained here that working-class leisure was not an entirely consistent entity since it was shaped by the competing categories of gender and generation. Studies that have dissected working communities in isolation, however, have often exaggerated the competition between working men, and stressed generational and gendered conflicts. Viewed from a wider perspective, male leisure manifests a discernible class dimension, in which cultural traditions and norms were dictated by social position. This study has argued that class continued as a principal determinant in the nature of working-class leisure between 1850–1945. Thus, although the urban elites set agendas regarding acceptable leisure patterns, the baseline was constantly being re-drawn as working men consistently transgressed and pushed the accepted norms of recreation. Clearly these challenges were not overt political responses to schemes of social citizenship. Nevertheless, they were meaningful to those involved and came from a tradition of active participation and contestation in popular culture stretching back into the nineteenth century. An independent male working-class culture continued to embrace and reject leisure opportunities, retaining a degree of autonomy that ensured that leisure was not a mere consolation for a culturally deprived class but an object of pleasure that working men could largely enjoy on their own terms.

Notes

1 M. Tebbutt, 'Women's talk? Gossip and "women's words"', in A. Davies and S. Fielding (eds), *Workers' Worlds. Cultures and Communities in Manchester and Salford, 1880–1939* (Manchester, Manchester University Press, 1992).

2 L. Senelick, 'Politics as entertainment: Victorian music-hall songs', *Victorian Studies*, 19 (1974); J. Clarke, C. Critcher and R. Johnson (eds), *Working Class Culture. Studies in History and Theory* (London, Hutchinson, 1979); R. Gray, 'Bourgeois hegemony in Victorian Britain', in T. Bennett et al. (eds), *Culture, Ideology and Social Process* (London, Batsford, 1981); B. Waites, T. Bennett and G. Martin (eds), *Popular Culture. Past and Present* (Beckenham, Croom Helm, 1981); R. Price, *Labour in British Society* (London, Routledge, 1986).

Bibliography

Primary sources

Manuscript sources

Birmingham Central Library

Osbourne Collection of newspaper cuttings
Various scrapbooks containing newspaper cuttings

British Newspaper Library, Colindale

Coventry Record Office

Acc 128/2, 'Coventry Religious and Useful Knowledge Society Minute Book 1839–1860'.
Acc CCA/1/4/13/8, 'Coventry Watch Committee Minute Book, 1914–1921'
Acc BA/C/Q/20/12, Freemen's Admissions, 1905–39.
CRO, Acc 240/2/9, 'Coventry Sports and Social Association Records', 1943–53.
ACC 135, Roland Barrett, 'Socialism made plain'.
ACC 835/2, Hugh Farren, 'Newspaper cuttings'.
Acc 91/1, 'Coventry Coffee Tavern Minute Book', 1878–1905.
Collection of Oral Histories

Coventry City Library, Local Studies

Cooper, E. W., 'Fifty Years of Reminiscences', unpublished scrapbook, 1928.
Coventry Corporation Boundary Commission Extension Act 1927. With Minutes of Evidence, 1927

Various scrapbooks containing newspaper cuttings
Trade Directories

Luton Central Library

Various scrapbooks containing newspaper cuttings
Trade Directories

Public Record Office, Kew

CAB 65 War Cabinet Minutes

MEPO Metropolitan Police Reports

HO 199 Intelligence reports on the effect of the Blitz during the Second World War

HO 207 Aftermath of Blitz

INF 1 Ministry of Information minutes, memoranda and correspondence, Home Office Intelligence reports and related propaganda material.

MUN 4 Intelligence reports on the working-class activities during the First World War

MUN 5 Munitions and Labour memoranda, correspondence and surveys

London School of Economics

Charles Booth Archive, researchers' notebooks.

Modern Records Centre, University of Warwick

Iron and Steel Trades Confederation
British Motor Industry Archive
National Cycle Archive
Peter Worm Automotive Industrial Relations Collection

University of Sussex

Tom Harrisson Mass-Observation Archive

Contemporary publications

Arnold, M., *Culture and Anarchy* (Cambridge, Cambridge University Press, 1932).

Baden-Powell, R., *Scouting for Boys* (London, C. Arthur Pearson, 1907).

Baden-Powell, R., *Yarns for Boy Scouts* (London, C. Arthur Pearson, 1909).

Bakke, E.W., *Unemployed Man. A Social Study* (London, Nesbit & Co., 1933).

Barker, E., 'Community centres and the uses of leisure', *Adult Education*, 11:1 (1938).

Besant, W., 'The amusements of the people', *Contemporary Review*, 45 (1884).

Blathwayt, R., 'Sentimental England', in I. Maris (ed.), *Essays on Duty and Discipline. A Series of Papers on the Training of Children in relation to Social and National Welfare* (London, Cassell & Co., 1910).

Booth, C., *Life and Labour of the People in London* (London, Macmillan, 1 vol. 1889; 2 vols 1891; 9 vols 1892–97; 17 vols 1902–03)).

Boyd, W. (ed.), *The Challenge of Leisure* (London, New Education Fellowship, 1936).

Bryan, H. S., *The Troublesome Boy* (London, A. C. Pearson, 1936).

Burt, C., *The Young Delinquent* (London, University of London Press, 1925).

Butterworth, J., *Clubland* (1932; London, Epworth Press, 1933).

Calvert, E. R. and T., *The Lawbreaker. A Critical Study of the Modern Treatment of Crime* (London, Routledge, 1933).

Cameron, C., A. Lush and G. Meara, *Disinherited Youth. A Report on the 18+ Age Group Enquiry Prepared for the Trustees of the Carnegie United Kingdom Trust* (Edinburgh, T. & A. Constable, 1943).

Carter, G. R., 'The cycle industry', in S. Webb and A. Freeman (eds), *Seasonal Trades* (London, Constable & Co., 1912).

Castle, E. B., A. K. C. Ottaway and W. T. R. Rawson, *The Coming of Leisure. The Problem in England* (London, New Education Fellowship, 1935).

Chamberlain, N. G., 'Labour exchanges and boy labour', *Economic Review* (1909).

Deedes, W., 'Social problems of the new housing estates', *Journal of State Medicine*, 45:1 (1937).

Erskine Clarke, J., 'The working man's Saturday night; its bane and an antidote', *Transactions of the National Association for the Promotion of Social Science* (1860).

Freeman, A., *Boy Life and Labour. The Manufacture of Inefficiency* (London, King and Son, 1914).

Greenwood, J., *The Wilds of London* (London, Chatto & Windus, 1874).

Greenwood, W., *Love on the Dole* (1933; Harmondsworth, Penguin, 1981).

Hatton, H. S., *London's Bad Boys* (London, Chapman & Hall, 1931).

Haw, G., *The Life Story of Will Crooks M.P.* (1907; Cassell, London, 1917).

Hyde, R. R., *The Boy in Industry and Leisure* (London, G. Bell & Sons, 1921).

Jay, A. O., *Life in Darkest London* (London, Webster & Cable, 1891).

Kuper, L. (ed.), *Living in Towns. Selected Research Papers in Urban Sociology of the Faculty of Commerce and Social Science University of Birmingham* (Cresset Press, London, 1953).

F. W. Lawrence 'The housing problem', in C. F. G. Masterman (ed.), *The Heart of the Empire* (London, Fisher Unwin, 1901).

Lawson, W., 'The drink difficulty', *Nineteenth Century*, 5 (1879).

Leavis, F. R., *Mass Civilisation and Minority Culture* (Cambridge, Minority Press, 1930).

Le Bon, G., *The Crowd. A Study of the Popular Mind* (1897; London, New Brunswick, 1995).

Lewis, M. A., *A Club for the Boys. Why Not Open One?* (London, Christian Knowledge Society, 1905).

Llewellyn Smith, H. (ed.), *The New Survey of London Life and Labour. Life and Leisure*, vol. 9 (London, P. S. King & Son, 1935).

Madge, C., and T. Harrisson, *Britain* (Harmondsworth, Penguin, 1939).

Manners Howe, T. H., 'Save the boys', in I. Maris (ed.), *Essays on Duty and Discipline. A Series of Papers on the Training of Children in Relation to Social and National Welfare* (London, Cassell & Co., 1910).

Marshall, F., 'Music and the people', *Nineteenth Century*, 8 (1880).

Marshall, T. H., *Citizenship and Social Class* (Cambridge, Cambridge University Press, 1950).

Masterman, C. F. G., 'Realities at home', in C. F. G. Masterman (ed.), *The Heart of the Empire* (London, Fisher Unwin, 1901).

Mayer, J. P., *British Cinemas and their Audiences* (London, Dennis Dobson, 1948).

Meath, Lord, 'Duty and discipline in the training of children', in I. Marris (ed.), *Essays on Duty and Discipline. A Series of Papers on the Training of Children in Relation to Social and National Welfare* (London, Cassell & Co., 1910).

Morgan, A. E., *The Needs of Youth. A Report to King George's Jubilee Trust Fund* (Oxford, Oxford University Press, 1939).

Morrison, A. A., *Child of the Jago* (London: MacGibbon & Key, 1969).

Muir, A., *75 Years of Progress. Smith's Stamping Works* (Tonbridge, Tonbridge Printers, 1958).

National Social Purity Crusade (ed.), *The Cleansing of a City* (London, Greening & Co., 1908).

Orwell, G., *Keep the Aspidistra Flying* (London, Secker & Warburg, 1936).

Orwell, G., *The Road to Wigan Pier* (1937; Harmondsworth, Penguin, 1974).

Orwell, G., 'Coming Up for Air', in *The Complete Novels* (1939; London, Penguin, 1983).

Owen, A. D. K., 'The social consequences of industrial transference', *Sociological Review*, 29 (1937).

Pelham, H. S., *The Training of a Working Boy* (London, Macmillan, 1914).

Poole, B., *Coventry and Its Antiquities* (London, John Russell Smith, 1869).

Priestley, J. B., *An English Journey* (1933; Harmondsworth, Penguin, 1977).

Rowntree, B. S., *Poverty. A Study of Town Life* (London, Macmillan, 1903).

Rowntree, B. S., *Poverty and Progress. A Second Social Survey of York* (London, Longman, 1941).

Russell, C. E. B. and L. M. Rigby, *Working Lad's Clubs* (1908; London, A. C. Black, 1932).

Secretan, H. A., *London Below Bridges. Its Boys and its Future* (London, Geoffrey Bles, 1931).

Shenfield, A. and P. S. Florence, 'Labour and the war industries. The experience of Coventry, 1943–5', *Review of Economic Studies*, 12:1 (1944–45).

Sinclair, R., *Metropolitan Man. The Future of the English* (London, Allen & Unwin, 1937).

Titmuss, R., *Problems of Social Policy* (London, HMSO, 1950).

Tressell, R., *The Ragged Trousered Philanthropists* (1914; London, Flamingo, 1993).

Turner, G., 'Amusements of the English people', *The Nineteenth Century*, 2 (1877).

Welldon, D. D., 'The early training of boys in citizenship', in I. Marris (ed.), *Essays on Duty and Discipline. A Series of Papers on the Training of Children in relation to Social and National Welfare* (London, Cassel, 1910).

Wright, T., *Some Habits and Customs of the Working Classes by a Journeyman Engineer* (London, Tinsley Brothers, 1867).

Yates, J. A., *Pioneers to Power. The Story of the Ordinary People of Coventry* (Coventry, Coventry Labour Party, 1950).

Zweig, F., *The British Worker* (Harmondsworth, Penguin, 1952).

Autobiographies, memoirs and diaries

Chancellor, V. E., *Master and Artisan in Victorian England. The Diary of William Andrews and the Autobiography of Joseph Gutteridge* (London, Evelyn, Adams & Mackay, 1969).

Donnelly, P. (ed.), *Mrs Milburn's Diaries. An Englishwoman's Day-to-Day Reflections 1939–45* (Glasgow, Collins, 1981).

Hodgkinson, G., *Sent to Coventry* (Bletchley, Maxwell, 1970).

Hoggart, R., *The Uses of Literacy* (Harmondsworth, Penguin, 1957).

Roberts, R., *The Classic Slum. Salford Life in the First Quarter of the Century* (Manchester, Manchester University Press, 1971).

Samuel, R., *East End Underworld. Chapters in the Life of Arthur Harding* (London, Routledge, 1981).

Symons, J., *The Thirties. A Dream Revolved* (London, Faber & Faber, 1960).

Webb, B., *My Apprenticeship*, vol. II (Harmondsworth, Penguin, 1938).

Woodruff, W., *The Road to Nab End. An Extraordinary Northern Childhood* (London, Abacus, 2002).

Newspapers, journals and trade directories

Aeroplane
Alfred Herbert News
Bedford and Hertfordshire Saturday Telegraph
The Clarion
Coventry Directory
Coventry Graphic
Coventry Herald
Cov Magazine
Coventry Standard
Coventry Times
Daily Graphic
Daily Mail
Era
Film Weekly
The Graphic
Harper's Magazine
The Limit
The Loudspeaker
Luton News
Luton Reporter

Midland Daily Telegraph
The New Statesmen
Northern Star
Pall Mall Magazine
The Rudge Record
The Spectator
Spinnel's Annual Directory, Coventry and District.
Siddeley Deasy Employers Quarterly
Stevens' Coventry Leamington, Nuneaton, Kenilworth and Warwickshire Directory.
The Times
Truth

British parliamentary papers

Report from the Select on Inquiry into Drunkeness, 5 August 1834.

First, Second and Third Reports from the Select Committee of the House of Lords on the Prevalence of Habits of Intemperance, sess. 8 February–14 August 1877, vol. XI.

Reports from the Commissioners, Inspectors and Others: Thirty Volumes, Technical Instruction, sess. 5 February–14 August 1884, Vol. XXXI.

Contemporary films

Things to Come, directed by W. Cameron Menzies, UK, 1936

Champagne Charlie, directed by A. Cavalcanti, UK, 1944.

Secondary sources

Addison, P., *The Road to 1945* (London, Pimlico, 1994).

Addison, P., *Now the War is Over* (London, Pimlico, 1995).

Aldgate, T., 'Comedy, class and containment: The British domestic cinema of the 1930s', in Curran and Porter (eds), *British Cinema History* (London, Weidenfeld & Nicolson, 1983).

Aldgate, A., and J. Richards, *Britain Can Take It. British Cinema During the Second World War* (Edinburgh, Edinburgh University Press, 1994).

August, A., 'A culture of consolation? Rethinking politics in working class London, 1870–1914', *Historical Research*, 74 (2001).

Bailey, P., *Leisure and Class in Victorian England. Rational Recreation and the Contest for Control 1830–1885* (London, Methuen, 1978).

Bailey, P., 'Champagne Charlie: Performance and ideology in the music hall swell song', in J.S. Bratton, *Music Hall. Performance and Style* (Milton Keynes, Open University Press, 1986).

Bailey, P., 'Conspiracies of meaning: Music hall and the knowingness of popular culture', *Past and Present*, 144 (August 1994).

Bailey, P., 'The politics and poetics of modern British leisure', *Rethinking History*, 3 (1999).

Bailey, V., 'Salvation Army riots, the "Skeleton Army" and legal authority in the provincial town', in A.P. Donajgrodzki (ed.), *Social Control in Nineteenth Century Britain* (London, Croom Helm, 1977).

Bailey, V., '"In Darkest England and the Way Out": The Salvation Army, social reform and the Labour movement 1885–1910', *International Review of Social History*, 29 (1984).

Barker, W.J., 'The making of a working-class football culture', *Journal of Social History*, 13 (1979).

Beaven, B., and D. Thoms, 'The Blitz and civilian morale in three northern cities, 1940–42', *Northern History*, 32 (1996).

Beaven, B., 'Shop floor culture in the Coventry motor industry, *c.* 1896–1920', in D. Thoms, L. Holden and T. Claydon (eds), *The Motor Car and Popular Culture in the 20th Century* (Aldershot, Ashgate, 1998).

Beaven, B., and J. Griffiths, 'The blitz, civilian morale and the city: Mass-Observation and working-class culture in Britain, 1940–41', *Urban History*, 26 (1999).

Beaven, B. and J. Griffiths, 'Urban elites, socialists and notions of citizenship in an industrial boomtown: Coventry *c.* 1870–1914', *Labour History Review*, 69:1 (2004).

Bevir, M., 'The Labour Church Movement', *Journal of British Studies*, 38 (1999).

Behagg, C., *Politics and Production in the Early Nineteenth Century* (Routledge, London, 1990).

Behagg, C., 'Narratives of control: Informalism and the workplace, 1800–1900', in O. Ashton, R. Fyson and S. Roberts (eds), *The Duty of Discontent. Essays for Dorothy Thompson* (London, Mansell, 1995).

Belchem, J., *Industrialization and the Working Class. The English Experience, 1750–1900* (Aldershot, Scolar Press, 1990).

Benson, J., *The Working Class in Britain, 1850–1939* (London, Longman, 1989).

Best, G., *Mid-Victorian Britain, 1851–75* (Glasgow, Collins, 1971).

Black, L. et al., *Consensus or Coercion. The State, the People and Social Cohesion in Post-War Britain* (Cheltenham, New Clarion Press, 2001).

Blanch, M., 'Imperialism, nationalism and organized youth', in J. Clarke, C. Critcher and R. Johnson (eds), *Working Class Culture. Studies in History and Theory* (London, Hutchinson, 1979).

Boyd, K., *Manliness and the Boys' Story Paper in Britain. A Cultural History, 1855–1940* (London, Palgrave, 2003).

Briggs, A., and A. Macartney, *Toynbee Hall. The First Hundred Years* (London, Routledge, 1984).

Burgess, K., 'Youth employment policy during the 1930s', *Twentieth Century British History*, 6 (1995).

Calder, A., 'Mass-Observation 1937–1949', in *Essays on the History of British Sociological Research*, ed. M. Bulmer (Cambridge, Cambridge University Press, 1984).

Calder, A., *The People's War. Britain 1939–1945* (1969; London, Pimlico, 1997).

Catterall, P., 'Morality and politics: The Free Churches and the Labour Party between the wars', *The Historical Journal*, 36 (1993).

Childs, M. J., *Labour's Apprentices. Working-Class Lads in Late Victorian and Edwardian England* (London, Hambledon Press, 1992).

Chinn, C., *They Worked All Their Lives. Women of the Urban Poor in England, 1880–1939* (Manchester, Manchester University Press, 1988).

Clapson, M., 'Working-class women's experiences of moving to new housing estates in England since 1919', *Twentieth Century History*, 10 (1999).

Clarke, J., C. Critcher and R. Johnson (eds), *Working Class Culture. Studies in History and Theory* (London, Hutchinson, 1979).

Constantine, S., 'Amateur gardening and popular recreation in the 19th and 20th centuries', *Journal of Social History*, 14 (1981).

Corrigan, P., 'Film entertainment as ideology and pleasure: A preliminary approach to a history of audiences', in J. Curran and V. Porter (eds), *British Cinema History* (London, Weidenfeld & Nicolson, 1983).

Croll, A., 'Street disorder, surveillance and shame: Regulating behaviour in the public spaces of the late Victorian town', *Social History*, 24 (1999).

Croll, A., *Civilizing the Urban. Popular Culture and Public Space in Merthyr, c. 1877–1914* (Cardiff, University of Wales Press, 2000).

Cross, G. (ed.), *Worktowners at Blackpool. Mass-Observation and Popular Leisure in the 1930s* (London, Routledge, 1990).

Crump, J., 'Recreation in Coventry between the wars', in B. Lancaster and T. Mason (eds), *Life and Labour in a 20th Century City. The Experience of Coventry* (Coventry, Cryfield Press, 1986).

Crump, J., 'Provincial Music Hall: Promoters and Public in Leicester, 1863–1929', in P. Bailey (ed.), *Music Hall. The Business of Pleasure* (Milton Keynes, Open University Press, 1986).

Cunningham, H., *Leisure in the Industrial Revolution, 1780–1880* (Beckenham, Croom Helm, 1980).

Davies, A., 'Police and the people: Gambling in Salford, 1900–39', *Historical Journal*, 34 (1991).

Davies, A., *Leisure, Gender and Poverty. Working-Class Culture in Salford and Manchester, 1900–1939* (Buckingham, Open University Press, 1992).

Davies, A., and S. Fielding (eds), *Workers' Worlds. Cultures and Communities in Manchester and Salford, 1880–1939* (Manchester, Manchester University Press, 1992).

Davies, A., 'Cinema and Broadcasting', in P. Johnson (ed.), *Twentieth Century Britain* (London, Longman, 1994).

Davis, J., 'Slums and the vote 1867–90', *Historical Research*, 64:155 (1991).

Dedman, M., 'Baden-Powell, militarism, and the "invisible contributors" to the Boy Scout scheme, 1904–1920', *Twentieth Century British History*, 4:3 (1993).

Dellheim, C., 'Imagining England: Victorian views of the north', *Northern History*, 22 (1986).

Dellheim, C., 'Business in time: The historian and corporate culture', *Public Historian*, 8 (1986)

Dingle, A., 'Drink and working-class living standards in Britain, 1870–1914', *Economic History Review*, 4 (1972).

Earl, J., 'Building the music halls', in P. Bailey (ed.), *Music Hall. The Business of Pleasure* (Milton Keynes, Open University, 1986).

Evans, R.A., 'The university and the city. The educational work of Toynbee Hall', *History of Education*, 11 (1982).

Featherstone, S., ''E dunno where 'e ave: Coster comedy and the politics of music hall', *Nineteenth Century Theatre*, 24:1 (1996).

Field, G., 'Perspectives on the working-class family in wartime Britain, 1939–1945', *International Labor and Working-Class History*, 38 (1990).

Field, G., 'Social patriotism and the British working class: Appearance and disappearance of a tradition', *International Labor and Working-Class History*, 42 (1992).

Fielding, S., *Class and Ethnicity. Irish Catholics in England, 1880–1939* (Buckingham, Open University Press, 1993).

Foster, J., *Class Struggle and the Industrial Revolution. Early Industrial Capitalism in Three English Towns* (London, Methuen, 1974).

Foulger, N., *Coventry. The Complete History of the Club* (Norwich, Wensum Books, 1979).

Fowler, D., 'Teenage consumers? Young wage earners and leisure in Manchester, 1919–1939', in A. Davies and S. Fielding (eds), *Workers' Worlds. Cultures and Communities in Manchester and Salford, 1880–1939* (Manchester, Manchester University Press, 1992).

Fowler, D., *The First Teenagers. The Lifestyle of Young Wage Earners in Interwar Britain* (London, Woburn Press, 1995).

Frayling, C., *Things to Come* (London, British Film Institute, 1995).

Freeman, M., '"No finer school than a Settlement": The development of the Educational Settlement Movement', *History of Education*, 31:3 (2002).

Gilbert, D., 'Community and municipalism: Collective identity in late Victorian and Edwardian mining towns', *Journal of Historical Geography*, 17:3 (1991).

Gillis, J.R., *Youth and History. Tradition and Change in European Age Relations, 1770–Present* (New York, Academic Press, 1974).

Glucksmann, M., *Women Assemble. Women Workers and the New Industries in Interwar Britain* (London, Routledge, 1990).

Gray, R., 'Bourgeois hegemony in Victorian Britain', in T. Bennett et al. (eds), *Culture, Ideology and Social Process* (London, Batsford, 1981); B. Waites, T. Bennett and G. Martin (eds), *Popular Culture. Past and Present* (Beckenham, Croom Helm, 1981).

Griffiths, J., '"Give my regards to uncle Billy": The rites and rituals of company life at Lever Brothers, c. 1900–1990', *Business History*, 37 (1995).

Griffiths, J., 'Exploring corporate culture: The potential of magazines for the business historian', *Business Archives*, 78 (1999).

Griffiths, P., 'Juvenile Delinquency in Time', in P. Cox and H. Shore (eds), *Becoming Delinquent. British and European Youth, 1650–1950* (Aldershot, Ashgate, 2002).

Griffiths, T., *The Lancashire Working Classes, c. 1880–1930* (Oxford, Clarendon Press, 2001).

Gunn, S., 'The "failure" of the Victorian middle class: A critique', in J. Wolff and J. Seed (eds), *The Culture of Capital, Art Power and the Nineteenth Century Middle Class* (Manchester, Manchester University Press, 1988).

Gutzke, D.W., *Protecting the Pub. Brewers and Publicans against Temperance* (London, Boydell Press, 1989).

Hargreaves, J., *Sport, Power and Culture* (Cambridge, Polity Press, 1987).

Harper, S., *Picturing the Past. The Rise and Fall of the British Costume Film* (London, British Film Institute, 1994).

Harris, J., 'War and social history: Britain and the home front during the Second World War', *Contemporary European History*, 1 (1992).

Harrison, B., and P. Hollis, 'Chartism, Liberalism and the life of Robert Lowery', *English Historical Review*, 82 (1967).

Harrison, B., *Drink and the Victorians. The Temperance Question in England, 1815–1872* (Keele, Keele University Press, 1994).

Harrisson, T., *Living through the Blitz* (London, Collins, 1976).

Haydu, J., *Between Craft and Class. Skilled Workers and Factory Politics in the United States and Britain, 1890–1922* (California, University of California Press, 1988).

Haynes, N., '"More than music-while-you-eat"? Factory and hostel concerts, "good culture" and the workers', in N. Haynes and J. Hill, *'Millions Like Us'? British Culture in the Second World War* (Liverpool, Liverpool University Press, 1999).

Hendrick, H., *Images of Youth. Age, Class and the Male Youth Problem, 1880–1920* (Oxford, Clarendon Press, 1990).

Hewitt, M., *The Emergence of Stability in the Industrial City. Manchester, 1832–67* (Aldershot, Scolar Press, 1996).

Hiley, N., '"Lets go to the pictures": The British cinema audience in the 1920s and 1930s, *Journal of Popular British Cinema*, 2 (1999).

Hill, J., 'Cup finals and community in the North of England', in J. Williams and S. Wagg (eds), *British Football and Social Change* (Leicester, University of Leicester Press, 1991).

Hill, J., 'When work is over: Labour, leisure and culture in wartime Britain', in N. Haynes and Hill, J., *'Millions Like Us'? British Culture in the Second World War* (Liverpool, Liverpool University Press, 1999).

Hill, J., *Sport, Leisure and Culture in Twentieth Century Britain* (London, Palgrave, 2002).

Hodgkinson, G., *Sent to Coventry* (Bletchley, Maxwell, 1970).

Hobsbawm, E.J., 'The making of the working class 1870–1914', in E.J. Hobsbawm, *Worlds of Labour. Further Studies in the History of Labour* (London, Weidenfeld & Nicolson, 1984).

Holt, R.J., 'Football and the urban way of life in nineteenth-century Britain', in J.A. Mangan (ed.), *Pleasure, Profit, Proselytism. British Culture and Sport at Home and Abroad, 1700–1914* (London, Frank Cass, 1988).

Holt, R., *Sport and the British. A Modern History* (Oxford, Clarendon Press, 1990).

Homer, A., Planned communities: The social objectives of the British new towns, 1945–65', in L. Black et al. *Consensus Or Coercion. The State, the People and Social Cohesion in Post-war Britain* (Cheltenham, New Clarion Press, 2001).

Hughes, A., and K. Hunt, 'A culture transformed? Women's lives in Wythenshawe in the 1930s', in A Davies and S. Fielding (ed.), *Workers' Worlds. Cultures and*

Communities in Manchester and Salford, 1880–1939 (Manchester, Manchester University Press, 1992).

Humphries, S., *Hooligan or Rebels? An Oral History of Working-Class Childhood and Youth, 1889–1939* (Oxford, Blackwell, 1981).

Johnson, P., 'Conspicuous consumption and working-class culture in late Victorian and Edwardian Britain', *Transactions of the Royal Historical Society*, 38 (1988).

Joicey, N., 'A paperback guide to progress: Penguin Books, 1935–1951', *Twentieth Century British History*, 4 (1993).

Jones, S. G., *Workers at Play. A Social and Economic History of Leisure, 1918–1939* (London, Routledge & Kegan Paul, 1986).

Jones, S. G., *Sport, Politics and the Working Class. Organised Labour and Sport in Inter-War Britain* (Manchester, Manchester University Press, 1992).

Joyce, P., *Visions of the People. Industrial England and the Question of Class, 1848–1914* (Cambridge, Cambridge University Press, 1990).

Joyce, S., 'Castles in the air: The People's Palace, cultural reformism, and the East End working class', *Victorian Studies* 39 (1996).

Kidd, A. J., and K. W. Roberts (eds), *City, Class and Cultures. Studies of Cultural Production and Social Policy in Manchester* (Manchester, Manchester University Press, 1985).

Kift, D., *The Victorian Music Hall. Culture, Class and Conflict* (Cambridge, Cambridge University Press, 1996).

Kirk, N., *Change, Continuity and Class. Labour in British Society, 1850–1920* (Manchester, Manchester University Press, 1998).

Kuhn, A., *Cinema, Censorship and Sexuality, 1909–1925* (London, Routledge, 1988).

Kuhn, A., 'Cinema-going in Britain in the 1930s: Report of a questionnaire survey', *Historical Journal of Film, Radio and Television*, 19 (1999).

Kuhn, A., *An Everyday Magic. Cinema and Cultural Memory* (London, I. B. Tauris, 2002).

Lancaster, B., 'Who's a real Coventry kid? Migration into twentieth century Coventry', in B. Lancaster and T. Mason (eds), *Life and Labour in a 20th Century City. The Experience of Coventry* (Coventry, Cryfield Press, 1986).

Langhamer, C., *Women's Leisure in England, 1920–1960* (Manchester, Manchester University Press, 2000).

Leventhal, F. M., 'The best for the most: CEMA and state sponsorship of the arts in war-time', *Twentieth Century British History*, 1 (1990).

Goldthorpe, J. H, D. Lockwood et al., *The Affluent Worker. Industrial Attitudes and Behaviour* (Cambridge, Cambridge University Press, 1968).

Lunn, K., and R. Thomas, 'Naval imperialism in Portsmouth 1905–14', *Southern History*, 10 (1988).

McAleer, J., *Popular Reading and Publishing in Britain, 1914–1950* (Oxford, Clarendon Press, 1992).

McG. Davies, J., 'A twentieth century paternalist: Alfred Herbert and the skilled Coventry workman', in B. Lancaster and T. Mason (eds), *Life and Labour in a 20th Century City. The Experience of Coventry* (Coventry, Cryfield Press, 1986).

McG. Eagar, W., *Making Men. The History of Boys' Clubs and Related Movements in Great Britain* (London, University of London Press, 1945).

Mackay, R., *Half the Battle. Civilian Morale in Britain during the Second World War* (Manchester, Manchester University Press, 2002)

McKibben, R., *The Ideologies of Class. Social Relations in Britain 1880–1950* (Oxford, Oxford University Press, 1991).

McKibbin, R., *Classes and Cultures. England, 1918–1951* (Oxford, Oxford University Press, 1998).

McLaine, I., *The Ministry of Morale* (London, Allen & Unwin, 1979).

Maloney, P., *Scotland and the Music Hall* (Manchester, Manchester University Press, 2003).

Mansfield, N., *English Farmworkers and Local Patriotism, 1900–1930* (Aldershot, Ashgate, 2001).

Mason, T., *Association Football and English Society* (Brighton, Harvester, 1980).

Mason, T., 'Sport and recreation', in P. Johnson (ed.), *Twentieth Century Britain. Economic, Social and Cultural Change* (London, Longman, 1994)

Marsh, J., *Back to the Land. The Pastoral Impulse in Victorian England, 1880–1914* (London, Quartet Books, 1982).

Marwick, A., *Britain in the Century of Total War. War, Peace and Social Change, 1900–1967* (Harmondsworth, Penguin, 1968).

Mayall, D., 'Palaces for entertainment and instruction: A study of early cinema in Birmingham, 1908–18', *Midland History*, 2 (1985).

Meacham, S., *Toynbee Hall and Social Reform, 1880–1914. The Search for Community* (New Haven, Yale University Press, 1987).

Meller, H., *Leisure and the Changing City, 1870–1914* (London, Routledge & Kegan Paul, 1976).

Meller, H. (ed.), *The Ideal City* (Leicester, Leicester University Press, 1979).

Meller, H., 'Urban renewal and citizenship: The quality of life in British cities, 1890–1990', *Urban History*, 22 (1995).

Miles, P., and M. Smith, *Cinema, Literature and Society* (Beckenham, Croom Helm, 1987).

Morgan, D., and M. Evans, *The Battle for Britain. Citizenship and Ideology in the Second World War* (London, Routledge, 1993).

Morris, R. J., 'The middle class and British towns and cities of the Industrial Revolution, 1780–1870', in D. Fraser and A. Sutcliffe (eds), *The Pursuit of Urban History* (London, Edward Arnold, 1983).

Mountjoy, P. R., 'Thomas Bywater Smithies, editor of the *British Workman*', *Victorian Periodicals Review*, 18 (1985).

Murdoch, N. H., 'Salvation Army disturbances in Liverpool, England 1879–1887', *Journal of Social History*, 25:3 (1992).

Nott, J. J., *Music for the People. Popular Music and Dance in Interwar Britain* (Oxford, Oxford University Press, 2002).

O'Connell, S., *The Car in British Society. Class, Gender and Motoring, 1896–1939* (Manchester, Manchester University Press, 1998).

Olechnowicz, A., *Working-Class Housing in England between the Wars. The Becontree Estate* (Oxford, Clarendon Press, 1997).

Olechnowicz, A., 'Civic leadership and education for democracy', *Contemporary British History*, 14 (2000).

Orr, N. G., 'Keep the home fires burning: Peace Day in Luton 1919', *Family and Community History*, 2 (1999).

Otter, C., 'Making liberalism durable: vision and civility in the late Victorian city', *Social History*, 27:1 (2002).

Pearson, G., *Hooligan. A History of Respectable Fears* (London, Macmillan, 1983).

Pearson, R., 'Knowing one's place: Perceptions of community in the industrial suburbs of Leeds, 1790–1890', *Journal of Social History*, 27:2 (1993).

Pennybacker, S. D., *A Vision of London 1889–1914. Labour, Everyday Life and the LCC Experiment* (London, Routledge, 1995).

Phillips, G., 'The social impact', in S. Constantine, M. W. Kirby and M. B. Rose (eds), *The First World War in British History* (London, Edward Arnold, 1995).

Picht, W., *Toynbee Hall and the English Settlement Movement* (London, G. Bell & Sons, 1914).

Pick, D., *Faces of Degeneration. A European Disorder, c. 1848–1918* (Cambridge, Cambridge University Press, 1989).

Pigou, A.C., *Memorials of Alfred Marshall* (New York, Augustus M. Kelley, 1966).

Pimlott, J. A. R., *Toynbee Hall. Fifty Years of Progress* (London, Dent, 1935).

Pivato, S., 'The bicycle as a political symbol: Italy, 1885–1955', *International Journal of the History of Sport*, 3:1 (1990).

Pope, R., 'Adjustment to peace: Educational provision for unemployed juveniles in Britain, 1918–19', *British Journal of Educational Studies*, 27 (1979).

Price, R. N., 'The Working Men's Club movement and Victorian social reform ideology', *Victorian Studies*, 17 (1971).

Price, R., *An Imperial War and the British Working Class. Working-Class Attitudes and Reactions to the Boer War, 1899–1902* (London, Routledge & Kegan Paul, 1972).

Proctor, T. A., '(Uni)forming youth: Girl Guides and Boy Scouts in Britain, 1908–39', *History Workshop Journal*, 45 (1998).

Pyke, S., 'The popularity of nationalism in the early British Boy Scout movement', *Social History*, 23:3 (1998).

Read, D., *England 1868–1914* (1979; London, Longman, 1985).

Reckett, M. B., *P.E.T. Widdrington. A Study in Vocation and Versatility* (London, SPCK, 1961).

Reid, D. A., 'The decline of St Monday, 1766–1876', *Past and Present*, 71 (1976).

Reid, D. A., 'Popular theatre in Victorian Birmingham, in D. Bradby, L. James and B. Sherratt (eds), *Performance and Politics in Popular Drama* (Cambridge, Cambridge University Press, 1980).

Richards, J., *The Age of the Dream Palace. Cinema and Society in Britain 1930–1939* (London, Routledge, 1984).

Richardson, K., *Twentieth Century Coventry* (Suffolk, Coventry Council, 1972).

Ridgwell, S., 'Pictures and proletarians: South Wales miners' cinemas in the 1930s', *Llafur*, 7:1 (1996).

Roberts, E., *A Women's Place. An Oral History of Working-Class Women 1890–1940* (Oxford, Oxford University Press, 1984).

Rose, J., *The Intellectual Life of the British Working Classes* (New Haven, Yale University Press, 2002).

Rose, S.O., 'Sex, citizenship, and the nation in World War II Britain', *American Historical Review*, October 1998.

Rosenthal, M., *The Character Factory. Baden-Powell and the Origins of the Boy Scout Movement* (New York, Pantheon Books, 1986).

Ross, E., 'Survival networks: Womens' neighbourhood sharing before the World War I', *History Workshop Journal*, 15 (1983).

Rubinstein, D., 'Cycling in the 1890s', *Victorian Studies*, 21 (1977).

Rubinstein, D., 'Sport and the sociologist, 1880–1914', *British Journal of Sports History*, 4 (1987).

Russell, D., *Football and the English. A Social History of Association Football in England, 1863–1995* (Preston, Carnegie Publishing, 1997).

Sandall, R., *The History of the Salvation Army*, vol. 1: *1865–1878* (London, Thomas Nelson & Sons, 1947).

Savage, M., and A. Miles, *The Remaking of the British Working Class, 1840–1940* (London, Routledge, 1994)

Scannell, P., and D. Cardiff, *A Social History of British Broadcasting*, vol. 1: *1922–1939, Serving the Nation* (Oxford, Blackwell, 1991).

Scott, P., 'The state, internal migration, and the growth of the new industrial communities in interwar Britain', *English Historical Review*, 461 (2000).

Sedgwick, J., *Popular Filmgoing in 1930s Britain. A Choice of Pleasures* (Exeter, University of Exeter, 2000).

Senelick, L., 'Politics as entertainment: Victorian music hall songs', *Victorian Studies*, 19 (1975–76).

Shore, H., *Artful Dodgers. Youth and Crime in Early 19th Century London* (London, Boydell Press, 2002).

Smith, M.A, 'Social usages of the public drinking house: changing aspects of class and leisure', *British Journal of Sociology*, 34:3 (1983).

Springhall, J., 'Lord Meath, youth and Empire', *Journal of Contemporary History*, 5:4 (1970).

Springhall, J., *Youth, Empire and Society. British Youth Movements, 1883–1940* (Beckenham, Croom Helm, 1977).

Springhall, J., 'Baden-Powell and the Scout movement before 1920: Citizenship training or soldiers of the future?', *English Historical Review*, 101 (Beckenham, Croom Helm, 1986).

Springhall, J., *Youth, Popular Culture and Moral Panics. Penny Gaffs to Gangster-Rap 1830–1996* (London, Macmillan, 1998).

Stedman Jones, G., *Outcast London. A Study in the Relationship Between the Classes in Victorian Society* (1971, Harmondsworth, Penguin, 1984).

Stedman Jones, G., 'Working class culture and working class politics in London 1870–1900: Notes on the remaking of a working class', *Journal of Social History*, 7 (1975).

Stephens, W.B., 'Crafts and industries', *A History of the County of Warwick*, vol. 8 (London, James St, 1969).

Stevenson, J., *British Society, 1914–45* (Harmondsworth, Penguin, 1984).

Stevenson, J., and C. Cook, *Britain in the Depression. Society and Politics, 1929–39* (London, Longman, 1994).

Summerfield, P., 'Mass-Observation: Social research or mass movement?', *Journal of Contemporary History*, 20 (1985).

Summerfield, P., 'The "leveling of class"', in H.L. Smith (ed.), *War and Social Change. British Society in the Second World War* (Manchester, Manchester University Press, 1986).

Taylor, M., 'Leisure and entertainment', in J. Bourne, P. Liddle and I. Whitehead (eds), *The Great World War, 1914–45. Who Won? Who Lost?* vol. 2: *The People's Experience* (London, HarperCollins, 2000).

Tebbutt, M., *Making Ends Meet. Pawnbroking and Working-class Credit* (Leicester, Leicester University Press, 1983).

Thomas, T., 'Representation of the Manchester working class in fiction, 1850–1900', in A.J. Kidd and K.W. Roberts (eds), *City, Class and Culture. Studies of Social Policy and Cultural Reproduction in Victorian Manchester* (Manchester, Manchester University Press, 1985).

Thoms, D., *War Industry and Society. The Midlands, 1939–45* (London, Routledge, 1989).

Thoms, D., and T. Donnelly, *The Coventry Motor Industry. Birth to Renaissance* (Aldershot, Ashgate, 2000).

Valverde, M., 'The dialectic of the familiar and the unfamiliar: "The jungle" in the early slum Travel writing', *Sociology*, 30:3 (1996).

Vamplew, W., *Pay Up and Play the Game. Professional Sport in Britain, 1875–1914* (Cambridge, Cambridge University Press, 1988).

Vincent, A., and R. Plant, *Philosophy, Politics and Citizenship. The Life and Thought of the British Idealists* (Oxford, Blackwell, 1984).

Vincent, D., 'Reading in the working-class home', in J.K. Walton and J. Walvin (eds), *Leisure in Britain, 1780–1939* (Manchester, Manchester University Press, 1983).

Wagg, S., *The Football World* (Brighton, Harvester, 1984).

Waites, B., T. Bennett and G. Martin (eds), *Popular Culture. Past and Present* (London, Croom Helm, 1981).

Waller, P.J., *Town, City and Nation. England, 1850–1914* (Oxford, Oxford University Press, 1983).

Warren, A., 'Sir Robert Baden-Powell, the Scout movement and citizen training in Great Britain 1900–1920', *English Historical Review*, 101 (1986).

Warren, A., 'Citizens of the Empire: Baden-Powell, Scouts and Guides, and an imperial idea', in J.M. Mackenzie, *Imperialism and Popular Culture* (Manchester, Manchester University Press, 1986).

Waters, C., 'Manchester morality and London capital: The battle over the Palace of Varieties', in P. Bailey (ed.), *Music Hall. The Business of Pleasure* (Milton Keynes, Open University Press, 1986).

Waters, C., *British Socialists and the Politics of Popular Culture, 1884–1914* (Manchester, Manchester University Press, 1990).

Weight, R., 'State intelligentsia and the promotion of national culture in Britain, 1939–45', *Historical Research*, 68 (1996).

Weight, R., and A. Beach (eds), *The Right to Belong. Citizenship and National Identity in Britain 1930–1960* (London, I. B. Tauris, 1998).

Weiner, D. E. B., 'The People's Palace. An image for East London in the 1880s', in D. Feldman and G. Stedman Jones (eds), *Metropolis London. Histories and Representations since 1800* (London: Routledge, 1989).

White, J., 'The summer riots of 1919', *New Society*, 13 August 1981.

Whitehand, J. W. R., and C. M. H Carr, 'England's interwar suburban landscapes: Myth and reality', *Journal of Historical Geography*, 25 (1999).

Whiting, A., *The View from Cowley. The Impact of Industrialisation upon Oxford, 1918–39* (Oxford, Clarendon Press, 1983).

Wiener, M. J., *English Culture and the Decline of the Industrial Spirit* (Harmondsworth, Penguin, 1981).

Wild, P., 'Recreation in Rochdale, 1900–1940', in J. Clarke, C. Critcher and R. Johnson (eds), *Working Class Culture. Studies in History and Theory* (London, Hutchinson, 1979).

Wilkinson, P., 'English youth movements, 1908–1930', *Journal of Contemporary History*, 4:2 (1969).

Williams, J., '"One could literally have walked on the heads of the people congregated there": Sport, the town and identity', in K. Laybourn (ed.), *Social Conditions, Status and Community, 1860–1920* (Stroud, Sutton Publishing, 1997).

Woollacott, A., '"Khaki-fever" and its control: Gender, class, age and sexual morality on the British homefront in the First World War', *Journal of Contemporary History*, 29 (1994).

Yeo, E. J., *The Contest for Social Science. Relations and Representations of Gender and Class* (London, Rivers Oram Press, 1996).

Yeo, S., 'A new life: The religion of Socialism in Britain, 1883–1896', *History Workshop*, 4 (1977).

Ziegler, P., *London at War 1939–1945* (London, Sinclair-Stevenson, 1995).

Zweig, F., *The British Worker* (Harmondsworth, Penguin, 1952).

Theses and unpublished papers

Abendstern, M., 'Expression and control: A study of working-class leisure and gender, 1918–39. A case study of Rochdale using oral history methods', Ph.D. thesis, University of Essex, 1986.

Badger, S., 'Household consumption, gender and the working class: The Black Country and Coventry, 1930–1970'. unpublished paper, Wolverhampton University, December 2000.

Beaven, B., 'The growth and significance of the Coventry car component industry, 1895–1939', Ph.D. thesis, De Montfort University, 1994.

Chapman, A., 'The Peoples' Palace for East London: A study of Victorian philanthropy', M.Phil. thesis, University of Hull, 1978.

North, N., 'Middle class suburban life styles and culture in England, 1919–1939', D.Phil. thesis, University of Oxford, 1989.

Sandler, C., 'Working-class adolescents in Birmingham: A study of social reform, 1900–14', Ph.D. thesis, University of Oxford, 1987.

Weller, P., 'Self-help and Provident Societies in Coventry in the nineteenth century, M.Phil. thesis, University of Warwick, 1990.

Index

Lightning Source UK Ltd.
Milton Keynes UK
UKOW051413231112

202642UK00002B/26/P